Comprehensive Math Review Actuarial Exams

First Edition

Written by: Digital Actuarial Resources, LLC

Publication Date: April 17, 2008
Format: Perfect-bound

Published by Digital Actuarial Resources, LLC
Saint Paul, Minnesota
www.digitalactuarialresources.com

Printed in the United States of America

ISBN 978-0-9798071-7-6

Table of Contents

Introduction

Math is evident in every part of the universe. Mathematics governs the physical laws and allows our reality to run smoothly. Our knowledge and applications of mathematical truths have allowed us to advance quickly. Humans progressed through the Atomic Age and Digital Age with the help of math. It contributes heavily to every science, and it is vital to industry. Engineers and computer scientists, for example, would not exist without our wide palette of math tools. Math also allows us to predict the future (in limited areas). I believe that the human mind is run by math, perhaps at a sub-conscious level for most people. We may actually have very advanced math running in our minds—math that helps us process inputs and compress memories. Math may also govern human logic and aid in decision-making.

This book is divided roughly in half between prerequisites for calculus and calculus itself. The math topics that precede calculus, such as trigonometry, are still powerful and have many applications in actuarial science. Logarithms, sequences, and complex numbers are also vital to understanding calculus. The calculus unit starts with derivatives, continues through single integrals and double integrals, and ends with partial derivatives. Calculus is an enormous field and usually spans several semesters in college. This text does not cover every topic in calculus but attempts to review just the topics required for the actuary exams. All the earlier types of math build up to calculus, and all the more advanced types of math depend on it.

This review manual is generally proof-free. Proofs tend to waste space in most math books, and students skip the proofs anyway. I would care more that a student can apply a math concept than understand its derivation. If a theorem is well-known and in a mathematics book, then it must be true. Math is only useful if a person applies it. A series of known facts is useless.

The math that we know is likely temporary and will be replaced by better forms of mathematics. Most of the math that we use is only a few centuries old, with the most archaic math being perhaps 3,000 years old. With mathematics evolving fast, we can expect the field to be completely different a thousand years from now. Our current form of math could limit our ability to advance as a civilization. We tend to describe the world with 4-sided shapes, and our traditional number system has only 10 digits. It is likely that life on other planets has a completely different way of working with numbers.

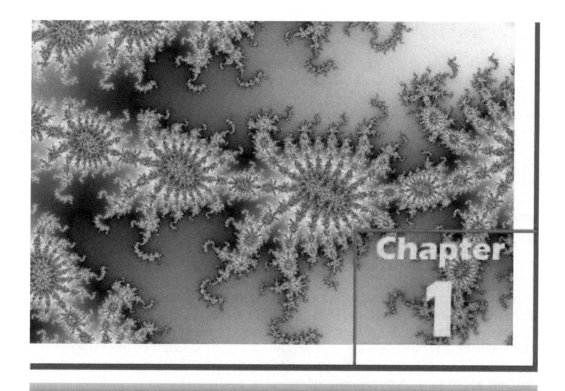

Chapter 1
Advanced Algebra

This book starts from the very beginning of knowledge needed for calculus. The first chapter covers algebra, which includes functions, logarithms, and factoring among other topics. Algebra is used extensively in actuarial science. Most of the material in this chapter is at a high school level. If you feel you already understand intermediate algebra, then you can skip ahead to the next chapter.

Numerous advancements in mathematics occurred during the "Golden Age" of the Islamic empire. Between the 7th and 14th centuries A.D., the people of the Middle East created the number system used globally today. They developed the digits 1 through 9. These digits have changed minimally in appearance since their original development. The citizens in the Middle East also created algebra. The word "algebra" actually stems from the Arabic phrase "al-jabr," meaning "balancing an equation." They even formalized the polynomial and created an efficient method of factoring. They used the new math to progress quickly in physics, chemistry, medicine, and economics.

Section 1-1 Classes of Numbers and Basic Operations

Types of Numbers:

Integers are all numbers that do not have a fractional component. They include negative and positive numbers. Examples of integers are -150, -2, 0, 1, 2, 3, 10, and 99. Examples of numbers that are not integers include -0.14, 3.14159, 7.25, 10.0, and 498.6.

Whole numbers are all the positive integers, along with zero. Examples of whole numbers are 0, 1, 2, 3, …. They are also referred to as *natural numbers*.

Real numbers essentially encompass all possible, non-imaginary values. A real number may or may not have a decimal point with a fractional component. All the integers are real numbers. Other examples of real numbers include 4.89, -1.424, 500, and 90.23.

A *rational number* is the ratio of two integers p and q: $\dfrac{p}{q}$. The bottom number, q, cannot be zero. Not all real numbers are rational numbers. For example, the constant π cannot be represented as a fraction. However, all integers are rational numbers. For instance, the number 8 can be written 8/1.

A *prime number* is an integer greater than 1 that is divisible only by itself and 1. The values 2, 3, 5, 7, and 11 are examples of primes. The value 11, for example, has no divisors but itself and 1.

Order of Operations:

The basic mathematical operations have a precise order of execution within an expression. Many expressions are quite complicated with parts added, divided, and so on, often without the guidance of parentheses. The order of operations from top to bottom is:

Parentheses
Exponents
Multiplication and **D**ivision
Addition and **S**ubtraction.

A common saying to memorize the order is "please excuse my dear aunt sally." You must first evaluate parentheses, then handle powers, then multiplication and division, and finally addition and subtraction.

Example
Calculate $70 * 8 \div 4 - 1 + 5 * (80 * 4 - 300)^2 + 700$

Solution:
$$70*8 \div 4 - 1 + 5*(20)^2 + 700$$
$$70*8 \div 4 - 1 + 5*400 + 700$$
$$560 \div 4 - 1 + 2000 + 700$$
$$140 - 1 + 2000 + 700$$
$$2839$$

Fractions:

A fraction has two components—a numerator and a denominator:

$$\frac{numerator}{denominator}$$

Proper and improper fractions:

-An *improper fraction* is of the form $\frac{a}{b}$, where the absolute value of 'a' is greater than the absolute value of 'b.' The fraction has a value greater than or equal to 1, or less than or equal to -1.

-A *mixed fraction* is of the form $C\frac{a}{b}$, where C is an integer and $\frac{a}{b}$ is less than 1. Mixed fractions are also improper fractions. However, with mixed fractions, the fraction completes the division, with the remainder term represented as $\frac{a}{b}$.

-A *proper fraction* is of the form $\frac{a}{b}$, where the absolute value of 'a' is less than the absolute value of 'b.' The fraction's value is between -1 and 1, exclusive.

Example
Are the following fractions proper or improper?

a. $\frac{5}{5}$ **b.** $22/7$ **c.** $5\frac{1}{4}$ **d.** $3/10$

Solutions:
a. Improper **b.** Improper **c.** Improper (mixed)
d. Proper

Adding two fractions:
-The fractions must have the same denominator. They don't necessarily need the lowest common denominator.

-Add the two numerators and keep the original common denominator

$$\frac{a}{b} + \frac{c}{b} = \frac{a+c}{b}$$

Subtracting two fractions:

-Just as in the addition of fractions, the two fractions need to have the same denominator.

-Subtract the two numerators in the order they appear, and keep the original common denominator.

Example

a. $\quad \frac{14}{3} + \frac{5}{6} = ?$

b. $\quad \frac{9}{4} - \frac{1}{5} = ?$

Solutions:

a. $\quad \frac{28}{6} + \frac{5}{6} = \frac{33}{6}$

b. $\quad \frac{9}{4} * \frac{5}{5} - \frac{1}{5} * \frac{4}{4} = \frac{45}{20} - \frac{4}{20} = \frac{41}{20}$

Multiplying two fractions:

-Multiply the two numerators together and the two denominators together.

$$\frac{a}{b} * \frac{c}{d} = \frac{a*c}{b*d}$$

Simplification of the quotient of two fractions:

$$\frac{\left(\dfrac{a}{b}\right)}{\left(\dfrac{c}{d}\right)} = \frac{a}{b} * \frac{d}{c} \quad, \text{ simply flip the fraction in the denominator}$$

Example

a. $\quad \frac{8}{15} * \frac{6}{11} = ?$

b. $\quad \frac{6}{(1/4)} = ?$

---

c. $\quad \dfrac{(12/19)}{3} = ?$

d. $\quad \dfrac{(7/18)}{(2/23)} = ?$

Solutions:

a. $\quad \dfrac{48}{165}$

b. $\quad \dfrac{6}{1} * \dfrac{4}{1} = \dfrac{24}{1} = 24$

c. $\quad \dfrac{12}{19} * \dfrac{1}{3} = \dfrac{12}{57}$

d. $\quad \dfrac{7}{18} * \dfrac{23}{2} = \dfrac{161}{36}$

Section 1-2 Coordinate Systems

A point is perhaps the simplest geometric object. It represents a single location in the universe. It has no length, no width, no area, and no volume. A dot is infinitely small and would not be visible to humans. In fact, a point is a zero-dimensional object. A point in n-dimensional space requires n coordinates to describe its location.

A line is the next simplest object. A line is essentially an infinite string of tangent points. If you choose any two points on the line, regardless of how close they are spaced, you can find another point on the line between the original two. A line adds the first dimension—length. However, lines have no width, and a true line would be invisible to humans.

A rectangle/plane then has length and width. A rectangle is really just an infinite number of lines stacked upon each other. Rectangles and similar two-dimensional polygons have areas but no volume. They are infinitely thin without any height.

A box has all three visible dimensions—length, width, and height. A box is essentially an infinite number of planes or rectangles stacked together. You could find the area of a cross section of the box, or you could find the volume of a certain region within the box.

As you can see, each object of a higher dimension builds upon the objects of the smaller dimensions. To recap,

first dimension = length
second dimension = width
third dimension = height
fourth dimension = time

Only the first three dimensions can be shown pictorially. The fourth dimension and any higher dimensions are theoretical and cannot be depicted in a single graph. The fourth dimension may describe parallel universes or repeating three-dimensional worlds. In other words, the fourth dimension gives the address of a single three-dimensional realm. It is possible to graph discrete parts of the fourth dimension, but you could not graph continuous changes in the fourth dimension. For example, you could build a 3D graph of a room, giving the coordinates of each object in the room. Assuming the room changes over time, you could provide separate 3D graphs of the room at perhaps times 5, 10, and 15. However, you could not show precisely how the setting changes from time 5 to 15. Any picture could not capture all the continuous changes.

The number line for 1-dimensional coordinates

The simplest coordinate system is the "number line," where points with only one coordinate can be graphed. A number line is generally a horizontal line with arrows at each end and several important values marked with ticks.

Plotting points involves finding the location of the single value along the number line.

Cartesian or 2-dimensional rectangular coordinates

Graphing points with two dimensions will entail using a coordinate system with a vertical and a horizontal axis. A two-dimensional point is in the format (x, y), where x is generally the value for the horizontal axis and y is the value in the vertical direction. The expression (x, y) is called an *ordered pair*. The 2D coordinates are also called Cartesian coordinates or rectangular coordinates. The point (0, 0) is the *origin*. The graphing plane is divided into four quadrants. The first quadrant is in the upper-right corner. The remaining quadrant numbers flow counter-clockwise.

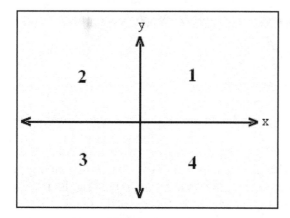

3-dimensional rectangular coordinates

Graphing points in three-dimensions will require a system with length, width, and height. 3D points have the syntax (x, y, z). An example of a 3D coordinate system is shown below:

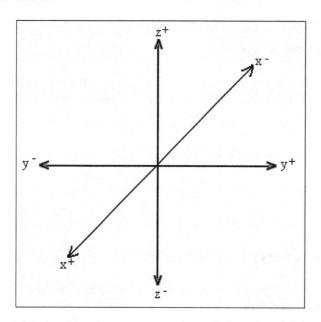

In this coordinate system, the 2D system, which is a plane, is essentially laid flat and stacked infinitely to add height. The z-axis represents the height element. Notice that the axes have been completely rearranged from the 2D graph. The y-axis now consumes the horizontal direction, z is vertical, and the x-axis runs diagonally. Functions in 3D are of the form $f(x, y) = z$, where x and y are the independent variables and the output corresponds to the height.

Section 1-3 Exponents

Consider the expression a^n. The value 'a' is the base, while 'n' is the exponent or power. The exponent n could be any real number. If n is an integer, then n signifies the number of times that 'a' should be multiplied by itself. The basic properties of exponents, which describe ways to simplify products and quotients of numbers raised to powers, are:

Properties of Exponents:

(1.) $a^0 = 1$

(2.) $a^b * a^c = a^{b+c}$

(3.) $\left(a^b\right)^c = a^{b*c}$

(4.) $\dfrac{a^b}{a^c} = a^{b-c}$

(5.) $(ab)^c = a^c * b^c$

(6.) $\left(\dfrac{a}{b}\right)^c = \dfrac{a^c}{b^c}$

Several other miscellaneous equations for exponents include:

(1.) $a^{-b} = \left(\dfrac{1}{a}\right)^b = \dfrac{1}{a^b}$

(2.) $a^{1/b} = \sqrt[b]{a}$

If you have an expression with a quotient, it is improper to have a negative exponent within the expression. If the term with the negative exponent is in the numerator, bring the term to the denominator and make the exponent positive. On the other hand, if the term with the negative exponent is in the denominator, bring the term to the numerator and make the exponent positive.

Example

Simplify the expression below:

$$\frac{x^2 * y^{-1} * z^{-3}}{x^{-4} * y * z^7}$$

Solution:

All terms with a negative exponent must switch sides of the quotient.

$$\frac{x^2 * y^{-1} * z^{-3}}{x^{-4} * y * z^7} = \frac{x^2 * x^4}{y * z^7 * y^1 * z^3} = \frac{x^6}{y^2 * z^{10}}$$

Example

Simplify the following expressions using the properties of exponents:

a. $\dfrac{x^6 y^9 x^2}{\left(y^2\right)^3}$

b. $\dfrac{(xy)^4 x^7 z^{-5}}{(xyz)^{-2}}$

c. $\dfrac{\left(\dfrac{a}{b}\right)^2 * b^{-4} * b^8}{(a^2)^5 * b}$

Solutions:

a. $\dfrac{x^8 y^9}{y^6} = x^8 y^3$

b. $\dfrac{x^4 y^4 x^7 z^{-5}}{x^{-2} y^{-2} z^{-2}} = \dfrac{x^4 y^4 x^7 x^2 y^2 z^2}{z^5} = \dfrac{x^{13} y^6}{z^3}$

c. $\dfrac{\dfrac{a^2}{b^2} * b^4}{a^{10} * b} = \dfrac{a^2 b^{-2} * b^4}{a^{10} * b} = \dfrac{a^2 b^2}{a^{10} b} = \dfrac{b}{a^8}$

Section 1-4 Polynomial Distribution

Distribution techniques are necessary when expanding a set of polynomials that are multiplied together. The expressions to be multiplied are usually in parentheses. Each expression could have any quantity of terms, such as a single constant or a full fourth-degree polynomial. When distributing, you start with a condensed expression and end with a long polynomial that has no parentheses. The degree of the expanded polynomial will equal the sum of the highest degrees from each individual expression.

The simplest distribution occurs when multiplying a constant through a polynomial. To perform the distribution, simply multiply each term in the larger polynomial by the constant.

Example

Distribute the outer constant with the larger polynomial:

$10(5x^2 - 4x + 13)$

Solution:

$10 * 5x^2 - 10 * 4x + 10 * 13 = 50x^2 - 40x + 130$

Another simple brand of distribution occurs when multiplying a single term of a polynomial, x^n, with a longer polynomial. As in the case of multiplying a constant through, multiply each term in the longer polynomial by x^n.

Example
Expand these expressions:
   a. $x^3(17x^2 + 45)$
   b. $8x^5(9x + 4)$

Solutions:
   a. $x^3 * 17x^2 + x^3 * 45 = 17x^5 + 45x^3$
   b. $8x^5 * 9x + 8x^5 * 4 = 72x^6 + 32x^5$

FOILing is a specific type of distribution in which you need to multiply two expressions within parentheses together, with each expression containing two terms. The term "FOIL" stands for "first, outside, inside, last." It is an acronym for the order in which the terms must be multiplied together. Consider the product $(a+b)(c+d)$. When FOILing, start by multiplying the "first" item in each set of parentheses—a and c. Then, multiply the "outside" terms a and d. Thirdly, multiply the "inside" terms, which are b and c. Lastly, multiply the "last" components together from each set of parentheses—b and d. These four individual products are summed up. You may need to add like terms together and perform other simplifications. The end result of the FOILing is a long polynomial with degree equal to or greater than the degree of each polynomial operand.

To summarize, with FOILing,
$(a + b)(c + d) = ac + ad + bc + bd$

Example
Consider the product of $(12x + 3)(10x + 8)$. To start foiling, multiply the "first" terms together, 12x and 10x. Then, multiply the "outside" terms 12x and 8. Then, multiply the "inside" items, which are 3 and 10x. Finally, multiply the "last" items 3 and 8.

$$(12x + 3)(10x + 8) = 12x * 10x + 12x * 8 + 3 * 10x + 3 * 8$$
$$= 120x^2 + 96x + 30x + 24$$
$$= 120x^2 + 126x + 24$$

Example
FOIL the following:
   a. $(x + 3)(x - 6)$

---

b. $(2x-10)(4x-9)$

c. $(11x-5)(16x+2)$

Solutions:

a.

$x*x+x(-6)+3*x+3(-6)$

$x^2-6x+3x-18$

$x^2-3x-18$

b. $2x*4x+2x(-9)+(-10)4x+(-10)(-9)$

$8x^2-18x-40x+90$

$8x^2-58x+90$

c. $11x*16x+11x*2+(-5)16x+(-5)*2$

$176x^2+22x-80x-10$

$176x^2-58x-10$

Example

Expand the following:

a. $x(4x^2+7x)$

b. $6x^2(5x^8+40)$

c. $(3x+5)(8x+2)$

Solutions:

a. $4x^3+7x^2$

b. $30x^{10}+240x^2$

c. First, multiply 3x by each of the values in the neighboring set of parentheses. Then, multiply 5 by each term in the neighboring parentheses. Sum all the products together.

$3x*8x+3x*2+5*8x+5*2$

$24x^2+6x+40x+10$

$24x^2+46x+10$

In calculus and higher types of math, most of the expressions to be multiplied are complicated polynomials with many components. Rather than just two terms existing in each set of parentheses, the parentheses could contain three or more items. To expand the polynomial, take the first term in the first expression and multiply it with all the terms in the second expression, adding the individual products together. Then, take the second item in the first expression and multiply it with all the elements in the second expression.

Continue this process until each term has been multiplied by all the other terms in the other expression. The equation for multiplying two polynomials, each with three terms, is:

$$(a+b+c)(d+e+f) = ad + ae + af + bd + be + bf + cd + ce + cf$$

Example
Perform distribution on the following expressions:

    a. $(5x + 7x^2 + 30)(6x + 3)$
    b. $(8x^3 + 14)(20x^4 + 15x - 1)$
    c. $(4x + 10)(6x^5 + 11x^3 + 2x + 5)$

Solutions:

    a. $5x * 6x + 5x * 3 + 7x^2 * 6x + 7x^2 * 3 + 30 * 6x + 30 * 3$

        $30x^2 + 15x + 42x^3 + 21x^2 + 180x + 90$

        $42x^3 + 51x^2 + 195x + 90$

    b. $8x^3 * 20x^4 + 8x^3 * 15x + 8x^3 * (-1) + 14 * 20x^4 + 14 * 15x + 14 * (-1)$

        $160x^7 + 120x^4 - 8x^3 + 280x^4 + 210x - 14$

        $160x^7 + 400x^4 - 8x^3 + 210x - 14$

    c.

      $4x * 6x^5 + 4x * 11x^3 + 4x * 2x + 4x * 5 +$

      $10 * 6x^5 + 10 * 11x^3 + 10 * 2x + 10 * 5$

      $24x^6 + 44x^4 + 8x^2 + 20x + 60x^5 + 110x^3 + 20x + 50$

      $24x^6 + 60x^5 + 44x^4 + 220x^3 + 8x^2 + 40x + 50$

Distribution can involve more than two sets of parentheses. To expand these polynomials, start by focusing on the first two sets of parentheses. Then, take the expanded result of the first two expressions and distribute it with the third expression. Continue expanding the expressions from left to right.

Example
Expand the following:
a. $5(7x + 14)(8x - 3)$
b. $(10x - 2)(x^2 + 1)(6x - 4)$

Solutions:
a. $(35x + 70)(8x - 3)$

$$35x * 8x + 35x * (-3) + 70 * 8x + 70 * (-3)$$
$$280x^2 - 105x + 560x - 210$$
$$280x^2 + 455x - 210$$

b. $(10x * x^2 + 10x * 1 - 2 * x^2 - 2 * 1)(6x - 4)$
$(10x^3 + 10x - 2x^2 - 2)(6x - 4)$

$10x^3 * 6x + 10x^3 * (-4) + 10x * 6x + 10x(-4) - 2x^2 * 6x - 2x^2 * (-4) +$
$(-2) * 6x - 2 * (-4)$

$60x^4 - 40x^3 + 60x^2 - 40x - 12x^3 + 8x^2 - 12x + 8$

$60x^4 - 52x^3 + 68x^2 - 52x + 8$

Section 1-5 Polynomial Factorization

Factorization is the reverse of distribution. When factoring, we start with an expanded polynomial and condense it. The end result is a collection of expressions within parentheses that are multiplied together. Most factoring examples use quadratics with integer coefficients. Beyond the third power, manual factoring becomes quite difficult. Factoring does not have a clear series of steps one can follow. Factoring requires logic and many unwritten tricks. With practice, factoring becomes easier.

Factoring will necessitate some trial and error. As a general rule when factoring, start with the highest power term. Create a mental list of the integers that, when multiplied together, would produce the coefficient for the highest power term. Draw two sets of parentheses, and place your initial guess for the coefficients as the first elements in each set of parentheses. Multiply these coefficients by combinations of x that, when multiplied together, yield the highest degree term. Then, examine the lowest power term, which is usually a constant. Create another mental list of the integers that can be multiplied together to create the constant. Place your guess in the second position within each set of parentheses. Finally, adjust the coefficients and their signs (positive versus negative) until the product of the factors yields the original polynomial.

Example
Factor the following polynomials into sets of parentheses with two elements per set:

a. $x^2 - 4$
b. $x^2 - 25$
c. $8x^2 - 10x - 12$
d. $4x^2 - 100$

Solutions:
a. $(x-2)(x+2)$
b. $(x-5)(x+5)$
c. $(4x+3)(2x-4)$

Check:
$4x*2x+4x(-4)+3(2x)+3(-4)=8x^2-16x+6x-12=8x^2-10x-12$

d. $4(x^2-25)$
   $4(x-5)(x+5)$

It is wise to perform a check after factoring each polynomial. Check your work by distributing your factors. If the distribution produces the original polynomial, then the factorization is correct.

Example
Factor the following:
a. $14x+21x+21xy$
b. $z(y+10)-9(y+10)$
c. $x^9+5x^4+yx^4$

Solutions:
a. $x(14+21+21y)=x(35+21y)=7x(5+3y)$
b. $(y+10)(z-9)$
c. $x^4(x^5+5+y)$

Section 1-6 Absolute Value

The *absolute value* provides the distance from x to zero. It will always be a positive number or zero. The symbol for the absolute value consists of two vertical bars around the original number. For example, $|x|$ is the absolute value of x.

Example
Find the absolute value of each expression below:
a. 8
b. -15
c. 0
d. -0.005
e. $\sqrt{18}-3$

Solutions:
    a. 8
    b. 15
    c. 0
    d. 0.005
    e. $\sqrt{18} - 3 \approx 1.24264$

Example
Solve for x in $|8x - 5| = 22$.

Solution:
The expression within the absolute value bars could have two values, which are ± 22.
We must solve for the two x-values that create the two y-values.

$$8x - 5 = 22 \quad \rightarrow \quad x = 3.375$$

$$8x - 5 = -22 \quad \rightarrow \quad x = -2.125$$

Example
Solve for x in $|-4x + 18| > 5$

Solution:
$$-4x + 18 > 5$$
$$-4x > -13$$
$$x < 3.25$$

*Remember that dividing by a negative number reverses the inequality sign.

$$-4x + 18 < -5$$
$$-4x < -23$$
$$x > 5.75$$

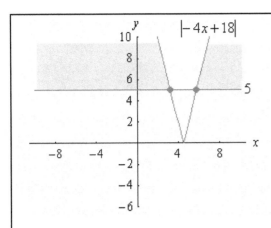

*The graph of an absolute value function typically has a 'v' shape.

Final Solutions: $x < 3.25$ OR $x > 5.75$

When finding the solutions to an inequality equation involving an absolute value expression, break the original equation into two separate equations. One equation should lack the absolute value signs and contain all mathematical operations in their initial forms. The second equation should have no absolute value signs, a rotated inequality sign, and the terms on the second half of the equation must be negated.

Section 1-7 Rounding with Step Functions

The *floor function*, also known as the *greatest integer function*, returns the largest integer that is less than or equal to the input x. The symbol for the floor function is $\lfloor x \rfloor$.

Example
Evaluate the following:
a. $\lfloor 10.9 \rfloor$ b. $\lfloor 2.8 \rfloor$ c. $\lfloor 0 \rfloor$
d. $\lfloor 20 \rfloor$ e. $\lfloor -30 \rfloor$ f. $\lfloor -6.3 \rfloor$

Solutions
a. 10   b. 2   c. 0
d. 20   e. -30 f. -7

The floor function is graphed below. The function has the appearance of a series of steps. Each segment has a closed circle on the left and an open circle on the right.

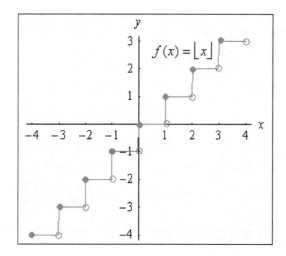

The *ceiling function*, or the *smallest integer function*, returns the lowest integer that is greater than or equal to the input x. The symbol for the ceiling function is $\lceil x \rceil$. The ceiling function will essentially round a value up to the next integer.

Example
Evaluate these:
a. $\lceil 20.4 \rceil$ **b.** $\lceil 150.01 \rceil$ **c.** $\lceil -14.2 \rceil$ **d.** $\lceil -75.25 \rceil$

Solutions:
a. 21   **b.** 151   **c.** -14   **d.** -75

The ceiling function is also a step function. Each segment is of length 1, and it has an open circle on the left and a closed circle on the right.

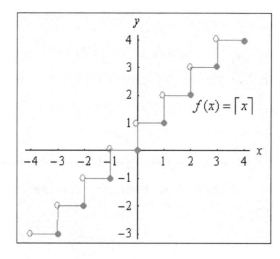

The domain for the floor and ceiling functions is the set of all reals. The range is the set of all integers.

Section 1-8 Factorials

The symbol for a *factorial* is an exclamation mark, !. The expression x! is read "x factorial." The value x must be an integer greater than or equal to zero. To compute x!, we must multiply all the positive integers that are less than or equal to x. Stated another way, $x! = 1*2*3*4*.....*(x-2)*(x-1)*x$. Several of the first factorials are listed here:

$$0! = 1$$
$$1! = 1$$
$$2! = 1*2 = 2$$
$$3! = 1*2*3 = 6$$
$$4! = 1*2*3*4 = 24$$
$$5! = 1*2*3*4*5 = 120$$

The first expression, $0!$, may be counterintuitive. According to the definition of the factorial, we should multiply zero perhaps by itself to get $0! = 0$. However, $0! = 1$ is a singularity in the factorial definition that you need to memorize. From the list above, you can see that to calculate the next factorial, simply take the previous factorial and multiply it by the current value of x. That is, $x! = (x-1)! * x$. In fact, factorials can be rewritten in many forms. For instance, 10! can be broken apart as:

$$10! = 1*2*3*...*10$$
$$10! = 7!*8*9*10$$
$$10! = 5!*6*7*8*9*10$$

Example

Evaluate these factorials:

a. $\dfrac{5000!}{4995!}$ **b.** $\dfrac{1500!*6!}{1498!}$ **c.** $\dfrac{15!*11!}{13!*16!}$

Solutions:

a.
$$\frac{5000!}{4995!} = \frac{4995!*4996*4997*4998*4999*5000}{4995!} \approx 3.11875*10^{18}$$

b.

$$\frac{1500!*6!}{1498!} = \frac{1498!*1499*1500*6!}{1498!} = 1499*1500*720 = 1,618,920,000$$

c.

$$\frac{15!*11!}{13!*16!} = \frac{15!*11!}{13!*(15!*16)} = \frac{11!}{13!*16} = \frac{11!}{(11!*12*13)*16} = \frac{1}{12*13*16} = \frac{1}{2496}$$

Section 1-9 Functions

A *function* is a system that takes at least one input parameter, processes the data in some manner, and returns output. A function should return only one segment of data for each set of input. The output could be a single value, a matrix of numbers, a word, or even a true/false value.

Consider a simple function defined as roundUp(x), which takes a single value x and rounds it up to the nearest integer. Suppose we apply the function as roundUp(23.105). The value 23.105 is the input parameter, the process the function performs is to round the input value up to the next integer, and the resulting output is 24.

Even simple mathematical expressions could be represented in functional form. The addition operator between two numbers could be written sum(number1, number2). The function would then add number1 and number2 together. Nearly every mathematical operation is actually a function.

An example of a Boolean expression is: $(m < n)$ AND $(m > p)$. Suppose m=12, n=25, and p=16. What is the result of the Boolean expression? The first sub-expression, $m < n$, becomes $12 < 25$, which is TRUE. The second sub-expression is FALSE, since m > p becomes $12 > 16$, which is FALSE. The full expression now becomes TRUE AND FALSE, which is FALSE.

Functions are used extensively in computer programming. For example, a programmer might create a function called "rectangle," which draws a rectangle on the monitor. To draw the rectangle, the function would need to know the vertices for the shape. The programmer could define the function as: rectangle(lowerLeftX, lowerLeftY, upperRightX, upperRightY). Whenever the program calls the function, it would need to provide the four coordinates—the lower left and upper right vertices—for the function to draw the rectangle. The four items in parentheses after the function name are called arguments, parameters, or independent variables. This function would not actually return a value, but would only perform an operation and send data to the video card.

Most functions that you will encounter in math will be labeled with single letters, such as f, g, or h. Functions differ slightly from expressions. A *mathematical expression* is simply a sequence of operators and operands without the use of the equal sign.

Examples of expressions include: $3 + 7$ and $3x^2 + 20x$. A function usually includes the equals sign "=" with assignment of the expression to a letter or word that identifies the function. A function in the form f(x) = y is read "f of x equals y." f(x) will provide the value of function f at x. Functions may also be scripted as $f : X \rightarrow Y$, which is equivalent to "f maps X onto Y."

The set of all possible numbers that can enter a function without generating an error within the function compose the *domain*. The set of all output values from the function, using the numbers in the domain, create the *range* of the function. In other words, the domain contains all valid x-values, and the range has all possible y-values. Typically, the input variable x is referred to as the *independent variable*, since the variable is free to be any value within its domain. The output variable y is called the *dependent variable*, since it depends on the value of x.

Example
Find the domain and range for the following functions:

a. $f(x) = 6x - 2$

b. $w(x) = \dfrac{5x^2}{x^2 - 100}$

c. $z(x) = x^3$, for x > 0

d. {(9, 18), (8, 25), (-2, 12), (0, 7), (-26, 7)}

Solutions:
a. Domain = all reals,   Range = all reals

b.

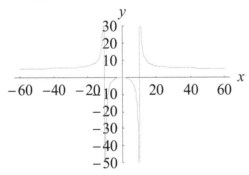

The function will fail when the denominator equals zero. The denominator will equal zero when x = 10 or x = -10. Therefore, the domain = all reals except 10 and -10. From the graph above, you can see that the function runs to positive and negative infinity around $x = \pm 10$. Determining the range requires a bit more work. While the graph does extend to $\pm \infty$ in the vertical direction, the plot

---

seems to have a gap in the y-interval (0, 5). Let's test the function in the three sub-intervals for x.

$w(-100) = 5.050505$
$w(0) = 0$
$w(100) = 5.050505$

The range for the central parabola is $(-\infty, 0]$. In the two outer wings, the range is $(5, \infty)$. Combining these ranges produces the final range for function w:
$\{(5, \infty), (-\infty, 0]\}$.

c. Domain = all reals greater than zero,   Range = all reals greater than zero

d. This relation has domain = {-26, -2, 0, 8, 9} and range = {7, 12, 18, 25}

In mathematics, a function must return exactly one value for each input value. That is, if you provide the value '5' to a function, it cannot return "10" in some cases and "20" in other instances. The *vertical line test* can determine whether a graphed equation is truly a function. If any vertical line crosses the graph in more than one location, the equation is not a function. That is, for a graph to be a function, every possible vertical line can intersect the graph no more than once.

Example
a. A graph that fails the vertical line test is the circle below:

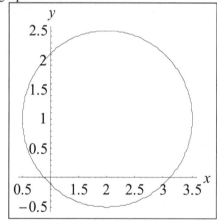

b. A graph that qualifies as a function is displayed here:

$$f(x)= (0.4\,x^3 + 1.2\,x^2 - x)$$

A function can be discrete or continuous. A *discrete function* has a domain with values that are never adjacent. The domain for a discrete function could still hold an infinite number of values. For instance, the domain could be the set of all positive integers. However, any finite interval cannot contain an infinite variety of input values. That is, a function is discrete iff there exists a constant $C > 0$ such that $|x_1 - x_2| > C$ $\forall$ $x_1, x_2 \in$ Domain. If you plot a discrete function, you would need to plot each point individually. You could not connect two points of the function with a line.

An example of a discrete function in automobile insurance is:

Number of speeding tickets (X)	Expected annual claims (Y)
0	$500
1	$760
2	$1,400
3	$2,950
4	$1,800

A *continuous function* has a domain that includes at least one continuous interval of real numbers. The domain for a continuous function has infinitely many values. Several examples of continuous functions include: $f(x) = 5x^3 + 2x + 50$, $g(x) = 7x + 8$, and $h(x) = 6$. These functions have a domain equal to the set of all reals.

Two broad categories of functions are the algebraic functions and transcendental functions. An *algebraic function* contains solely algebraic operations. An algebraic function may feature roots, polynomials, and exponents. *Transcendental functions* are those that include operations other than algebra, such as logarithms and trigonometric expressions.

Roots

A *root* of a function f(x) is an x-value that, when plugged into the function, produces zero. In other words, the roots are the x-intercepts. You can find the roots by solving for the x-value(s) that fit the equation $f(x) = 0$. A function can have any quantity of roots. Some functions have no roots, while others have imaginary roots (this topic will be discussed later).

Interval Notation

The endpoints of an interval can be designated with parentheses or square brackets. A square bracket signifies inclusion, while a parenthesis means exclusion.

> ") " = is less than
> " (" = is greater than
> "] " = is less than or equal to
> " [" = is greater than or equal to

Example
    a. (3, 5) → The interval of all real numbers between 3 and 5, not including the endpoints.
    b. [4, 10] → The interval from 4 to 10, including the endpoints
    c. (-2, 8] → The interval from -2 to 8, excluding -2 but including 8
    d. $(-\infty, \infty)$ → The interval of all real numbers

Piecewise Functions

A *piecewise function* has a different expression assigned to the function name depending on the value of the independent variable. An example of a piecewise function and its graph are shown below:

$$f(x) = \begin{cases} 0.3x^2 + 2x + 1, & \text{if } x \geq 2 \\ \sqrt{x}, & \text{if } x < 2 \end{cases}$$

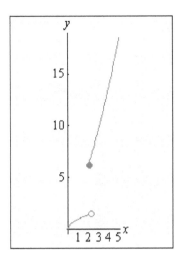

In the above graph, notice that the leftmost endpoint of ($0.3x^2 + 2x + 1$) is solid black, while the rightmost endpoint of $\sqrt{x}$ is an empty circle. The filled circle means the function includes the endpoint, and the empty circle signifies that the function runs up to but does not include the endpoint.

Movement of Functions

A function can have one of three states between two x-values. The function can be increasing, decreasing, or flat. You can describe a function over its entire domain or a subset of the domain with four possible descriptors:

A function f is *strictly increasing* iff $x_1 < x_2$ and $f(x_1) < f(x_2)$.

A function f is *strictly decreasing* iff $x_1 < x_2$ and $f(x_1) > f(x_2)$.

A function f is *nondecreasing* iff $x_1 < x_2$ and $f(x_1) \le f(x_2)$. The function is either increasing or horizontally level but never falling.

A function f is *nonincreasing* iff $x_1 < x_2$ and $f(x_1) \ge f(x_2)$. The function is either decreasing or horizontally level but never rising.

Section 1-10 One-To-One Functions

A *one-to-one function* generates a unique output value for each input value. That is, the output values are never repeated. You can invert a one-to-one function and obtain a new function. A function is 1-1 if it passes the horizontal line test. If any horizontal line intersects the graph in more than one location, then the function is not 1-1 and cannot be inverted.

Example
Suppose an expression has the following input and output values. Is the expression a function? Is it a 1-1 function?

x	f(x)
0	8
1	2
2	-4
3	11
4	2

Solution:
Each input value for x has only one associated output value. Therefore, f is a function. However, since the output value of '2' repeats twice for different input values, the function is not 1-1.

Example
Are the following functions 1-1?

    a. $f(x) = \dfrac{4}{x^2}$

    b. $g(x) = 2x^3 - 3x + 1.5$

Solutions:
    a.

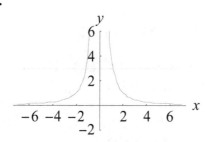

    This function fails the horizontal line test many times, so f(x) is not 1-1.

    b.

Function g also fails the horizontal line test innumerably. Therefore, g(x) is not 1-1.

Section 1-11 Polynomials

Polynomials are a special class of functions. A polynomial is in the format: $f(x) = c_0 + c_1 x^1 + c_2 x^2 + c_3 x^3 + ... + c_n x^n$, where n is an integer. The polynomial is the sum of a variety of terms, each consisting of a coefficient c_i that is multiplied by x^i. Some of the c_i's could be zero or one, simplifying the function. The highest power within the function is the *degree* of the polynomial. A polynomial of n degrees has n roots. Typically, each of the exponents is a positive integer. The domain for all polynomials is the set of all real numbers.

The trivial polynomial is created when the degree of the function is zero. That is, the polynomial of degree 0 is $f(x) = c_0$. The graph is a horizontal line of height c_0.

Another simple polynomial is a line. Recall that a line has the equation $y = mx + b$, where m is slope and b is the y-intercept. The general line is a first degree polynomial, since it contains the independent variable raised to the power of 1. The slope of a line is simply rise over run:

$$m = \frac{y_2 - y_1}{x_2 - x_1} = \frac{\Delta y}{\Delta x}$$

Y-Intercept Formula for a Line
$y = mx + b$

If you have two points within a line, you can find the equation for the line by first calculating the slope (m) between the two points. Then, place the (x, y) values from one of the points, along with the slope, in the y-intercept formula and solve for b.

Example
What is the equation for a line that includes points (3, 8) and (7, 2)?

Solution
$$m = \frac{2-8}{7-3} = \frac{-6}{4} = -1.5$$

$$y = mx + b \quad \rightarrow \quad 8 = -1.5*3 + b \quad \rightarrow \quad b = 12.5$$

$$y = -1.5x + 12.5$$

The point-slope formula for a line is useful when you have one point (x_1, y_1) on the line and the slope. Place the values of x_1, y_1, and m in the formula below, and simplify to transform the equation into the y-intercept format.

Point-Slope Formula for a Line
$$y - y_1 = m(x - x_1)$$

Example
Find the formula for a line that includes the point (-5, 1) and has slope 2.

Solution:
$$y - 1 = 2(x + 5)$$
$$y - 1 = 2x + 10$$
$$y = 2x + 11$$

Second degree polynomials are called *quadratics* or parabolas. A quadratic has the syntax $f(x) = ax^2 + bx + c$. Parabolas are perfectly symmetric vertical-wise. The coefficient 'a' determines how the parabola opens. If 'a' is positive, then the parabola opens upwards. If 'a' is negative, the parabola opens downwards. The absolute value of 'a' determines how steep the graph opens. If 'a' is relatively small, such as 0.25, the parabola will open very gradually. On the other hand, if 'a' is large, such as 8, the parabola will be very steep. The value 'c' is the y-intercept for the quadratic. When x = 0, the function will equal c.

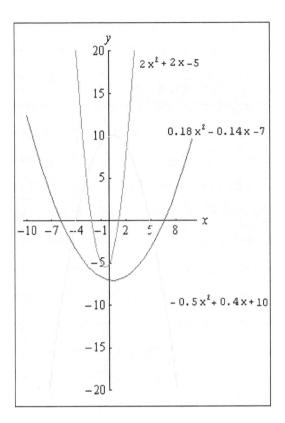

The quadratic formula is used to find the roots of a parabola. That is, the formula returns the x-values where the parabola crosses the x-axis.

Quadratic Formula: $\quad x = \dfrac{-b \pm \sqrt{b^2 - 4ac}}{2a}$

Example

Find the x-intercepts for $f(x) = 1.5x^2 - 4x + 1$

Solution:
a = 1.5, b = –4, c = 1

$$x = \frac{4 \pm \sqrt{(-4)^2 - 4 * 1.5 * 1}}{2 * 1.5} = \frac{4 \pm \sqrt{16 - 6}}{3} = \frac{4 \pm \sqrt{10}}{3}$$

$x \approx 2.38743 \quad$ and $\quad x \approx 0.27924$

Example

Suppose a parabola crosses through the points (-6, -7), (-9, 11.75), and (2, 9). What is the equation of the parabola?

Solution:

Each of the given points must satisfy the equation $ax^2 + bx + c$. Since we have three unknown—a, b, and c, we need the three points to find the final parabola equation. The three points, when placed in the basic parabola equation, create a system of three equations:

$$\begin{cases} -7 = a(-6)^2 + b(-6) + c \\ 11.75 = a(-9)^2 + b(-9) + c \\ 9 = a(2)^2 + b(2) + c \end{cases}$$

We need to solve for a, b, and c.

$$\begin{cases} -7 = 36a - 6b + c \\ 11.75 = 81a - 9b + c \\ 9 = 4a + 2b + c \end{cases}$$

Subtract the first equation from the second equation:

$$11.75 = 81a - 9b + c$$
$$- \quad -7 = 36a - 6b + c$$
$$\overline{18.75 = 45a - 3b}$$

Subtract the second equation from the third equation:

$$9 = 4a + 2b + c$$
$$- \quad 11.75 = 81a - 9b + c$$
$$\overline{-2.75 = -77a + 11b}$$

We have a new system featuring variables a and b:

$$\begin{cases} 18.75 = 45a - 3b \\ -2.75 = -77a + 11b \end{cases}$$

Solve for b in the first equation:

$$18.75 - 45a = -3b \quad \rightarrow \quad b = \frac{18.75 - 45a}{-3} \quad \rightarrow \quad b = -6.25 + 15a$$

Place the expression for b in the second equation:

$$-2.75 = -77a + 11(-6.25 + 15a)$$
$$-2.75 = -77a - 68.75 + 165a$$
$$66 = 88a \quad \rightarrow \quad a = 0.75$$

Place the value for a into the first equation, and solve for b:

$18.75 = 45 * 0.75 - 3b$

$18.75 = 33.75 - 3b$

$-15 = -3b \quad \rightarrow \quad b = 5$

Put the values of a and b into the very first equation, and solve for c:

$-7 = 36 * 0.75 - 6 * 5 + c$

$-7 = 27 - 30 + c$

$-4 = c$

The final quadratic equation is $f(x) = 0.75x^2 + 5x - 4$

The *cubic* function is a third degree polynomial. The usual form for this function is $f(x) = ax^3 + bx^2 + cx + d$. The value 'a' controls which arm of the cubic is up and which is down, along with the vertical sheer. Lower values of 'a' in absolute value make the graph open more gradually. When 'a' is positive, the left arm is pointing down and the right arm is up. The opposite is true if 'a' is negative. The coefficients 'b' and 'c' influence the curvature. Last of all, 'd' governs the vertical shift.

To summarize,

        degree 0 = horizontal line

        degree 1 = line

        degree 2 = quadratic

        degree 3 = cubic

The plot below shows examples of polynomials with degrees zero through three.

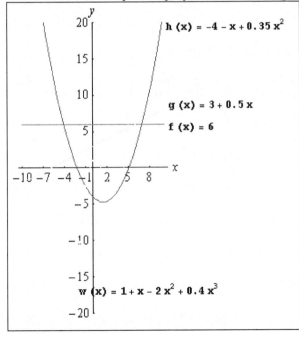

Again consider a general polynomial of the syntax
$f(x) = c_0 + c_1 x^1 + c_2 x^2 + c_3 x^3 + ... + c_n x^n$. Several general observations can be made about the appearance of the graph based on the coefficient c_n and the value n (the degree of the polynomial). First, if c_n is positive, then the right arm of the function curves upwards to positive infinity. On the other hand, if the coefficient is negative, then the right arm curves downwards to negative infinity. An even value for n means that both arms will be up or down. When n is odd, one arm will curve up while the other curves down.

Rational Functions

A *rational function* is the quotient of two polynomials. The polynomials could be of any degree with any quantity of terms. Rational functions are used extensively in limit analysis and integrals.

Example
Examples of rational functions:

    a. $f(x) = \dfrac{27x^3 + 6x^2 + 40x}{97x^6 + 42x^4 + 3x}$

    b. $f(x) = \dfrac{4x^3 + 70}{65x^{10} + 4x^8 + 6}$

Section 1-12 Even and Odd Functions

An *even function* is symmetric about the y-axis. You can fold the graph of the function along the y-axis, and the right side of the graph will coincide perfectly with the left side. Function f is even iff $f(x) = f(-x)$ for all x in the domain of f.

Example
A parabola centered on the y-axis is a common example of an even function. Consider the quadratic $f(x) = 0.4x^2 + 3$.

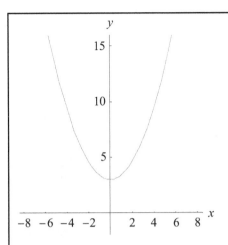

To prove f is an even function, we must show that in general, $f(x) = f(-x)$.
$$f(-x) = 0.4(-x)^2 + 3 = 0.4x^2 + 3 = f(x)$$
$$f(-x) = f(x)$$
∴ f is even

An *odd function* is symmetric about the origin. You could rotate the graph 180 degrees, and obtain the same image. In mathematical terms, a function is odd iff $f(-x) = -f(x)$ for all x in the domain of f.

Example
The cubic function $f(x) = x^3$ is odd.

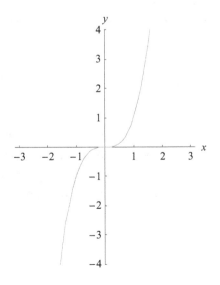

Proof:

$$f(-x) = (-x)^3 = -\left(x^3\right)$$
$$-f(x) = -\left(x^3\right)$$
$$f(-x) = -f(x)$$
$\therefore$ f is odd

Example
Are the following functions even, odd, or neither?

    a. $f(x) = 7x^2 + 18x$

    b. $g(x) = 24x^7 - 5x^3 + 4x$

    c. $h(x) = 16x^6 + 14x^2$

Solutions:

    a. $f(-x) = 7(-x)^2 + 18(-x) = 7x^2 - 18x$

        $f(-x) \neq f(x)$ and $f(-x) \neq -f(x)$

        $\therefore$ f is not even and f is not odd

    b. $g(-x) = 24(-x)^7 - 5(-x)^3 + 4(-x) = 24(-(x^7)) - 5(-(x^3)) - 4x$

           $= -24x^7 + 5x^3 - 4x = -g(x)$

        $g(-x) = -g(x)$

        $\therefore$ g is odd

    c. $h(-x) = 16(-x)^6 + 14(-x)^2 = 16x^6 + 14x^2 = h(x)$

        $h(-x) = h(x)$

        $\therefore$ h is even

The degree of a single-term polynomial (such as $f(x) = ax^n$) reveals whether the function is even or odd. If the degree is an even integer, then the polynomial is even. If the degree is an odd number, then the polynomial is odd.

The powers within a multi-term polynomial affect the function's even or odd nature. If a polynomial has terms with only odd exponents, such as x^1, x^3, x^5, etc., then the function is odd. Similarly, if the polynomial has only even exponents, such as x^2, x^4, and x^6, then the equation is even. If the polynomial has a mix of even and odd exponents, then the function will be neither even nor odd.

Section 1-13 Continuity

In simple terms, a function is continuous between two x-values in its domain if you can graph the function between these two points without lifting a pencil. More mathematically, a function f(x) is *continuous* at x = a iff $\lim\limits_{x \to a} f(x) = f(a)$. That is, the limit of f(x) as x approaches 'a' must exist and be finite. In addition, the function must be defined at 'a' with 'a' in the function's domain. The function must equal its limit at x = a.

An illustration of a continuous function is:

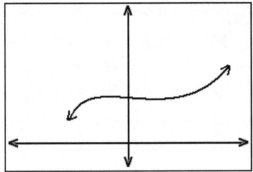

Common examples of continuous functions for all values in their domains (the set of all reals): polynomials, absolute value function (i.e., $f(x) = |x|$), and cos(x) and sin(x). The function f(x) is continuous over the interval (a, b) if f is continuous $\forall \; x \in (a,b)$.

Two types of discontinuities exist for functions. With *removable discontinuity*, the gap can be removed by simply adding a single point. A function with a removable discontinuity will appear quite similar to a fully continuous function except for an empty circle at the discontinuity:

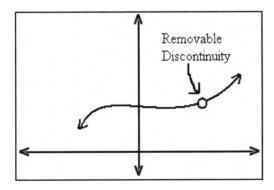

Removable Discontinuity

A *jump or essential discontinuity* cannot be easily repaired. If function f exhibits an essential discontinuity at x = a, then $\lim\limits_{x \to a} f(x)$ does not exist. In other words, the limit of the function at the discontinuity is different from the right and left.

Example

Find the discontinuities in this function: $f(x) = \dfrac{10}{x^4 - 81}$

Solution:
The plot of the function is

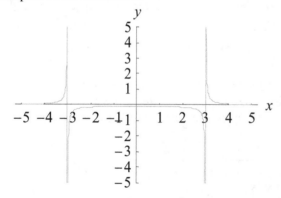

The function seems to have discontinuities around $x = \pm 3$. We can verify these discontinuities by examining the denominator of the function. The function is undefined when the denominator is zero. We need to solve the succeeding equation to find the true gaps:

$$x^4 - 81 = 0$$
$$x^4 = 81$$
$$x = \sqrt[4]{81} = \pm 3$$

The function has essential discontinuities (actually vertical asymptotes) at $x = \pm 3$.

Example

Find the discontinuities in: $f(x) = \dfrac{\sin(x)^2}{\sin(x)}$

Solution:

While the function could be reduced to just $f(x) = \sin(x)$, the original function still had a sine operator in the denominator and thus possibilities for divide-by-zero errors. Recall that $\sin(x) = 0$ when $x = \pi * n$ for all integers n. Correspondingly, function f has jump discontinuities for $x = \pi * n$.

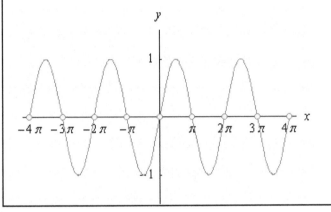

Example

For which values of $x \in R$ is the following function discontinuous?:

$$f(x) = \begin{cases} \sin(x), & \text{if } x \le 0 \\[2mm] \dfrac{5x - 20}{x^2 - 16}, & \text{if } 0 < x < 10 \\[2mm] \dfrac{1}{7}x - \dfrac{15}{14}, & \text{if } x \ge 10 \end{cases}$$

Solution:

The first function, sin(x), is continuous for all real numbers, so f(x) is continuous for x<0.

A split then occurs between the sub-functions at $x = 0$. It is true that f is defined at $x = 0$, since $f(0) = \sin(0) = 0$. However, the limit of f(x) at $x = 0$ does not exist:

$$\lim_{x \to 0^-} f(x) = \lim_{x \to 0^-} \sin(x) = \sin(0) = 0$$

$$\lim_{x \to 0^+} f(x) = \lim_{x \to 0^+} \left(\frac{5x - 20}{x^2 - 16} \right) = \frac{5*0 - 20}{0^2 - 16} = \frac{-20}{-16} = 5/4$$

$$\lim_{x \to 0^-} f(x) \neq \lim_{x \to 0^+} f(x)$$

$$\therefore \lim_{x \to 0} f(x) \quad \text{d.n.e.}$$

Since lim f(x) as $x \to 0$ is non-existent, f(x) has a discontinuity at x = 0.

The second function can be written $\frac{5x - 20}{(x - 4)(x + 4)} = \frac{5(x - 4)}{(x - 4)(x + 4)}$.

The function will produce an error for x = 4 and x = -4. Since x = -4 belongs in the domain of sin(x), we just need to examine the rational function with x = 4.

$$f(4) = \frac{5*4 - 20}{4^2 - 16} = \frac{20 - 20}{0} = \text{undefined}$$

$$\lim_{x \to 4} \left(\frac{5x - 20}{x^2 - 16} \right) = \lim_{x \to 4} \left(\frac{5(x - 4)}{(x - 4)(x + 4)} \right) = \lim_{x \to 4} \left(\frac{5}{(x + 4)} \right) = 5/8$$

$$\lim_{x \to 4} f(x) = 5/8 \text{, but f(4) = undefined.}$$

∴ f is discontinuous at x = 4.

The next possible discontinuity occurs around x = 10 when the functions switch again.

$$f(10) = \frac{1}{7} * 10 - \frac{15}{14} = 5/14 \text{ ; f is defined at x = 10}$$

$$\lim_{x \to 10^-} f(x) = \lim_{x \to 10^-} \left(\frac{5x - 20}{x^2 - 16} \right) = \left(\frac{5*10 - 20}{10^2 - 16} \right) = 5/14$$

$$\lim_{x \to 10^+} f(x) = \lim_{x \to 10^+} \left(\frac{1}{7}x - \frac{15}{14} \right) = \frac{1}{7} * 10 - \frac{15}{14} = 5/14$$

$$\lim_{x \to 10^-} f(x) = \lim_{x \to 10^+} f(x) = 5/14$$

$$\therefore \lim_{x \to 10} f(x) = 5/14$$

f(10) is defined and the limit exists.
∴ f is continuous at x = 10.

To summarize, discontinuities exist at x = 0 and x = 4.

The Intermediate Value Theorem describes the nature of continuous functions between two points. Consider a function that is continuous between points (a, y_1) and (b, y_2). Within the x-interval (a, b), the function must span every possible y-value between y_1 and y_2. Some of the y-values in the interval (y_1, y_2) might be repeated, but every value in that interval must be covered by the function. The continuous line below shows the theorem in action. When traveling from (-4, -1.8) to (4, 3.8), you will cross all the intermediate y-values, including y = 0, y =1, and y = 2. You can trace the function without lifting a pencil.

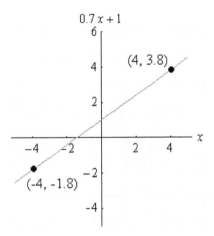

Intermediate Value Theorem
Suppose function f is continuous over the interval [a, b], and y is any value between f(a) and f(b). Then, a value c exists in interval (a, b) with f(c) = y.

Section 1-14 Composite Functions

A *composite function* is a single function that contains at least one other nested function. The symbol for the composition of two functions is a small circle, ∘ . The expression $f \circ g$ reads "f composed with g." Another expression for the composition of two functions f and g is $f(g(x))$, which reads "f of g of x." In other words, the output

---

from function g becomes the input for function f. You are simply providing the result of g(x) as the parameter for function f.

Example

Consider the function $h(x) = \ln(x^3)$. This function appears to have two nested sub-functions. x^3 could be a function by itself, and $\ln(x)$ might be another sub-function. The cubic expression is the input to the natural log. If we let $g(x) = x^3$ and $f(x) = \ln(x)$, then the composition of the two functions is $f(g(x)) = \ln(g(x)) = \ln(x^3)$, which also equals the original function h. In summary, h(x) is the composite of two simpler functions f and g.

Example

You are given that $f(x) = 14x - 8$ and $g(x) = x^4$. Find...
a. Function f composed with g
b. Function g composed with f

Solutions:
a. $f(g(x)) = 14 * g(x) - 8 = 14x^4 - 8$

*Note that all instances of x within f(x) are replaced with the new input, which is function g(x).

b. $g(f(x)) = (14x - 8)^4$

*All instances of x in g(x) are replaced with function f(x).

*Note also that $f(g(x)) \neq g(f(x))$.

Example

Consider the function $h(x) = e^{70x^4 + 8x^2 + 52}$

Function h is actually the composition of two functions:

$f(x) = e^x$
$g(x) = 70x^4 + 8x^2 + 52$

If function g is used as the input for function f, the result is function h. That is, $h = f \circ g$.

Other Combinations of Functions
(1.) $(f + g)(x) = f(x) + g(x)$

(2.) $(f-g)(x) = f(x) - g(x)$

(3.) $(f*g)(x) = f(x)*g(x)$

(4.) $\left(\dfrac{f}{g}\right)(x) = \dfrac{f(x)}{g(x)}$

Example

You are given that $f(x) = 9x^2 + 10x + 11$ and $g(x) = 8x^5$. Find the following:

a. $(f+g)(x)$ **b.** $(f-g)(x)$ **c.** $(f*g)(x)$ **d.** $\left(\dfrac{f}{g}\right)(x)$

Solutions:

a. $8x^5 + 9x^2 + 10x + 11$ **b.** $9x^2 + 10x + 11 - 8x^5$ **c.** $72x^7 + 80x^6 + 88x^5$

d. $\dfrac{9x^2 + 10x + 11}{8x^5} = \dfrac{9}{8}x^{-3} + \dfrac{10}{8}x^{-4} + \dfrac{11}{8}x^{-5} = \dfrac{9}{8x^3} + \dfrac{10}{8x^4} + \dfrac{11}{8x^5}$

Section 1-15 Inverting Functions

The *inverse* of function f(x) is represented as $f^{-1}(x)$, with the -1 after and above the function name. A common misconception is that the inverse is obtained by simply raising the function to the power of -1. That is, $f^{-1}(x) \neq \dfrac{1}{f(x)}$. Instead, the inverse is obtained by essentially switching the dependent and independent variables. However, the inverted function will still be defined in terms of the original independent variable. Another way of creating the inverse of a function is to reflect it over the line y = x.

To invert a function, it must be a 1-1 function. In other words, the original function must pass the horizontal line test in order for its inverse to be a function. The horizontal line test for the initial function becomes the vertical line test for the inverse. Consider a simple parabola $0.35x^2 + 4$. This quadratic fails the horizontal line test at all points except for its vertex.

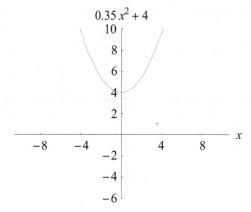

To invert the function graphically, we need to reflect it over y = x. The inverse would appear as:

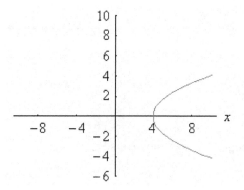

This graph fails the vertical line test and is thus not a function. Again, since the original function failed the horizontal line test, the inverse failed its vertical line test.

Example
You are given the original function $y = 4x + 6$. Find the inverse.

Solution:
In the original equation, x is the independent variable and y is the dependent variable. These two variables must be switched, so that y now becomes the independent variable. We must solve for x.

$$y = 4x + 6$$
$$y - 6 = 4x$$
$$x = \frac{y - 6}{4} = 0.25y - 1.5$$

The inverse is the line $y = 0.25x - 1.5$. After solving for the original independent variable, we must flip the x and y.

Suppose function f has domain X and range Y. The inverse of f will have domain Y and range X. If the point (a, b) is in the original function, the point (b, a) is in the inverse function. If f was not 1-1, the domain (set Y) for f^{-1} would contain at least one repeated input value that would produce multiple output values, and thus f^{-1} would fail to be a function.

The inverse of f applied with the original f equals the independent variable, and the original f applied with the inverse of f produces x:

$$f^{-1}(f(x)) = x \quad \text{and} \quad f(f^{-1}(x)) = x$$

Another way of illustrating the canceling effect of f and its inverse applied to each other is to use composite notation:

$$f \circ f^{-1} = x = f^{-1} \circ f$$

Steps for inverting the function f(x):
  (1.) Substitute f(x) with the variable 'y.'
  (2.) Solve for x in terms of y.
  (3.) Replace x with $f^{-1}(x)$, and replace y with x.

Example
Invert the following functions:
  a. $f(x) = 8x^3$
  b. $g(x) = \sin(3x)$
  c. $h(x) = \dfrac{\sqrt{x+50}}{4}$
  d. $m(x) = \dfrac{5}{x^2} - 4$

Solutions:
  a. $y = 8x^3$

  $\dfrac{y}{8} = x^3$

  $\sqrt[3]{\dfrac{y}{8}} = x$

$$f^{-1}(x) = \sqrt[3]{\frac{x}{8}}$$

b. $y = \sin(3x)$

$\sin^{-1}(y) = 3x$

$$x = \frac{\sin^{-1}(y)}{3} \quad \rightarrow \quad f^{-1}(x) = \frac{\sin^{-1}(x)}{3}$$

c. $y = \frac{\sqrt{x+50}}{4} \quad \rightarrow \quad 4y = \sqrt{x+50} \quad \rightarrow \quad (4y)^2 = x + 50$

$16y^2 - 50 = x \quad \rightarrow \quad f^{-1}(x) = 16x^2 - 50$

d. $y = \frac{5}{x^2} - 4$

$$y + 4 = \frac{5}{x^2} \quad \rightarrow \quad \frac{1}{y+4} = \frac{x^2}{5} \quad \rightarrow \quad x^2 = \frac{5}{y+4} \quad \rightarrow \quad x = \sqrt{\frac{5}{y+4}}$$

$$f^{-1}(x) = \sqrt{\frac{5}{x+4}}$$

Example

Prove that $f^{-1}(x) = \sqrt{3{,}375x^3 - 8}$ is an inverse of function f, which is $f(x) = \dfrac{\sqrt[3]{8+x^2}}{15}$ for x > 0.

Solution:

$$f(f^{-1}(x)) = \frac{\sqrt[3]{8 + \left(f^{-1}(x)\right)^2}}{15} = \frac{\sqrt[3]{8 + \left(\sqrt{3{,}375x^3 - 8}\right)^2}}{15} = \frac{\sqrt[3]{8 + 3{,}375x^3 - 8}}{15}$$

$$= \frac{\sqrt[3]{3{,}375x^3}}{15} = \frac{15x}{15} = x$$

$$f^{-1}(f(x)) = \sqrt{3{,}375(f(x))^3 - 8} = \sqrt{3{,}375\left(\frac{\sqrt[3]{8+x^2}}{15}\right)^3 - 8}$$

$$= \sqrt{3{,}375\left(\frac{8+x^2}{3{,}375}\right) - 8} = \sqrt{8 + x^2 - 8} = \sqrt{x^2} = x$$

$f(f^{-1}(x)) = f^{-1}(f(x)) = x$

∴ $f^{-1}(x)$ is an inverse of f(x).

If you need to prove that two functions are inverses of each other, you must show that $f(f^{-1}(x)) = x$ and $f^{-1}(f(x)) = x$. Rather than using an actual value for x, leave the independent variable in its abstract form.

Section 1-16 Complex Numbers

A plane of theoretical existence lies outside the realm of real numbers. Imaginary numbers are the complements of real numbers. Recall that a polynomial of degree n has exactly n roots. Consider the quadratic function graphed below:

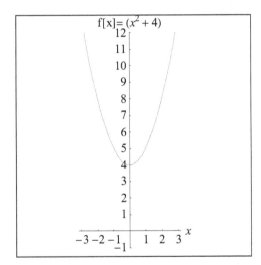

The parabola should have two roots, but it never intersects the x-axis. The two roots still exist but must be imaginary.

Solving for the roots yields:
$$x^2 + 4 = 0 \quad \rightarrow \quad x^2 = -4$$

No known real numbers when squared produce -4. In fact, attempting to compute $\sqrt{-4}$ will produce an error on most calculators. The square root of a negative number can be calculated with imaginary numbers, nonetheless.

Imaginary numbers, also known as complex numbers, contain the letter 'i,' which equals the square root of negative 1. The first few powers of i are:

$$i = \sqrt{-1}$$
$$i^2 = -1$$
$$i^3 = i^2 * i = -\sqrt{-1} = -i$$
$$i^4 = 1$$

The above pattern repeats forever, with $i^5 = \sqrt{-1}$, $i^6 = -1$, and so on.

Back to the example with the quadratic, the roots become $\pm\sqrt{-4} = \pm\sqrt{-1} * \sqrt{4} = \pm i\sqrt{4} = \pm 2i$. To find these solutions, we first need to break the square root of the negative number into two other square roots: one being $\sqrt{-1}$ and the other is the square root of the positive version of the original number. The negative component is essentially pulled outside the root with the help of $\sqrt{-1}$. Replace the square root of -1 with i. In the end, the quadratic has two imaginary roots at $x = \pm 2i$. Some of the roots might be real, while others are imaginary.

Example
Write the following numbers in complex form:

a. $\sqrt{-80}$ **b.** $\sqrt{-16}$ **c.** $5 + \sqrt{-144}$

Solutions:

a. $\sqrt{-1} * \sqrt{80} = i\sqrt{80}$ **b.** $4i$ **c.** $5 + 12i$

Example
Calculate i^{35}

Solution:
$$i^{35} = \left(i^4\right)^8 * i^3 = 1^8 * (-i) = -i$$

Complex numbers can be represented in a variety of formats. The formats that will be covered below include the traditional "rectangular" format and polar form. Another syntax for complex values—the Euclidean form—is usually not featured on the actuary tests and thus is excluded from this manual.

Complex-Rectangular Syntax

A complex number in rectangular form has the syntax $z = a + bi$. 'a' is the *real part* of z; Re(z) = a. 'b' is the *imaginary part* of z; Im(z) = b. Nonetheless, 'a' and 'b' are still real numbers. Complex numbers may be graphed on a 2D plot. The horizontal x-axis becomes the *real axis*. The vertical y-axis corresponds to the *imaginary axis*. The 2D point (x, y) corresponds to point (a, b). The axes and several plotted points appear below:

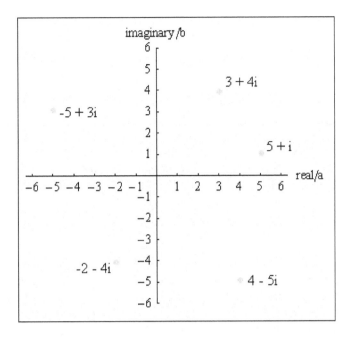

The mathematical operations involving complex numbers are very similar to the operations with real numbers. The operations break apart the complex numbers into their constituents. A complex number is not a rigid object; the real and imaginary parts may be pulled off a complex number and dealt with separately. Additionally, the 'i' is treated like a variable.

Basic Mathematical Operations with Complex Numbers

(1.) Addition: $(a + bi) + (c + di) = (a + c) + (b + d)i$

(2.) Subtraction: $(a + bi) - (c + di) = (a - c) + (b - d)i$

(3.) Multiplication: $(a + bi) * (c + di) = ac + adi + bci + bdi^2$
$$= (ac - bd) + (ad + bc)i$$

(4.) Division: $\dfrac{(a + bi)}{(c + di)} = \dfrac{(a + bi)}{(c + di)} * \dfrac{(c - di)}{(c - di)}$

When adding and subtracting complex numbers, you must add or subtract like terms. All the real parts are added together, and all the imaginary parts are added separately. The multiplication of complex numbers is essentially distribution. Division is the most difficult operation. You need to find the complex conjugate of the denominator. If the denominator is $z = c + di$, then the complex conjugate is $\bar{z} = c - di$. Note that when finding the complex conjugate, the real part is not changed but the imaginary part is negated. Place a bar over the 'z' to designate a complex conjugate. You then multiply the top and bottom by this conjugate. Finally, you need to perform complex multiplication on the numerator and denominator, simplifying the expression into one fraction.

Properties of Complex Conjugates

(1.) $\overline{c+d} = \overline{c} + \overline{d}$

(2.) $\overline{cd} = \overline{c} * \overline{d}$

(3.) $\overline{c^n} = (\overline{c})^n$

The *modulus* of a complex number is the distance from the origin to the number when graphed. The symbol for a modulus is two vertical bars. The modulus of complex number z is: $|z| = \sqrt{a^2 + b^2}$.

Complex-Polar Syntax

Polar, complex numbers are treated much like traditional polar values. Recall that a polar point has a radius and angle theta. These polar coordinates can be plotted on a regular 2D plane, and they may be converted to rectangular coordinates and back to polar form. Complex numbers in polar syntax also utilize an angle and radius. Every rectangular, complex number has an associated polar point, so you can plot complex numbers in both formats on the same plane. The equations for converting between polar and rectangular coordinates for complex numbers are identical to the formulas for real numbers. A complex number in polar form is $z = r(\cos(\theta) + i * \sin(\theta))$.

Example

Find the polar coordinates of $z = 8 - 5i$.

Solution:

In rectangular form, this complex number corresponds to point (8, -5), which is in the fourth quadrant.

$$r = \sqrt{8^2 + (-5)^2} = \sqrt{89}$$

$$\theta = \tan^{-1}\left(\frac{b}{a}\right) = \tan^{-1}\left(\frac{-5}{8}\right) = -0.5586$$

$(8, -5) \rightarrow (\sqrt{89}, -0.5586) \quad \rightarrow \quad z = \sqrt{89}(\cos(-0.5586) + i * \sin(-0.5586))$

*Simplifying the above expression for z would result in the original rectangular syntax.

Example

You are given the point $(\sqrt{74}, 110°)$. Find $z = a + bi$.

Solution:

$$a = r * \cos(\theta) = \sqrt{74} * \cos(110°) \approx -2.94217$$
$$b = r * \sin(\theta) = \sqrt{74} * \sin(110°) \approx 8.08354$$

$$z = -2.94217 + 8.08354i$$

Multiplying Complex Numbers in Polar Form
$$r_1(\cos(\theta_1) + i * \sin(\theta_1)) * r_2(\cos(\theta_2) + i * \sin(\theta_2))$$
$$\downarrow$$
$$r_1 r_2(\cos(\theta_1 + \theta_2) + i * \sin(\theta_1 + \theta_2))$$

AND

$$(r_1, \theta_1) * (r_2, \theta_2) = (r_1 r_2, \theta_1 + \theta_2)$$

Dividing Complex Numbers in Polar Form
$$r_1(\cos(\theta_1) + i * \sin(\theta_1)) \div r_2(\cos(\theta_2) + i * \sin(\theta_2))$$
$$\downarrow$$
$$\left(\frac{r_1}{r_2}\right)(\cos(\theta_1 - \theta_2) + i * \sin(\theta_1 - \theta_2))$$

AND

$$(r_1, \theta_1) \div (r_2, \theta_2) = (r_1 / r_2, \theta_1 - \theta_2)$$

De Moivre, a mathematician living in France and England during the 17th and 18th centuries, created an equation for raising a complex number to a power. The theorem makes use of complex numbers in polar form. The theorem basically states that the point (r, θ) raised to the power of n is $(r^n, n\theta)$.

De Moivre's Theorem for Complex Numbers
   Let $z = r(\cos(\theta) + i * \sin(\theta))$. Then, $z^n = r^n(\cos(n\theta) + i * \sin(n\theta))$

Example
You are given $z = 3 + 7i$. Find z^5 in rectangular form.

Solution:
First, we need to convert from rectangular to polar.

$$r = \sqrt{3^2 + 7^2} = \sqrt{58}$$

$$\theta = \tan^{-1}\left(\frac{7}{3}\right) \approx 1.1659$$

$$z^5 = r^5(\cos(5\theta) + i*\sin(5\theta)) = \sqrt{58}^5(\cos(5*1.1659) + i*\sin(5*1.1659))$$
$$= 25,619.46073(\cos(5.8295) + i*\sin(5.8295))$$

Next, simplify the polar syntax into rectangular format.
$$z^5 = 23,027.74509 - 11,228.52279i$$

Complex Roots of Polynomials

As shown in the first example of this section, a polynomial of degree n can have a mix of real and complex roots. The polynomial will not necessarily cross the x-axis n times. In fact, the polynomial may never cross the horizontal axis. Imaginary roots always appear in conjugate pairs. That is, if $6i$ is a root, then $-6i$ is also a root. The number of complex roots must be an even value. On the other hand, the amount of real roots could be odd or even.

Example
Find all the roots for $f(x) = (x^4 - 121)(3x^2 - 13x + 14)$

Solution:
Expand the function as follows:
$$f(x) = (x^2 - 11)(x^2 + 11)*(3x - 7)(x - 2)$$

Find solution(s) for each set of parentheses.
$$x^2 - 11 = 0 \quad \rightarrow \quad x^2 = 11 \quad \rightarrow \quad x = \pm\sqrt{11}$$

$$x^2 + 11 = 0 \quad \rightarrow \quad x^2 = -11 \quad \rightarrow \quad x = \pm\sqrt{-11} = \pm i\sqrt{11}$$

$$3x - 7 = 0 \quad \rightarrow \quad x = 7/3$$

$$x - 2 = 0 \quad \rightarrow \quad x = 2$$

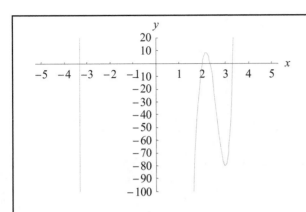

In the end, we have 6 roots for a sixth degree polynomial.

Section 1-17 Exponential Functions

Exponential functions take the form $f(x) = a^x$. 'a' must be a positive real number. The domain for an exponential function is the set of all reals, and the range is the set of all reals greater than zero. The base 'a' can fit in one of three classes of values. If 0<a<1, then f→∞ as x→−∞, and f→0 as x→∞. If a=1, then the graph is a straight horizontal line at y=1. If a>1, then f→0 as x→−∞, and f→∞ as x→∞.

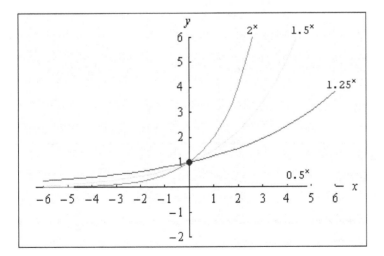

All exponential functions cross the point (0, 1), since $a^0 = 1 \; \forall$ a. Additionally, the x-axis is a horizontal asymptote for these functions.

The exponential function is perhaps most commonly used with a base equal to 'e' or roughly 2.71828. The function $f(x) = e^x$ is shown below:

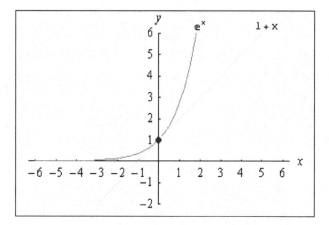

At (0, 1), the tangent line has a slope of precisely 1. Each base 'a' will have a unique tangent line at point (0, 1).

Exponential functions are utilized extensively in models of continuous change. The class of functions has applications in finance, such as computing the balance of an account that accrues interest continuously. Exponential equations are also used in half-life problems.

Example
A radioactive isotope has a half-life of 200 years. A sample of the isotope today has mass 50 grams. What is the sample's mass in 470 years?

Solution:
mass = m(t)
$m(t) =$ (starting amount) * (rate of change) ^ (t/amount of time for 1 cycle of change)
$m(t) = 50 * 0.5^{t/200}$
$m(470) = 50 * 0.5^{470/200} \approx 9.8073$ grams

Formula for continuous change: $a(t) = a_0 e^{rt}$
 *a(t) is the current amount at time t
 *a_0 is the starting amount at time t = 0
 *r is the rate of change per unit of time

Example
A banking client deposits $30,000 today in an account that earns 6% annual interest compounded continuously. What is the value of the account in 4.5 years?

Solution:
$a(4.5) = 30,000 * e^{0.06*4.5} \approx \$39,298.93$

Section 1-18 Logarithmic Functions

The equation $\log_b(x) = y$ reads "log base b of x equals y." The value 'b' is the base of the logarithm. 'x' is the input into the logarithm, and 'y' is the output. Shown below is a graph of several log functions with different bases. The domain for a logarithm is $(0, \infty)$ and the range is the set of all reals. Note that the functions are undefined for $x \leq 0$. Additionally, the y-axis is a vertical asymptote for these functions.

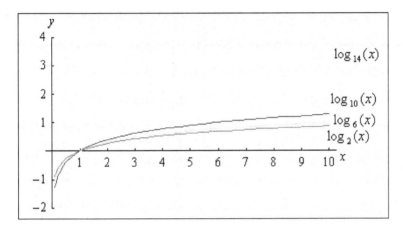

The functions approach positive infinity as x becomes very large. Lastly, all logs cross the point $(1, 0)$.

The concept of logarithms is based on the property below:

Fundamental Theorem of Logs
$\log_b(x) = y$ translates to $b^y = x$

Logarithms are closely tied to exponential functions. Assuming x>0, $\log_b(x)$ yields the exponent to which the base 'b' must be raised to finally produce x. A common saying to remember this theorem is "little to the big equals the middle." We take the little number (the base), raise it to the big number on the right side, and produce the middle value x.

Example
Compute $\log_2 256$.

Solution:
The problem asks you to find the exponent for the base 2 that will produce 256. 2 raised to what power will produce 256? 2 raised to the 7th power produces 128, and 2 raised to the 8th produces 256. So, the final answer is 8.

The logarithmic function and the exponential function are inverses of each other. Taking the logarithm of an exponential function yields the central input parameter. Likewise, using an exponential function as the outermost expression and placing the logarithm in the power position creates the innermost parameter.

Log Cancellation Equations

(1.) $\log_a(a^x) = x$

(2.) $a^{\log_a x} = x$

Natural Logarithm

When the logarithm has a base equal to e^1 (or 2.71828), a *natural logarithm* occurs. The natural logarithm is typically written as $\ln(x)$. Two properties of the natural log, which make use of the fact that the exponential and logarithmic functions are inverses of one another, are:

(1.) $\ln(e^x) = x$
(2.) $e^{\ln x} = x$

The base could be any positive real number other than 0 and 1. Usually the base is an integer between 2 and 10. Most calculators will only process base-10 logarithms or base-e logarithms. That is, most calculators are unable to perform a computation such as $\log_4(35)$. A shortcut formula exists for computing logs with bases other than 10 or e:

Change of Base Formula

$$\log_b(x) = \frac{\log_{10}(x)}{\log_{10}(b)} = \frac{\ln(x)}{\ln(b)}$$

Example
Compute the following logarithms:

    a. $\log_8(64)$

    b. $\log_3(528)$

    c. $\log_7(891)$

Solutions:

---

a. $\dfrac{\ln(64)}{\ln(8)} = \dfrac{4.15888}{2.07944} = 2$

b. $\dfrac{\ln(528)}{\ln(3)} = 5.70638$

c. $\dfrac{\ln(891)}{\ln(7)} = 3.49057$

Example

Solve for y in the following equations:

      a. $4^y = 25$

      b. $7^y = 100$

      c. $2^y = 32$

Solutions:

      a. Using the previous translation, b = 4, x = 25, and y = ?

$$\log_4(25) = y \quad \rightarrow \quad y = \frac{\ln(25)}{\ln(4)} \approx 2.32193$$

      b. b = 7, x = 100, y = ?

$$\log_7(100) = y \quad \rightarrow \quad y = \frac{\ln(100)}{\ln(7)} \approx 2.36659$$

      c. b = 2, x = 32, y = ?

$$\log_2(32) = y \quad \rightarrow \quad y = \frac{\ln(32)}{\ln(2)} = 5$$

Logarithms are powerful tools when trying to force the independent variable out of an exponential location. In these situations, take the natural log of both sides of the equation. The independent variable should "roll" out of the power position and down next to the logarithm. You can then evaluate the logarithms with a calculator and replace them with constants. Simple algebra then follows.

Example

Solve for y using only natural logs:

      a. $4^y = 25$

      b. $7^y = 100$

      c. $2^y = 32$

Solutions:

---

a. $\ln(4^y) = \ln(25)$ **First, take the natural log of both sides**

$\ln(4)^y = \ln(25)$ **The y will "roll" down next to the natural log expression**

$y * \ln(4) = \ln(25)$

$y = \dfrac{\ln(25)}{\ln(4)} \approx 2.32193$

b. $\ln(7^y) = \ln(100)$

$\ln(7)^y = \ln(100)$

$y * \ln(7) = \ln(100)$

$y = \dfrac{\ln(100)}{\ln(7)} \approx 2.36659$

c. $\ln(2^y) = \ln(32)$

$\ln(2)^y = \ln(32)$

$y * \ln(2) = \ln(32)$

$y = \dfrac{\ln(32)}{\ln(2)} = 5$

Example

Solve for the unknown variable in the following equations:

     a. $\log_6(x) = 4$

     b. $\log_5(125) = y$

     c. $\log_b(75) = 9$

Solutions:

     a. $6^4 = x \quad \rightarrow \quad x = 1{,}296$

     b. $y = \dfrac{\ln(125)}{\ln(5)} = 3$

     c. $b^9 = 75$

        $\left(b^9\right)^{1/9} = 75^{1/9}$

        $b = 75^{1/9} = 1.61562$

     Properties exist for simplifying an equation with many logarithmic expressions. The first property shows how to eliminate an exponent. Taking the log of an exponential expression causes the power to roll down in front of the logarithm. The second property states that the difference between two logs with the same base is equivalent to a single log with input equal to the quotient of the two prior inputs. The third law claims that the sum of two logs with the identical base equals one logarithm with the two inputs multiplied together.

Properties of Logarithms:

(1.) $\log_b(x^n) = n * \log_b(x)$

(2.) $\log_b(a) - \log_b(c) = \log_b\left(\dfrac{a}{c}\right)$

(3.) $\log_b(a) + \log_b(c) = \log_b(a * c)$

Example

Simplify the expressions below:

    a. $\log_{10}(25) + \log_{10}(4)$

    b. $\log_{12}(90) - \log_{12}(15)$

Solutions:

    a. $\log_{10}(25 * 4) = \log_{10}(100)$

    b. $\log_{12}\left(\dfrac{90}{15}\right) = \log_{12}(6)$

Example

Remove the exponents from the following:

    a. $\log_8(5^{15})$ **b.** $(\log_{14}(6))^2$

Solutions:

    a. $15 * \log_8(5)$ **b.** $2 * \log_{14}(6)$ **OR** $\log_{14}(36)$

Example

Evaluate the expressions below without using a calculator:

    a. $\log_4(32) + 3 * \log_4(2)$

    b. $\ln(e^6) * \log_3(81)$

    c. $e^{3*\ln(9)} * (\log_{11}(242) - \log_{11}(2))$

Solutions:

    a. $\log_4(32) + \log_4(2^3) = \log_4(32 * 8) = \log_4(256) = 4$

    b. $\ln(e^6) = 6$

        $\log_3(81) = 4$

        $\ln(e^6) * \log_3(81) = 24$

---

c. $e^{3*\ln(9)} = e^{\ln(9^3)} = 9^3 = 729$

$$\log_{11}(242) - \log_{11}(2) = \log_{11}\left(\frac{242}{2}\right) = \log_{11}(121) = 2$$

$$e^{3*\ln(9)} * (\log_{11}(242) - \log_{11}(2)) = 729 * 2 = 1,458$$

Example

A nuclear core has a half-life of 32 years. The core decays continuously at rate r. Find r, and compute the mass of a sample in 45 years that currently has a mass of 500 grams.

Solution:

In 32 years, the sample of initial amount a_0 grams will be reduced in half. That is, a(32) will equal $0.5a_0$.

$$\frac{1}{2}a_0 = a_0 * e^{r*32}$$

$$\frac{1}{2} = e^{r*32}$$

$$\ln\left[\frac{1}{2}\right] = \ln\left[e^{r*32}\right]$$

$$\ln\left[\frac{1}{2}\right] = r*32 \quad \rightarrow \quad r = -0.02166$$

$$a(45) = 500 * e^{-0.02166*45} \approx 188.64555g.$$

Section 1-19 Nth Roots

Roots come into play when the exponent of an expression is a fraction. The nth root is written as $\sqrt[n]{x}$. The nth root is equivalent to the exponent (1/n). That is, if $x \geq 0$, then $\sqrt[n]{x} = x^{1/n}$.

Fundamental Property of Roots

$$\sqrt[n]{f(x)} = (f(x))^{1/n}$$

The value n is an integer greater than or equal to 2. The root has a canceling effect against its reciprocal. For instance, the square root will cancel out the second power: $\sqrt{(x^2)} = (x^2)^{1/2} = x^{2*(1/2)} = x$. Another basic definition of the nth root is: $y = \sqrt[n]{x}$ iff

---

$y^n = x$. You can eliminate an exponent of an expression by raising the expression to the inverse of the original exponent:

$$\left(f(x)^n\right)^{1/n} \quad \rightarrow \quad f(x)$$

Roots are useful tools when trying to isolate a variable that is raised to an exponent.

Example
Solve for x: $4 = x^2$

Solution:
$x = \pm 2$

We can solve for x without explicitly using roots. We need to ask, what numbers, when raised to the second power, produce 4?" We know that $2^2 = 4$, so x = 2 is one solution. Another solution is x = -2, since $(-2)^2$ is also 4.

The analytical approach to solving the problem is to isolate x by raising each side to the reciprocal of x's exponent. That is, we need to take the square root of both sides:

$$\sqrt{4} = \sqrt{x^2} \quad \rightarrow \quad x = \pm\sqrt{4} = \pm 2$$

In a math problem of the nature $c = x^n$, where c and n are known real numbers and we need to solve for x, we could either implicitly or explicitly use roots to find x. The implicit method would entail guessing values of x and checking if x^n produces c. The explicit, analytical method requires raising each side of the equation to 1/n (that is, we take the nth root of both sides). The nth root eliminates the exponent over x, and results in $x = \sqrt[n]{c}$, which you can evaluate with a calculator.

Example
Solve for x: $800 = x^5$

$$\sqrt[5]{800} = \sqrt[5]{x^5} \quad \rightarrow \quad x = \sqrt[5]{800} \approx 3.80731$$

The table below shows the number of roots depending on the even/odd nature of the root and the value of x:

Value of n	Value of x	Number of real roots
odd	positive or negative	1

---

even	positive	2	
even	negative	0	

Example

Compute the following without a calculator:

a. $\sqrt{400}$ **b.** $\sqrt[3]{64}$ **c.** $\sqrt[3]{343}$ **d.** $\sqrt[8]{256}$

Solutions:

For each of these expressions, you must ask, "What number raised to the reciprocal of the root will yield the value within the root?"

a. For this problem, we ask, "What number squared yields 400?" The obvious answer is 20.

b. What number cubed equals 64? Answer: 4

c. What number cubed equals 343? Answer: 7

d. What number raised to the power of 8 yields 256? Answer: 2

Rules of Roots

(1.) $\sqrt[n]{a*b} = \sqrt[n]{a} * \sqrt[n]{b}$

(2.) If the exponent is a rational number (of the form m/n), then

$$x^{m/n} = \left(x^m\right)^{1/n} = \sqrt[n]{x^m} = \left(\sqrt[n]{x}\right)^m.$$

      The second rule for roots provides several ways to write an expression x that is raised to a rational power. The value 'n' represents the root, while 'm' is the power. The expression $x^{m/n}$ could read "the nth root of x to the mth power."

Example

Write the following with radical signs:

a. $x^{3.5}$ **b.** $x^{1/9}$ **c.** $(7xy)^{5/6}$

Solutions:

a. $x^{3.5} = x^{7/2} = \left(\sqrt{x}\right)^7$

b. $\sqrt[9]{x}$

c. $\sqrt[6]{(7xy)^5} = \sqrt[6]{(7^5 x^5 y^5)} = \sqrt[6]{16,807 x^5 y^5}$

Example

Write the following without radical signs:

a. $\sqrt[7]{\sqrt[3]{w}}$ **b.** $\sqrt[4]{4{,}096x^3}$ **c.** $\sqrt{x^7 y^2}$

Solutions:

a. $\sqrt[7]{w^{1/3}} = \left(\sqrt[7]{w}\right)^{1/3} = \left(w^{1/7}\right)^{1/3} = w^{(1/7)(1/3)} = w^{1/21}$

b. $\sqrt[4]{4{,}096} * \sqrt[4]{x^3} = 8 * \sqrt[4]{x^3} = 8 * x^{3/4}$

c. $\sqrt{x^7} * \sqrt{y^2} = x^{7/2} * y$

Most large roots can be reduced to a simpler expression. You can calculate nearly any root without a calculator. The first step in computing a root is to find the divisors of the number under the root. Try to choose at least one divisor that has an integral root. For example, the square roots of 16, 25, 36, and 49 produce integers. You should use the property that $\sqrt[n]{a*b} = \sqrt[n]{a} * \sqrt[n]{b}$. Try to find a value 'a' such that its nth root is an integer. The nth root of b may require further simplification. If 'b' does not have an integral root, you should attempt to break down the root separately. Once you have sufficiently simplified the second root, multiply it by the root of the first divisor.

The best strategy for computing a square root is to progress through the perfect squares, starting with 4. If the number is not divisible by 4, then go up to 9. If it is not divisible by 9, then move up to 16. Work through the perfect squares, starting low, until you find a square that divides evenly into the input value without a remainder. If none of the perfect squares divide into the input value, then the initial square root cannot be simplified.

Example

Calculate $\sqrt{270}$

Solution:
What positive integers divide evenly into 270? Which of these divisors are perfect squares?

1 and 270 are divisors, but the square roots of these numbers do not move us past $\sqrt{270}$. Other divisors include 3 and 90, 5 and 54, 6 and 45, and 9 and 30.
We found our first perfect square, 9. The expression now becomes:

$$\sqrt{270} = \sqrt{9} * \sqrt{30} = 3\sqrt{30}$$

Since the second divisor is not a perfect square, we must attempt to break down its root separately. The divisors of 30 include 2 and 15, 3 and 10, 5 and 6. None of these divisors are perfect squares, so the simplification ends here.

Final answer: $\sqrt{270} = 3\sqrt{30}$

A similar strategy applies to cube roots. Create a list of the first few integers cubed, and check if they divide nicely into the original value under the root. The second divisor will probably not be a perfect cube and may require separate simplification.

Example

Evaluate $\sqrt[3]{1,728}$

Solution:
The first perfect cubes are 8, 27, 64, 125, and 216.
8 divides evenly into 1,728.

$$\sqrt[3]{1,728} = \sqrt[3]{8} * \sqrt[3]{216}$$

Both 8 and 216 are perfect cubes, so the final answer is an integer.

$$\sqrt[3]{1,728} = 2 * 6 = 12$$

Example

Reduce the following:

  a. $\sqrt{200}$ **b.** $\sqrt{1,296}$ **c.** $\sqrt[3]{750}$

Solutions:

a. $\sqrt{200} = \sqrt{100} * \sqrt{2} = 10\sqrt{2}$

b. $\sqrt{1,296} = \sqrt{4} * \sqrt{324} = 2\sqrt{324}$

$$\sqrt{324} = \sqrt{4} * \sqrt{81} = 2 * 9 = 18$$

$$\sqrt{1,296} = 2 * 18 = 36$$

c. The first few positive integers cubed include 8, 27, 64, and 125.
    125 divides evenly into 750.

$$\sqrt[3]{750} = \sqrt[3]{125} * \sqrt[3]{6} = 5 * \sqrt[3]{6}$$

Rationalizing Denominators

The technique of rationalizing denominators is useful when reducing a fraction that holds a square root in the denominator. To simplify an expression by rationalizing the denominator, first find the reciprocal of the denominator. The reciprocal or conjugate of $a + \sqrt{b}$ is $a - \sqrt{b}$. You only need to negate the sign of the second operand to reciprocate an expression of roots. Then, multiply that conjugate by the numerator and denominator.

Example

Simplify the following expressions by rationalizing the denominator:

a. $\dfrac{11 - \sqrt{17}}{8 + \sqrt{12}}$
b. $\dfrac{40 + \sqrt{30}}{14 - \sqrt{34}}$

Solutions:

a.

$$\frac{11 - \sqrt{17}}{8 + \sqrt{12}} = \frac{11 - \sqrt{17}}{8 + \sqrt{12}} * \frac{8 - \sqrt{12}}{8 - \sqrt{12}} = \frac{88 - 11\sqrt{12} - 8\sqrt{17} + \sqrt{204}}{64 - 8\sqrt{12} + 8\sqrt{12} - \sqrt{144}} = \frac{88 - 11\sqrt{12} - 8\sqrt{17} + \sqrt{204}}{52}$$

b.

$$\frac{40 + \sqrt{30}}{14 - \sqrt{34}} = \frac{40 + \sqrt{30}}{14 - \sqrt{34}} * \frac{14 + \sqrt{34}}{14 + \sqrt{34}} = \frac{560 + 40\sqrt{34} + 14\sqrt{30} + \sqrt{1020}}{196 + 14\sqrt{34} - 14\sqrt{34} - 34}$$

$$= \frac{560 + 40\sqrt{34} + 14\sqrt{30} + \sqrt{1020}}{162}$$

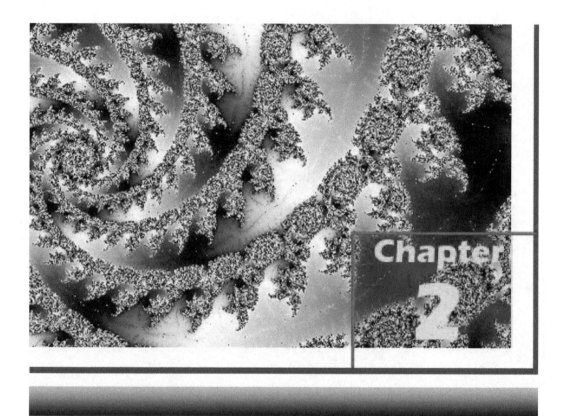

Chapter 2
Trigonometry

Trigonometry is the study of triangles. This type of math provides ways to solve for unknown elements in a triangle, such as missing angles, side lengths, or slopes of sides. If you have several measurements of a triangle, such as a few sides and angles, you can find the remaining parts of the triangle with trigonometry.

Section 2-1 Introduction to Triangles

Types of Triangles and Angles

A triangle has three internal angles and three corresponding sides. The angles within the triangle must add up to $180°$. In a polygon of 'S' sides, the sum of all the internal angles must be $180(S-2)$. An *acute angle* measures less than $90°$. An *obtuse angle* is more than $90°$ and less than $180°$. In addition, a *right angle* is $90°$. The size of an angle affects the length of the edge opposite that angle. The largest angle will be opposite from the largest side, and the smallest angle will correspond with the shortest edge.

A *right triangle* has one angle that is $90°$. The 90-degree angle is marked with a small box.

An *isosceles triangle* has two angles of the same degree. The two sides opposite the angles will be the same length. Hash marks along the sides are used to illustrate that two edges have the identical length. Angles use small curves to show that two angles are of the same degree.

An *acute triangle* has three angles that are all less than $90°$:

An *obtuse triangle* has one angle that is over $90°$:

An *equilateral triangle* has three sides that are equal and three angles that are all the same. Every angle is exactly 60 degrees.

Solving Unknown Sides in a Right Triangle

The *Pythagorean Theorem* states that given a right triangle, the square of the hypotenuse equals the sum of the squares of the two legs. Using the picture below, $a^2 + b^2 = c^2$.

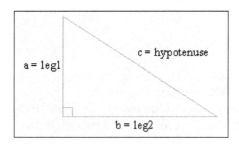

Example
Find the missing side in each triangle below:

    a.

    b.

Solutions:

a. $a^2 + b^2 = c^2$
$8^2 + 13^2 = c^2$
$c^2 = 233 \quad \rightarrow \quad c = \sqrt{233} \approx 15.26434$

b. $a^2 + b^2 = c^2$
$(4b)^2 + b^2 = 17^2$
$16b^2 + b^2 = 17^2$
$17b^2 = 17^2$
$b^2 = 17 \quad \rightarrow \quad b = \sqrt{17} \approx 4.12311 \quad \rightarrow \quad a = 4b \approx 16.49242$

Section 2-2 The Three Basic Trig Functions

Trigonometry relies on three primary functions—sine, cosine, and tangent. The triangle under examination must be a right triangle. When using the three trig functions, the diagram below will apply. The angle in question is usually denoted theta. The side directly opposite the angle theta is called "opposite." The side opposite the right angle is called the "hypotenuse." The remaining side is the "adjacent" side to theta.

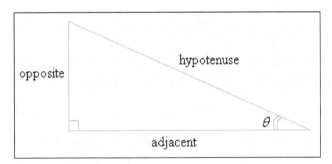

Each of the basic trig functions requires an angle for the input parameter.

Sine, Cosine, and Tangent Functions

$$\text{sine} = \sin(\theta) = \frac{\text{opposite}}{\text{hypotenuse}}$$

$$\text{cosine} = \cos(\theta) = \frac{\text{adjacent}}{\text{hypotenuse}}$$

$$\text{tangent} = \tan(\theta) = \frac{\text{opposite}}{\text{adjacent}}$$

Another equation for the tangent of an angle is: $\tan(\theta) = \dfrac{\sin(\theta)}{\cos(\theta)}$

A popular acronym for memorizing the three elementary trig functions is:

SOH-CAH-TOA

For example, "SOH" means sine equals opposite over hypotenuse.

Graphical Representations of the Basic Trig Functions

A set of terms describe the behavior of a sine wave. The *period* of a sine wave is the horizontal distance between two crests of the wave. It is the distance required for one full cycle of the function. The lowest points along the wave are called troughs. The *amplitude* is the height of the wave. The *phase shift* is the horizontal translation of the entire wave. If the phase shift is positive, the graph slides rightwards. On the other hand, a negative phase shift means the graphs slides leftwards. The *vertical shift* is the vertical displacement of a wave. A graph might be shifted up or down from its default position.

A sine wave follows the "OHOLO" pattern—zero, high, zero, low, zero. The sine wave intersects the origin. The unmodified sine function has a period of 2π radians; the graph will repeat again after each segment of 2π radians along the x-axis. The amplitude is the distance from the x-axis to a crest, which is 1. Note that the graph is bounded by $y = 1$ and $y = -1$. The domain for the sine function is the set of all reals.

A cosine wave follows the "HOLOH" pattern—high, zero, low, zero, high. A cosine wave is identical to a sine wave except that the cosine wave is moved backwards $\pi/2$ radians along the horizontal axis. It also has an amplitude of 1 and period of 2π radians. The domain is all real numbers.

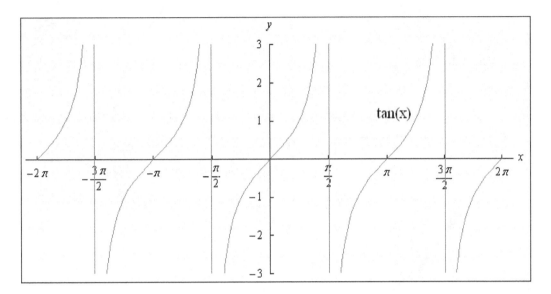

The tangent function produces a unique wave pattern. Tangent graphs have a period of π radians, with the first period in the x-interval $(-\pi/2, \pi/2)$. The function is undefined at the ends of a period. Vertical asymptotes exist at $x = \dfrac{\pi}{2} + \pi n$, where n is any integer. These graphs repeat forever in both directions along the x-axis. With a range encompassing all real numbers, the amplitude of a tangent wave is undefined.

The Unit Circle

The *unit circle* has heavy uses in trigonometry. The unit circle is a circle of radius 1 centered at the origin of a 2D rectangular coordinate system. The circle provides a graphical representation of the basic trigonometric functions—sin, cos, and tan.

In the diagram below, the angles are specified inside the circle (in degrees and radians). The angle measurements start along the positive horizontal axis and increase counterclockwise. A full revolution of the circle is 2π radians or $360°$. If you travel around the circle twice, you end up at 4π radians or $720°$, which is again along the positive x-axis. When dealing with negative angles, you must measure clockwise from the positive x-axis. For example, $-45°$ is equivalent to $315°$. Radian measurements are nearly always specified in terms of pi.

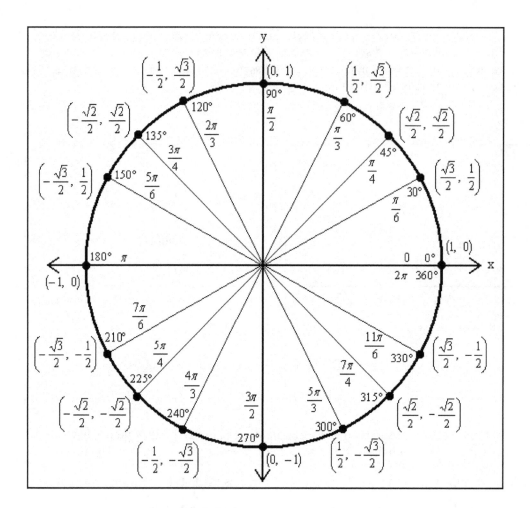

Two convenient equations exist for converting angles between degrees and radians. When translating from degrees to radians, simply multiply the degree measurement by $\pi/180$. If you need to convert from radians to degrees, multiply the radian value by $180/\pi$. Notice that the targeted unit is in the numerator. If we need radians, remember that π should be in the numerator of the conversion ratio.

Equation for converting degrees to radians

$$radians = degrees * \frac{\pi}{180}$$

Equation for converting radians to degrees

$$degrees = radians * \frac{180}{\pi}$$

The unit circle also has a variety of points labeled with (x, y) coordinates. The x-value corresponds to the result of the cosine function, while the y-value equals the result of the sine function. For example, when angle θ is zero radians, the cosine function yields 1 and the sine function produces 0. Consequently, we receive the point (1, 0) at zero radians. Moving up to $\pi/6$ radians, the cosine operator is $\sqrt{3}/2$ and sine yields 0.5, so we end up with the point ($\sqrt{3}/2$, 1/2). At $\pi/2$ radians, we have the point (0, 1). We then know that $\cos(\pi/2) = 0$ and $\sin(\pi/2) = 1$.

If you memorize just the first quadrant of the unit circle, you can deduce the sine and cosine values of any other point in the circle. For instance, suppose we need to calculate the two trig functions at $5\pi/4$ radians. This angle is half a unit circle from the angle $\pi/4$ radians, and the point lies in the third quadrant where x and y are negative. We know that $\cos(\pi/4) = \sqrt{2}/2$ and $\sin(\pi/4) = \sqrt{2}/2$. Negating these two values creates the coordinates for the point at $5\pi/4$ radians—$\left(-\sqrt{2}/2,\ -\sqrt{2}/2\right)$. When you are given an angle, try to visualize the angle on the unit circle. Decide which quadrant the point lies within. Adjust the cosine and sine values from the first quadrant to match the coordinates for the new quadrant.

The second unit circle below includes the tangent values. The tangent function corresponds to slope. Notice that along the horizontal axis, where a line segment is perfectly flat with zero slope, the tangent function equals zero. As you increase in angle measurement within the first quadrant, the slope quickly increases. At $\pi/4$ radians, a line drawn from the origin has slope 1. When you reach $\pi/2$ radians, a ray connecting the origin and point (0, 1) has an infinitely large slope. Rays in the second quadrant have a negative rise over run. Just beyond $\theta = \pi/2$, the slope is a large, negative number. The slope approaches zero as the angle nears π. At $3\pi/2$ radians, the tangent function equals negative infinity.

values of the tangent function
(slope)

Example

Find the (x, y) coordinates and slope at these angles:

a. $-210°$ **b.** $495°$ **c.** 3π **d.** $-5\pi/3$ **e.** $19\pi/6$

Solutions:

a. $(-\sqrt{3}/2, 0.5)$, slope $= -\sqrt{3}/3$

b. $(-\sqrt{2}/2, \sqrt{2}/2)$, slope $= -1$

c. $(-1, 0)$, slope $= 0$

d. $(0.5, \sqrt{3}/2)$, slope $= \sqrt{3}$

e. $(-\sqrt{3}/2, -0.5)$, slope $= \sqrt{3}/3$

The repeating nature of the sine, cosine, and tangent functions is defined more formally in the next theorem:

Periodicity Theorem

∀ angles θ specified in radians, the following equalities hold:

$$\sin(\theta) = \sin(\theta + 2\pi n)$$
$$\cos(\theta) = \cos(\theta + 2\pi n)$$
$$\tan(\theta) = \tan(\theta + \pi n)$$

where n is any integer.

Example

Use the basic trig functions to find the missing sides in the triangles below:

a.

b.

c.

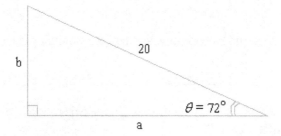

Solutions:

    a. First, let's solve for side a...

Side 'a' is opposite angle theta, and we already have the hypotenuse. Since we are working with the opposite and hypotenuse sides, we need to use $\sin(\theta)$.

$$\sin(50°) = \frac{a}{12} \quad \rightarrow \quad 12 * \sin(50°) = a \quad \rightarrow \quad a \approx 9.19253$$

Side 'b' is adjacent to theta, and we already have the hypotenuse. The cosine function will work with the adjacent and hypotenuse sides.

$$\cos(50°) = \frac{b}{12} \quad \rightarrow \quad 12 * \cos(50°) = b \quad \rightarrow \quad b \approx 7.71345$$

We can use Pythagorean's Theorem as a final check:

$$a^2 + b^2 = c^2 \quad \rightarrow \quad 9.19253^2 + 7.71345^2 = 12^2 \quad \rightarrow \quad 143.9999 \approx 144$$

b. Side 'a' is the adjacent side to angle theta. And, we already have the opposite side. Adjacent and opposite sides mean we should use the tangent function to find 'a.'

$$\tan(18°) = \frac{5}{a} \quad \rightarrow \quad \frac{1}{\tan(18°)} = \frac{a}{5} \quad \rightarrow \quad a = \frac{5}{\tan(18°)} \approx 15.38842$$

From an engineering perspective, it is unwise to use the new angle or side in solving for the other remaining unknowns. If one of the new angles or sides you computed is incorrect, you will be building on wrong answers. If possible, you should use the information given in the problem for finding all the unknowns.

Finding side c involves the use of the opposite and hypotenuse sides. The sine function will work.

$$\sin(18°) = \frac{5}{c} \quad \rightarrow \quad \frac{1}{\sin(18°)} = \frac{c}{5} \quad \rightarrow \quad c = \frac{5}{\sin(18°)} \approx 16.18034$$

Check with Pythagorean's Theorem...

$$15.38842^2 + 5^2 = 16.18034^2 \quad \rightarrow \quad 261.80347 \approx 261.80340$$

c. Side 'a' is the adjacent side, and we already have the hypotenuse. Use the cosine function.

$$\cos(72°) = \frac{a}{20} \quad \rightarrow \quad a \approx 6.18034$$

Side 'b' is opposite, and we already know the hypotenuse. Use the sine function.

$$\sin(72°) = \frac{b}{20} \quad \rightarrow \quad b \approx 19.02113$$

Check...

$$6.18034^2 + 19.02113^2 = 20^2$$
$$399.99999 \approx 400$$

Section 2-3 Morphing Sine Waves

The three basic trigonometric functions have a general syntax. The waves can be stretched horizontally or vertically, they can be compressed, and they can be shifted up and down. The general format for a sine function is shown here:

Sine Function Formula
$$f(x) = A * \sin(Bx + C) + D$$

where

$$A = \frac{(\text{max} - \text{min})}{2}$$

$$B = \frac{2\pi}{period}$$

$$C = -\left(\frac{2\pi}{period} * (\text{phase shift}) \right)$$

$D = $ vertical translation of the graph in radians

Corollaries from the Sine Function Formula:

(1.) amplitude $= |A|$

(2.) period $= \left| \dfrac{2\pi}{B} \right|$

(3.) phase shift $= -\dfrac{C}{B}$

Variable A provides the amplitude (height) of the wave. The amplitude is half the vertical change from trough to crest. When A is negative, the parent function must be flipped vertically. The B factor helps to determine the period. The value C influences the horizontal shift, but C has no impact on the wave's period. Finally, D governs the vertical shift.

Example

Find the function for a sine wave with amplitude 4, period π, no phase shift, and a vertical shift of 1.

Solution:

A = amplitude = 4

$B = \dfrac{2\pi}{period} = \dfrac{2\pi}{\pi} = 2$

$C = -\left(\dfrac{2\pi}{period} * 0 \right) = 0$

D = 1

$f(x) = A * \sin(Bx + C) + D = 4 * \sin(2x) + 1$

Example

Find the function for a sine wave of amplitude 3, period 6 radians, phase shift of 8, and vertical shift of -2.

Solution:

A = amplitude = 3

$B = \dfrac{2\pi}{period} = \dfrac{2\pi}{6} = \dfrac{\pi}{3}$

$C = -\left(\dfrac{2\pi}{6} * 8 \right) = -\left(\dfrac{16\pi}{6} \right) = -\dfrac{8\pi}{3}$

D = -2

$f(x) = A * \sin(Bx + C) + D = 3 * \sin\left(\dfrac{\pi}{3}x - \dfrac{8\pi}{3} \right) - 2$

Example
Find the amplitude, period, phase shift, and vertical shift for the following function:
$$f(x) = -5 * \sin(10x - 4) + 12$$

Solution:
A = -5, B = 10, C = -4, D = 12

$$\text{amplitude} = |A| = |-5| = 5$$

$$\text{period} = \left|\frac{2\pi}{B}\right| = \left|\frac{2\pi}{10}\right| = \frac{\pi}{5}$$

$$\text{phase shift} = -\frac{C}{B} = -\frac{(-4)}{10} = \frac{4}{10} = \frac{2}{5}$$

vertical shift = D = 12

Section 2-4 Inverse Trig Functions

Like most other math functions, the three trigonometric functions have inverses. These functions are vital to solving equations that have trigonometric functions. The inverse function essentially works in reverse. Remember that for the original trig functions, we provide an angle for input and receive an x-value, y-value, or slope. For the inverse trig functions, we must provide an x-value for arccos, a y-value for arcsin, or a slope for arctan and receive the angle measurement as output. Stated differently, the inverse trig functions allow us to find the angle that produced a certain cosine, sine, or tangent value. The inverses of the common trigonometry functions appear below. The "arc" prefix or the inverse sign (-1) is used for these inverse functions.

$$\arcsin(\theta) = \sin^{-1}(\theta)$$

$$\arccos(\theta) = \cos^{-1}(\theta)$$

$$\arctan(\theta) = \tan^{-1}(\theta)$$

The original trig functions, when applied in conjunction with their inverses, cancel out both functions:

$$\arcsin(\sin(\theta)) = \theta \quad \text{and} \quad \sin(\arcsin(\theta)) = \theta$$
$$\arccos(\cos(\theta)) = \theta \quad \text{and} \quad \cos(\arccos(\theta)) = \theta$$
$$\arctan(\tan(\theta)) = \theta \quad \text{and} \quad \tan(\arctan(\theta)) = \theta$$

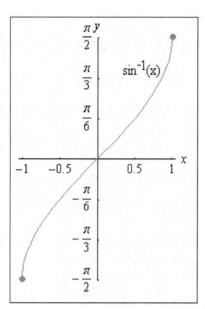

The inverse sine function has a domain [-1, 1], which equals the range of the original sine function. The range of the inverse sine function is $\left[-\frac{\pi}{2}, \frac{\pi}{2} \right]$. The graph includes the two endpoints $\left(-1, -\frac{\pi}{2} \right)$ and $\left(1, \frac{\pi}{2} \right)$. The inverse sine function utilizes only the right half of the unit circle.

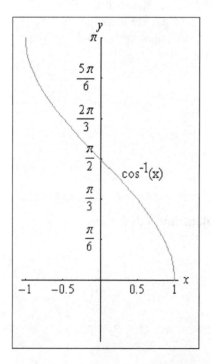

The original cosine function outputs values between -1 and 1, so the domain of the inverse cosine function must be [-1, 1]. The inverse cosine function uses just the top half of the unit circle. Its output ranges from 0 to pi, inclusive.

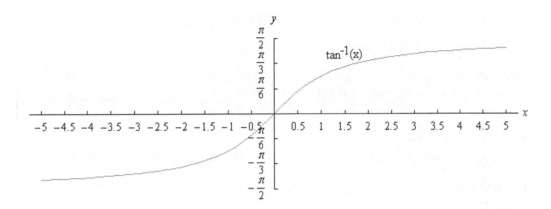

The inverse tangent function has the domain $(-\infty, \infty)$ and range $(-\pi/2, \pi/2)$. It has horizontal asymptotes at $y = -\pi/2$ and $y = \pi/2$. As in the case of the arcsin function, the inverse tangent function uses only the right half of the unit circle.

The inverse trig functions are essential when solving for an unknown angle. As shown directly above, applying the inverse function to the original function will force out the angle.

Example
Solve for angle theta
   a.

   b.

$\theta = ?$

11

7.5

Solutions:

a. Since we have the opposite and hypotenuse sides, the sine function is appropriate.

$$\sin(\theta) = \frac{10}{22} \approx 0.45455$$

$\arcsin(\sin(\theta)) \approx \arcsin(0.45455)$

$\theta \approx \arcsin(0.45455)$

$\theta \approx 0.47187$ radians ≈ 27.03598 degrees

b. We are given the adjacent and opposite sides relative to the angle, so we need to use the tangent function.

$$\tan(\theta) = \frac{11}{7.5} \approx 1.46667$$

$\arctan(\tan(\theta)) \approx \arctan(1.46667)$

$\theta \approx \arctan(1.46667)$

$\theta \approx 0.97238$ radians ≈ 55.71312 degrees

Example

A ferris wheel has malfunctioned and left Uriah 60 feet above the ground. The wheel is 100 feet in diameter, touches the ground, and rotates only counter-clockwise (relative to the viewer). Uriah can safely jump from the ride when his cart is 30 feet from the ground. How many radians must the ride rotate before he can jump, if the ride must rotate Uriah through its highest point?

Solution:

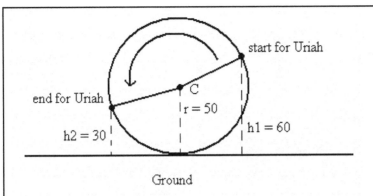

Consider the ferris wheel to be the unit circle with radius 50 feet. His starting height is 60 feet from the ground or 10 feet above the x-axis centered at C.

$$\sin(\theta) * 50 = 10$$
$$\sin(\theta) = 0.2 \quad \rightarrow \quad \theta = \sin^{-1}(0.2) \approx 0.20136$$

Uriah's starting angle on the ride is roughly 0.20136 radians.

He must end 30 feet above the ground in quadrant 3, which translates to 20 feet below the negative x-axis.

$$\sin(\theta) * 50 = -20$$
$$\sin(\theta) = -0.4 \quad \rightarrow \quad \theta = \sin^{-1}(-0.4) \approx -0.41152$$
$$\theta \approx 0.41152 + \pi \approx 3.55311$$

total rotation needed = $3.55311 - 0.20136 \approx 3.35175$ radians

Example
In a rectangular coordinate system, a boat is located at (3, 7), and the port the boat is trying to reach is at (12, 1). What bearing should the boat take to reach the port in a straight line?

Solution:

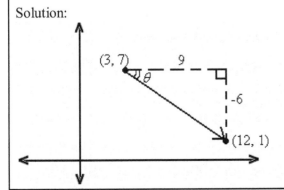

The boat and the port form a right triangle with the distances between them. The horizontal distance is 9, and the vertical change from the boat to the port is -6. Angle theta is the required bearing.

$$\tan(\theta) = \frac{\text{opposite}}{\text{adjacent}} = \frac{-6}{9} = \frac{-2}{3}$$

$$\theta = \tan^{-1}\left(-\frac{2}{3}\right) \approx -0.588 \text{ radians}$$

Example

Dredge is at the base of a hill with an incline of $37°$. The horizontal distance to the top of the hill is 650 m. What is the vertical distance to the top?

Solution:

We are working with the opposite and adjacent sides of the triangle relative to angle theta, so the tangent function is needed to find y.

$$\tan(37°) = \frac{y}{650} \quad \rightarrow \quad y = 489.81$$

Section 2-5 Law of Cosines and Law of Sines

These two laws are convenient when solving for unknown sides and angles in a non-right triangle. The vertices (or angles) of the triangle are labeled A, B, and C (with capital letters). The sides are designated with lowercase letters. The side opposite angle A is labeled 'a,' the side opposite angle B is labeled 'b,' and so on.

You can use the law of cosines when you are given SSS or SAS within a triangle. (S means "side" and A means "angle.") A triangle at work under the law of cosines is shown below. We are only concerned about one angle—theta. However, we need to work with all the sides of the triangle.

Law of Cosines

$$x^2 = a^2 + b^2 - 2ab\cos(\theta)$$

where θ is the angle of interest, x is the side opposite θ, and a and b are sides adjacent to θ.

The law of cosines clearly uses the cosine function.

Example
Find the angles in the triangle below:

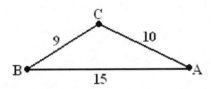

Solution:
First, let's find angle A.
$$9^2 = 10^2 + 15^2 - 2*10*15*\cos(A)$$
$$81 = 100 + 225 - 300*\cos(A)$$
$$-244 = -300*\cos(A)$$
$$244 = 300*\cos(A)$$
$$\cos(A) = \frac{244}{300} \approx 0.81333 \qquad \rightarrow \quad A \approx \cos^{-1}(0.81333) \approx 35.5771°$$

Finding angle B...
$$10^2 = 9^2 + 15^2 - 2*9*15*\cos(B)$$
$$100 = 81 + 225 - 270*\cos(B)$$
$$-206 = -270*\cos(B)$$
$$206 = 270*\cos(B)$$
$$\cos(B) = \frac{206}{270} \approx 0.76296 \qquad \rightarrow \quad B \approx \cos^{-1}(0.76296) \approx 40.27389°$$

Using the fact that the angles in a triangle must sum to 180 degrees, angle C must be 104.149°.

Example
Find side b in the triangle below:

Solution:

$a^2 = 5^2 + 6^2 - 2*5*6*\cos(32°)$

$a^2 = 25 + 36 - 60*0.84805$

$a^2 = 10.11711 \quad \rightarrow \quad a \approx 3.18074$

The law of sines is helpful when you are given ASA or AAS. That is, we need two angles and just one side to find the other parts of the triangle. A diagram of the law of sines is displayed here:

The law of sines depends on the sine function:

Law of Sines

$$\frac{\sin(A)}{a} = \frac{\sin(B)}{b} = \frac{\sin(C)}{c}$$

Only two of these ratios are required.

Example
Use the law of sines to find the missing sides in the triangle:

Solution:
We are given AAS and must find sides a and c.

Angle A must be 31 degrees. To find side a, use the following part of the law of sines:

$$\frac{\sin(A)}{a} = \frac{\sin(B)}{b} \rightarrow \frac{\sin(31°)}{a} = \frac{\sin(29°)}{14} \rightarrow \frac{0.51504}{a} = \frac{0.48481}{14} \rightarrow a \approx 14.87297$$

To find side c,
$$\frac{\sin(C)}{c} = \frac{\sin(B)}{b} \rightarrow \frac{\sin(120°)}{c} = \frac{\sin(29°)}{14} \rightarrow \frac{0.86603}{c} = \frac{0.48481}{14} \rightarrow c \approx 25.0086$$

Example
Apply the law of sines to the following triangle to find side c:

Solution:
Angle B must be 40 degrees.

$$\frac{\sin(B)}{b} = \frac{\sin(C)}{c} \rightarrow \frac{\sin(40°)}{16} = \frac{\sin(94°)}{c} \rightarrow 0.04017 \approx \frac{0.99756}{c} \rightarrow c \approx 24.83346$$

Section 2-6 Additional Trig Functions

The co- trigonometric functions are reciprocals of the original trig functions. To generate these functions, we simply divide 1 by each of the basic trig functions. The three new functions are shown here:

$$\text{cosecant: } \csc(\theta) = \frac{1}{\sin(\theta)} = \frac{\text{hypotenuse}}{\text{opposite}}$$

$$\text{secant: } \sec(\theta) = \frac{1}{\cos(\theta)} = \frac{\text{hypotenuse}}{\text{adjacent}}$$

$$\text{cotangent: } \cot(\theta) = \frac{1}{\tan(\theta)} = \frac{\cos(\theta)}{\sin(\theta)} = \frac{\text{adjacent}}{\text{opposite}}$$

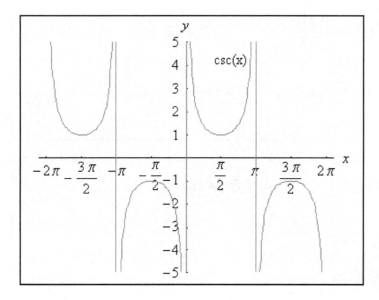

The cosecant function has the appearance of repeating parabolas. The vertices of the parabolas occur at $y = 1$ and $y = -1$. The graph has vertical asymptotes that repeat every pi radians, starting with zero radians.

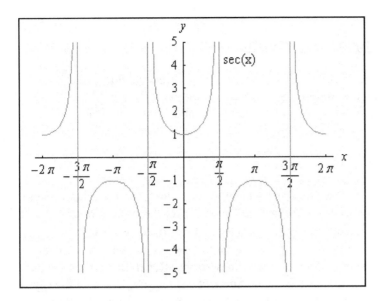

The secant function is also a sequence of repeating parabolas. The secant graph is identical to the cosecant version except the plot is translated $-\pi/2$ radians. Vertical asymptotes are present every pi radians starting at $x = -\pi/2$.

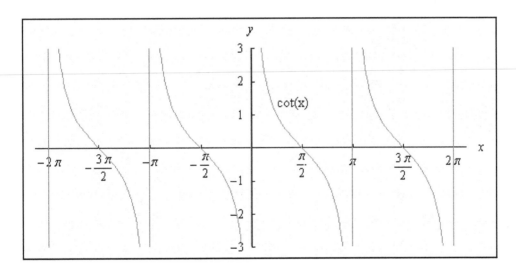

The cotangent function is remarkably similar to the original tangent wave. Each segment of the tangent function has been reflected about a vertical line and translated rightward by $\pi/2$ radians. Vertical asymptotes are still present every pi radians.

Section 2-7 Polar and Spherical Coordinates

Polar and spherical coordinates rely on the basic trigonometric functions. These systems use angles and distances to describe points. Trigonometry is helpful in converting between the traditional rectangular coordinates and polar-spherical coordinates.

Polar Coordinates

Polar coordinates are used to represent a point in 2 dimensions. Polar coordinates are similar to rectangular coordinates, but they use two different descriptors to plot a point. Polar coordinates are in the form (r, θ), where r is the radius (or distance) of the point from the origin, and θ is the bearing (or direction) of the point. These coordinates have applications in physics, especially when plotting vectors. Recall that a vector must have a directional component and a magnitude component. Often, the length of the ray represents speed (a longer vector for higher speeds), and the angle is the direction of movement.

The angle theta follows the same method of measuring angles as seen in the unit circle. Theta is usually measured in radians rather than degrees. The angle is measured between an arbitrary ray starting at the origin and the positive x-axis. A ray pointing directly rightward along the positive x-axis is at 0 radians. A ray pointing straight up is at $\pi / 2$ radians. The angle increases as you move counterclockwise around the unit circle. The angle decreases as you move clockwise. One revolution of the unit circle is $360°$ or 2π radians.

Several points with polar coordinates are plotted on the graph below:

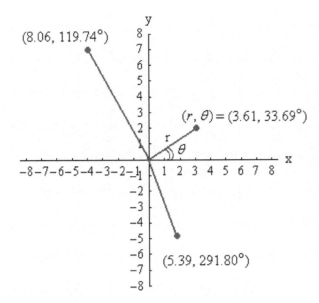

You can convert from rectangular coordinates to polar coordinates using the formulas below:

$$r = \sqrt{x^2 + y^2}$$

$$\theta = \tan^{-1}\left(\frac{y}{x}\right)$$

You can also convert polar coordinates into rectangular coordinates:

$$x = r * \cos(\theta)$$

$$y = r * \sin(\theta)$$

Example
Convert the rectangular coordinates below to polar coordinates:

        a. (4, 4)
        b. (-3, 10)
        c. (6, -1)

Solutions:

        a. $r = \sqrt{4^2 + 4^2} = \sqrt{32}$

$$\theta = \tan^{-1}\left(\frac{4}{4}\right) = \tan^{-1}(1) = \frac{\pi}{4}$$

$(\sqrt{32},\ \pi/4)$

b. $r = \sqrt{(-3)^2 + 10^2} = \sqrt{109}$

$$\theta = \tan^{-1}\left(\frac{10}{-3}\right) = -1.27934$$

The current angle theta describes a point in the fourth quadrant. However, the point (-3, 10) is in the second quadrant. We need to add pi onto the angle measurement to find the corresponding angle in the correct second quadrant.

$$\theta = -1.27934 + \pi = 1.86225$$

$(\sqrt{109},\ 1.86225)$

c. $r = \sqrt{6^2 + (-1)^2} = \sqrt{37}$

$$\theta = \tan^{-1}\left(\frac{-1}{6}\right) = -0.16515$$

$(\sqrt{37},\ -0.16515)$

Example
Convert the polar coordinates to rectangular coordinates:
    a. $(12,\ \pi/3)$
    b. $(20,\ (7\pi)/6)$
    c. $(4,\ (7\pi)/4)$

Solutions:
    a.
$$x = 12 * \cos(\pi/3) = 6$$
$$y = 12 * \sin(\pi/3) \approx 10.3923$$

    b.
$$x = 20 * \cos((7\pi)/6) \approx -17.32051$$
$$y = 20 * \sin((7\pi)/6) = -10$$

    c.
$$x = 4 * \cos((7\pi)/4) \approx 2.82843$$
$$y = 4 * \sin((7\pi)/4) \approx -2.82843$$

You should perform several quick checks when converting between polar and rectangular coordinates. First, check that the original point and new point are in the same quadrant. Remember that the inverse tangent function only returns values from $-\pi/2$ to $\pi/2$. If the actual point is on the left side of the unit circle, you need to add pi onto the angle returned from the arctan function, since the tangent function has a period of pi. Secondly, you can try to convert your new point into the original coordinates. For example, if you initially need to convert from polar to rectangular, check that the rectangular coordinates convert back into the original polar form.

Example
Suppose Uriah fires a gun at the origin of a 2D coordinate system. The bullet has a launch angle of $40°$. The speed of the bullet is a constant 400 m/s. Assume gravity and other forces do not affect the speed and trajectory of the bullet. What is the location of the bullet in rectangular coordinates after 5 seconds?

Solution:
The bullet has a vector with length 400 m/s (the "radius") and angle $40°$ (theta). After 5 seconds of motion, the bullet's polar coordinates are (r=2000 meters, $\theta = \frac{2\pi}{9}$). We must convert these polar coordinates to rectangular coordinates:

$$x = 2000 * \cos(\frac{2\pi}{9}) = 1{,}532$$

$$y = 2000 * \sin(\frac{2\pi}{9}) = 1{,}286$$

Many problems in math can be better solved using polar coordinates rather than rectangular points. You may need to convert between the two systems several times when solving a problem.

Spherical Coordinates

Spherical coordinates compose the three-dimensional version of polar coordinates. To describe a 3D point, we need two angles and the distance of the point from the origin. A spherical point is labeled (ρ, θ, φ). Rho is the radius (or distance) of the point from (0, 0, 0). Theta is the angle measured counter-clockwise from the positive x-axis. The point will cast a "shadow" on the x-y plane. Theta is the angle between this shadow and the x-axis. Theta can be any possible angle measurement but is usually between 0 and 2π. The second angle is denoted phi, which is measured out from the positive z-axis. Phi should be between 0 and π. The succeeding diagram illustrates the three coordinates:

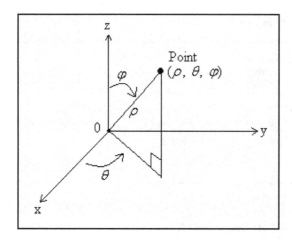

Spherical coordinates may be converted to or from rectangular coordinates. The conversion theorems are outlined below:

Converting spherical to rectangular

$x = \rho * \sin(\varphi) * \cos(\theta)$

$y = \rho * \sin(\varphi) * \sin(\theta)$

$z = \rho * \cos(\varphi)$

Converting rectangular to spherical

$\rho = \sqrt{x^2 + y^2 + z^2}$

$\theta = \tan^{-1}\left(\dfrac{y}{x}\right)$

$\phi = \cos^{-1}\left(\dfrac{z}{\rho}\right)$

Example

Convert the point $\left(5, \dfrac{2\pi}{3}, \dfrac{\pi}{6}\right)$ into rectangular coordinates.

Solution:
The original point is in spherical coordinates with values

$\rho = 5, \quad \theta = \dfrac{2\pi}{3}, \quad \phi = \dfrac{\pi}{6}$

$x = \rho * \sin(\varphi) * \cos(\theta) = 5 * \sin\left(\dfrac{\pi}{6}\right) * \cos\left(\dfrac{2\pi}{3}\right) = -1.25$

$$y = \rho * \sin(\varphi) * \sin(\theta) = 5 * \sin\left(\frac{\pi}{6}\right) * \sin\left(\frac{2\pi}{3}\right) = 2.16506$$

$$z = \rho * \cos(\varphi) = 5 * \cos\left(\frac{\pi}{6}\right) = 4.33013$$

Point (-1.25, 2.16506, 4.33013)

Example
Convert the point (4, -2, -5) into spherical coordinates.

Solution:

$$\rho = \sqrt{4^2 + (-2)^2 + (-5)^2} = \sqrt{45}$$

$$\theta = \tan^{-1}\left(\frac{-2}{4}\right) \approx -0.46365$$

$$\phi = \cos^{-1}\left(\frac{-5}{\sqrt{45}}\right) \approx 2.41186$$

Point $(\sqrt{45},\ -0.46365,\ 2.41186)$

Chapter 3
Linear Algebra

Linear algebra is a field of math using matrices to solve systems of linear equations. A *linear equation* is a polynomial with arbitrarily many variables each with degree 1. An example of a linear equation is $5 = 6w + 15x + 24y - 21z$. This equation has four unknown variables each raised to the power of 1. Linear algebra is a very large branch. The linear algebra presented in this section will empower you to solve systems of equations.

The dominant feature of linear algebra is the heavy use of matrices. A *matrix* is a collection of numbers arranged in a rectangular pattern, with each number identified by a unique address. Matrices could have any number of dimensions, but most of the matrices used in linear algebra are one- or two-dimensional. Matrices are enclosed with square brackets.

Section 3-1 Introduction to Vectors and Matrices

A one-dimensional matrix is also called a *vector*. Vectors are written vertically and thus have only the row dimension (and not the column dimension). A vector is represented by a lowercase letter with an arrow over the top. In addition, individual elements within any matrix are represented by lowercase letters. An example of a vector is

$$\vec{x} = \begin{bmatrix} x_1 \\ x_2 \\ x_3 \\ \vdots \\ x_n \end{bmatrix}$$

The first element is x_1 and is written at the top.

A two-dimensional matrix has rows and columns of elements. A 2D matrix is represented by a capital letter. A 2D matrix might have the form:

$$A = \begin{bmatrix} x_{11} & x_{12} & x_{13} & \cdots & x_{1n} \\ x_{21} & x_{22} & & & x_{2n} \\ x_{31} & & \ddots & & x_{3n} \\ \vdots & & & \ddots & \vdots \\ x_{m1} & x_{m2} & x_{m3} & \cdots & x_{mn} \end{bmatrix}$$

The above matrix is m x n, with m rows and n columns. The cell at row i and column j is denoted by x_{ij}.

Example

(a.) An example of a 2x2 matrix is $\begin{bmatrix} 10 & 6 \\ 42 & 0 \end{bmatrix}$

(b.) An example of a 2x4 matrix is $\begin{bmatrix} 17 & 1 & -8 & 11 \\ -3 & 12 & 4 & 20 \end{bmatrix}$

(c.) An example of a 5x2 matrix is
$$\begin{bmatrix} 2 & 1 \\ 15 & -4 \\ 0 & 7 \\ 52 & 0 \\ 3 & -2 \end{bmatrix}$$

The value 52 is at cell x_{41}, and the value 7 is at cell x_{32}.

Identity Matrix

An *identity matrix* has ones along the main diagonal and zeros elsewhere. The matrices are square in shape and identified with the letter "I." The subscript after "I" signifies the dimensions of the matrix.

$$I_n = \begin{bmatrix} 1 & 0 & 0 & \cdots & 0 \\ 0 & 1 & 0 & & 0 \\ 0 & 0 & 1 & & \vdots \\ \vdots & & & \ddots & 0 \\ 0 & 0 & \cdots & 0 & 1 \end{bmatrix}$$

Some common identity matrices include:

$$I_2 = \begin{bmatrix} 1 & 0 \\ 0 & 1 \end{bmatrix} \qquad I_3 = \begin{bmatrix} 1 & 0 & 0 \\ 0 & 1 & 0 \\ 0 & 0 & 1 \end{bmatrix} \qquad I_4 = \begin{bmatrix} 1 & 0 & 0 & 0 \\ 0 & 1 & 0 & 0 \\ 0 & 0 & 1 & 0 \\ 0 & 0 & 0 & 1 \end{bmatrix}$$

Section 3-2 Matrix Operations

Matrix Addition

To add two matrices A and B, the matrices must have the same dimensions. Suppose $A + B = C$. If A and B have dimensions m x n, then matrix C also has dimensions m x n. Element i, j in matrix C is computed by adding the corresponding elements i, j in matrices A and B. That is, $c_{ij} = a_{ij} + b_{ij}$. In matrix form,

$$A + B = C = \begin{bmatrix} a_{11} + b_{11} & a_{12} + b_{12} & \cdots & a_{1n} + b_{1n} \\ a_{21} + b_{21} & a_{22} + b_{22} & \cdots & a_{2n} + b_{2n} \\ a_{31} + b_{31} & & & \vdots \\ \vdots & & & \vdots \\ a_{m1} + b_{m1} & \cdots & \cdots & a_{mn} + b_{mn} \end{bmatrix}$$

Example

Add the matrices:

a. $\begin{bmatrix} 16 & 1 \\ 9 & 22 \end{bmatrix} + \begin{bmatrix} 8 & 25 \\ 0 & 18 \end{bmatrix}$

b. $\begin{bmatrix} 20 & 62 \\ 31 & 4 \\ 14 & 0 \\ 1 & 50 \end{bmatrix} + \begin{bmatrix} 26 & 0 \\ 30 & 54 \\ 19 & 7 \\ 37 & 43 \end{bmatrix}$

Solutions:

a. $\begin{bmatrix} 16+8 & 1+25 \\ 9+0 & 22+18 \end{bmatrix} = \begin{bmatrix} 24 & 26 \\ 9 & 40 \end{bmatrix}$

b.

$\begin{bmatrix} 20+26 & 62+0 \\ 31+30 & 4+54 \\ 14+19 & 0+7 \\ 1+37 & 50+43 \end{bmatrix} = \begin{bmatrix} 46 & 62 \\ 61 & 58 \\ 33 & 7 \\ 38 & 93 \end{bmatrix}$

Matrix Subtraction

Matrix subtraction is very similar to matrix addition. If $A - B = C$, all three matrices must have the same dimensions m x n. In the resulting matrix, element $c_{ij} = a_{ij} - b_{ij}$. In matrix form,

$$A - B = C = \begin{bmatrix} a_{11} - b_{11} & a_{12} - b_{12} & \cdots & a_{1n} - b_{1n} \\ a_{21} - b_{21} & a_{22} - b_{22} & \cdots & a_{2n} - b_{2n} \\ a_{31} - b_{31} & & & \vdots \\ \vdots & & & \vdots \\ a_{m1} - b_{m1} & \cdots & \cdots & a_{mn} - b_{mn} \end{bmatrix}$$

Example

Subtract the matrices:

a. $\begin{bmatrix} 42 & 18 & 6 & 5 \end{bmatrix} - \begin{bmatrix} 29 & 0 & 9 & 40 \end{bmatrix}$

b. $\begin{bmatrix} 13 & 55 & 35 \\ 53 & 97 & 98 \\ 68 & 1 & 49 \end{bmatrix} - \begin{bmatrix} 86 & 36 & 4 \\ 2 & 76 & 98 \\ 62 & 79 & 85 \end{bmatrix}$

Solutions:

a. $\begin{bmatrix} 13 & 18 & -3 & -35 \end{bmatrix}$

b. $\begin{bmatrix} -73 & 19 & 31 \\ 51 & 21 & 0 \\ 6 & -78 & -36 \end{bmatrix}$

Constant Matrix Multiplication

To multiply a constant value, c, by a matrix A, simply multiply each element in A by c. In matrix form,

$$cA = \begin{bmatrix} ca_{11} & ca_{12} & ca_{13} & \cdots & ca_{1n} \\ ca_{21} & ca_{22} & & & ca_{2n} \\ ca_{31} & & \ddots & & ca_{3n} \\ \vdots & & & \ddots & \vdots \\ ca_{m1} & ca_{m2} & ca_{m3} & \cdots & ca_{mn} \end{bmatrix}$$

The size of the new matrix is unchanged from that of A.

Example

Compute the following:

a.

$5 * \begin{bmatrix} 1 & -2 & -7 \\ 0 & 6 & -6 \\ -5 & -7 & -3 \end{bmatrix}$

b.

$$-8 * \begin{bmatrix} 10 \\ -6 \\ 4 \\ -1 \end{bmatrix}$$

Solutions:

a.

$$\begin{bmatrix} 5 & -10 & -35 \\ 0 & 30 & -30 \\ -25 & -35 & -15 \end{bmatrix}$$

b.

$$\begin{bmatrix} -80 \\ 48 \\ -32 \\ 8 \end{bmatrix}$$

Matrix Multiplication

Suppose A is a m x n matrix, and B is a n x p matrix. Then, A*B = C, where C is a m x p matrix. Notice that the number of columns in the left-hand matrix equals the number of rows in the right-hand matrix.

$$m \times n \quad * \quad n \times p \ = \ m \times p$$

In the resulting matrix, cell $c_{ij} = \sum_{k=1}^{n} a_{ik} * b_{kj}$. Stated differently, cell c_{ij} equals the sum of the elements in row i of matrix A multiplied by the corresponding elements in column j of matrix B.

Example
Perform the following matrix multiplications:

a.

$$\begin{bmatrix} 13 & 1 \\ 4 & 11 \end{bmatrix} * \begin{bmatrix} 9 & 19 & 13 \\ 5 & 8 & 4 \end{bmatrix} = C$$

b.

$$\begin{bmatrix} 11 & 13 & -7 & -1 \end{bmatrix} * \begin{bmatrix} 19 & 0 \\ -6 & -3 \\ 0 & 16 \\ 18 & 9 \end{bmatrix} = C$$

Solutions:

a.

$(2 \times 2)*(2 \times 3) = 2 \times 3$ matrix

$c_{11} = $ (row 1 from A) * (column 1 from B) $= 13 * 9 + 1 * 5 = 122$
$c_{12} = $ (row 1 from A) * (column 2 from B) $= 13 * 19 + 1 * 8 = 255$
$c_{13} = $ (row 1 from A) * (column 3 from B) $= 13 * 13 + 1 * 4 = 173$

$c_{21} = $ (row 2 from A) * (column 1 from B) $= 4 * 9 + 11 * 5 = 91$
$c_{22} = $ (row 2 from A) * (column 2 from B) $= 4 * 19 + 11 * 8 = 164$
$c_{23} = $ (row 2 from A) * (column 3 from B) $= 4 * 13 + 11 * 4 = 96$

$$C = \begin{bmatrix} 122 & 255 & 173 \\ 91 & 164 & 96 \end{bmatrix}$$

b.

$(1 \times 4)*(4 \times 2) = 1 \times 2$ matrix

$c_{11} = 11*19 + 13(-6) + (-7)*0 + (-1)*18 = 113$
$c_{12} = 11*0 + 13(-3) + (-7)*16 + (-1)*9 = -160$

$$C = \begin{bmatrix} 113 & -160 \end{bmatrix}$$

Transposing Matrices

The symbol for a transpose operation is a capital 'T' above and to the right of the matrix. For example, A^T means "matrix A transposed." When transposing a matrix, the rows and columns of the original matrix essentially switch positions. If matrix A is m x n, its transpose is n x m (the number of columns and rows flip). Row 1 of matrix A will become column 1 of A^T. Row 2 of A becomes column 2 of A^T, and so on. Another way to visualize the transposition is column 1 of A becomes row 1 of A^T, column 2 of A becomes row 2 of A^T, etc. Cell a_{ij} from matrix A will be cell a_{ji} in A^T.

Example

Transpose the following:

a.

$$A = \begin{bmatrix} -9 & 5 & 4 \\ 11 & 0 & 3 \end{bmatrix}$$

b.

$$B = \begin{bmatrix} -1 & 3 & 6 & 11 \end{bmatrix}$$

c.

$$C = \begin{bmatrix} 14 & 19 \\ 21 & -9 \\ -5 & 15 \\ 26 & 12 \end{bmatrix}$$

Solutions:

a.

$$A^T = \begin{bmatrix} -9 & 11 \\ 5 & 0 \\ 4 & 3 \end{bmatrix} \quad 3 \times 2$$

b.

$$B^T = \begin{bmatrix} -1 \\ 3 \\ 6 \\ 11 \end{bmatrix} \quad 4 \times 1$$

c.

$$C^T = \begin{bmatrix} 14 & 21 & -5 & 26 \\ 19 & -9 & 15 & 12 \end{bmatrix} \quad 2 \times 4$$

Rather than writing vectors as space-consuming columns of numbers, you can transpose the vector into a row of values. For instance, instead of writing vector x in the regular column form, you could illustrate the vector with $\vec{x}^T = \begin{bmatrix} x_1 & x_2 & x_3 & \cdots & x_n \end{bmatrix}$. Many mathematicians write vectors as rows with angle brackets, such as $\vec{x} = < x_1, \ x_2, \ x_3, \ ...., \ x_n >$.

Section 3-3 Systems of Linear Equations

A *system* is a set of two or more equations that contain two or more of the same unknown variables. To solve a system of linear equations containing n unknown variables, the system must have at least n equations. We essentially need one equation for each variable. To solve for 3 variables, we must have 3 or more equations.

Example

Solve for x and y given the following relations:

$$\begin{cases} 3x - 2y = 7 \\ 8x + y = 4 \end{cases}$$

Solution:

To solve for x and y without using matrices, first pick one of the equations and solve for one variable in terms of the other variables.

$$3x - 2y = 7$$
$$\downarrow$$
$$3x = 7 + 2y$$
$$x = \frac{7 + 2y}{3}$$

Next, place the definition for x into the second equation.

$$8\left(\frac{7 + 2y}{3}\right) + y = 4$$
$$18.6667 + 5.3333y + y = 4$$
$$6.3333y = -14.6667 \quad \rightarrow \quad y = -2.31579$$

Next, place the value for y into the first equation, and solve for x.

$$3x - 2y = 7$$
$$3x + 4.63158 = 7$$
$$x \approx 0.78947$$

$$\begin{cases} x = 0.78947 \\ y = -2.31579 \end{cases}$$

The above method for solving a system works well with a small number of variables and equations. However, the "brute force" method becomes very challenging with a large system. We need a more efficient method to solve systems of any size.

Systems of linear equations are ideal candidates for matrix operations. A system even has the appearance of containing several matrices. Consider the system below:

$$\begin{cases} 2x_1 + 17x_2 + 13x_3 + 18x_4 = -2 \\ 10x_1 + 13x_2 - 1x_3 + 6x_4 = -4 \\ -2x_1 + 18x_2 - 10x_3 + 15x_4 = 15 \\ -3x_1 + 19x_2 - 5x_3 - 9x_4 = 20 \end{cases}$$

First, note that all the solutions on the right side form a column vector. Let's call $\vec{b}$ the vector of solutions. This system has 4 unknown variables. Each variable in each equation has a real-valued coefficient. These coefficients form another matrix, called matrix A, which is 4x4. Lastly, let's store the 4 variables in $\vec{x}$. For this problem,

$$A = \begin{bmatrix} 2 & 17 & 13 & 18 \\ 10 & 13 & -1 & 6 \\ -2 & 18 & -10 & 15 \\ -3 & 19 & -5 & -9 \end{bmatrix} \qquad \vec{x} = \begin{bmatrix} x_1 \\ x_2 \\ x_3 \\ x_4 \end{bmatrix} \qquad \vec{b} = \begin{bmatrix} -2 \\ -4 \\ 15 \\ 20 \end{bmatrix}$$

Multiplying matrix A and vector x will create the left half of the preceding system. That is,

$$A\vec{x} = \begin{bmatrix} 2x_1 + 17x_2 + 13x_3 + 18x_4 \\ 10x_1 + 13x_2 - 1x_3 + 6x_4 \\ -2x_1 + 18x_2 - 10x_3 + 15x_4 \\ -3x_1 + 19x_2 - 5x_3 - 9x_4 \end{bmatrix}$$

We can then set the above matrix equal to vector b. In a more concise form, $A\vec{x} = \vec{b}$. To summarize,

---

A = matrix of coefficients

$\vec{x}$ = vector of unknowns

$\vec{b}$ = vector of solutions

$A\vec{x} = \vec{b}$

When solving systems using linear algebra, the primary objective is to simplify matrices A and b. Ideally, if matrix A was an identity matrix, then vector b would contain the values for all the unknown variables. Reducing matrix A to an identity matrix requires a great amount of work. The second best option is for A to be a diagonal matrix (with non-zero entries along the main diagonal and zeros elsewhere). You could then solve for the lone unknown variable in each row. This routine also requires much effort. The third and most practical option entails transforming A into an upper triangular matrix. This matrix has a mix of non-zero and zero elements along the main diagonal and upper-right corner, and it has only zeros in the lower-left corner. You solve for the unknowns in reserve, starting with x_n and using the values for the unknowns to find the remaining variables.

To transform a system to upper triangular form, you must use *Gaussian elimination*. This type of elimination contains three operations you can perform on matrices A and b. The operations are performed at a row level rather than with columns or the entire matrix. The operations are stated here:

Gaussian Elimination

(1.) Permutation -- Switch rows i and j.
Syntax: $R_i \leftrightarrow R_j$

(2.) Constant Multiplication -- Multiply row i by a constant c.
Syntax: cR_i

(3.) Row Addition -- Multiply row i by a constant and add it to row j.
Syntax: $cR_i + R_j$

These operations do not change the values of the unknowns. The resulting upper triangular system is in *row echelon form* (or REF). If you need to convert the coefficient matrix to a perfect diagonal, then you must also perform column operations of the same nature. A system in which A has been simplified to an identity matrix is in *reduced row echelon form* (or RREF).

You should follow several other details when using Gaussian Elimination. First, matrices A and b are typically combined into one large matrix. The two matrices are separated by a vertical bar, as in $\left[A \mid \vec{b}\right]$. The same Gaussian Elimination operations apply to both A and $\vec{b}$. The goal is to obtain zeros in all cells below the main diagonal of matrix A. Even though you are performing row operations, work on the matrix column by column. Start with the leftmost column and reduce it so that all the elements below the first row are zero. Then move on to the second column and create zeros below the cell (2, 2). The end result for a 3x3 matrix would be similar to:

$$\begin{bmatrix} 5 & -1 & 3 & 6 \\ 0 & 8 & 7 & 3 \\ 0 & 0 & 2 & 4 \end{bmatrix}$$

You should not be concerned about the end result of vector b. Focus only on transforming matrix A into upper triangular form.

Example
Reduce the succeeding matrices to upper triangular form with Gaussian elimination.

a.

$$\left[A \mid \vec{b}\right] = \begin{bmatrix} 2 & 17 & 13 & 18 & -2 \\ 10 & 13 & -1 & 6 & -4 \\ -2 & 18 & -10 & 15 & 15 \\ -3 & 19 & -5 & -9 & 20 \end{bmatrix}$$

$$\downarrow -5R_1 + R_2, \quad R_1 + R_3, \quad \frac{3}{2}R_1 + R_4$$

$$\begin{bmatrix} 2 & 17 & 13 & 18 & -2 \\ 0 & -72 & -66 & -84 & 6 \\ 0 & 35 & 3 & 33 & 13 \\ 0 & 44.5 & 14.5 & 18 & 17 \end{bmatrix}$$

$$\downarrow \frac{35}{72}R_2 + R_3, \quad \frac{44.5}{72}R_2 + R_4$$

$$\begin{bmatrix} 2 & 17 & 13 & 18 & -2 \\ 0 & -72 & -66 & -84 & 6 \\ 0 & 0 & -29.083 & -7.833 & 15.917 \\ 0 & 0 & -26.292 & -33.917 & 20.708 \end{bmatrix}$$

$$\downarrow -0.904R_3 + R_4$$

$$\begin{bmatrix} 2 & 17 & 13 & 18 & -2 \\ 0 & -72 & -66 & -84 & 6 \\ 0 & 0 & -29.083 & -7.833 & 15.917 \\ 0 & 0 & 0 & -26.836 & 6.319 \end{bmatrix}$$

b.

$$\left[A \mid \vec{b}\right] = \begin{bmatrix} 0 & 1 & 4 & 7 \\ 6 & 0 & 5 & 3 \\ 2 & 7 & 10 & 4 \end{bmatrix}$$

$$\downarrow R_1 \leftrightarrow R_3$$

$$= \begin{bmatrix} 2 & 7 & 10 & 4 \\ 6 & 0 & 5 & 3 \\ 0 & 1 & 4 & 7 \end{bmatrix}$$

$$\downarrow -3R_1 + R_2$$

$$= \begin{bmatrix} 2 & 7 & 10 & 4 \\ 0 & -21 & -25 & -9 \\ 0 & 1 & 4 & 7 \end{bmatrix}$$

$$\downarrow \frac{1}{21}R_2 + R_3$$

$$= \begin{bmatrix} 2 & 7 & 10 & 4 \\ 0 & -21 & -25 & -9 \\ 0 & 0 & 2.8095 & 6.5714 \end{bmatrix}$$

Continuing the example in this section (from part 'a' above), the system is now

$$\begin{cases} 2x_1 + 17x_2 + 13x_3 + 18x_4 = -2 \\ -72x_2 - 66x_3 - 84x_4 = 6 \\ -29.083x_3 - 7.833x_4 = 15.917 \\ -26.836x_4 = 6.319 \end{cases}$$

After performing Gaussian Elimination, the final step of solving a system is to use *back substitution*. Start with the bottommost equation and solve for the single unknown variable, x_n. Then move up to the second-to-last equation, plug the value for x_n into the expression, and solve for x_{n-1}. Continue moving up the equation list, using the solutions for unknowns to find the next variable. Back substitution applied to this example takes the form:

$$-26.836x_4 = 6.319 \quad \rightarrow \quad x_4 = -0.23547$$

$$-29.083x_3 - 7.833x_4 = 15.917$$
$$-29.083x_3 + 1.84444 = 15.917 \quad \rightarrow \quad x_3 = -0.48388$$

$$-72x_2 - 66x_3 - 84x_4 = 6$$
$$-72x_2 + 31.93608 + 19.77948 = 6 \quad \rightarrow \quad x_2 = 0.63494$$

$$2x_1 + 17x_2 + 13x_3 + 18x_4 = -2$$
$$2x_1 + 10.79398 - 6.29044 - 4.23846 = -2 \quad \rightarrow \quad x_1 = -1.13254$$

To check the solutions, place the values for the 4 unknowns into one of the original equations. The last equation becomes

$$-3x_1 + 19x_2 - 5x_3 - 9x_4 = 20$$
$$20.00011 \approx 20$$

Example

Solve this system:

$$\begin{cases} 4x_1 + x_3 = 7 \\ -2x_2 + 6x_3 = 4 \\ 8x_1 - 4x_2 + 9x_3 = 1 \end{cases}$$

Solution:

$$[A \mid \vec{b}] = \begin{bmatrix} 4 & 0 & 1 & 7 \\ 0 & -2 & 6 & 4 \\ 8 & -4 & 9 & 1 \end{bmatrix}$$

$$\downarrow -2R_1 + R_3$$

$$\begin{bmatrix} 4 & 0 & 1 & 7 \\ 0 & -2 & 6 & 4 \\ 0 & -4 & 7 & -13 \end{bmatrix}$$

$$\downarrow -2R_2 + R_3$$

$$\begin{bmatrix} 4 & 0 & 1 & 7 \\ 0 & -2 & 6 & 4 \\ 0 & 0 & -5 & -21 \end{bmatrix}$$

$$\begin{cases} 4x_1 + x_3 = 7 \\ -2x_2 + 6x_3 = 4 \\ -5x_3 = -21 \end{cases}$$

$$-5x_3 = -21 \quad \rightarrow \quad x_3 = 4.2$$

$$-2x_2 + 6x_3 = 4$$
$$-2x_2 + 25.2 = 4 \quad \rightarrow \quad x_2 = 10.6$$

$$4x_1 + x_3 = 7$$
$$4x_1 + 4.2 = 7 \quad \rightarrow \quad x_1 = 0.7$$

The vector of solutions is $< x_1 = 0.7, \ x_2 = 10.6, \ x_3 = 4.2 >$

Chapter 4
Derivatives

Many fields require tracking the change in a phenomenon over time or with respect to a similar independent variable. Perhaps the simplest application of derivatives appears in the motion of objects. For example, you might have discrete data on the location of an object traveling in a straight line at various times. Suppose time is on the horizontal axis and distance is on the vertical axis, and the various points are connected with segments. When the graph spikes upwards, the object must be moving quickly, but when the graph levels off, the object must be traveling slowly. In other words, the slope of the graph corresponds to the speed of the object. If the graph turns downwards, the object must be traveling in reverse (with negative speed). The slope of a graph is the first derivative of the graph. Recall that the slope simply reports the magnitude of change over 1 unit of independent variable increment. In this example, speed is the first derivative of distance. You can also take the derivative of derivatives. The derivative of speed is acceleration. Just as speed measures the change in distance per unit of time, acceleration measures the change in speed per unit of time. The object will have positive acceleration if the next segment in time is steeper than the previous segment. On the other hand, the object will be decelerating if the next segment has a smaller slope than the previous segment. Acceleration is the second derivative of distance. You can even find the derivative of acceleration, called jerk, creating a third order derivative of distance.

Section 4-1 Sequences and Series

A *sequence* is a list of terms generated by a common function. The terms of a sequence are generally represented by lowercase letters and a subscript indicating the address of the term in the sequence. Sequences typically begin with subscript n equal to 1 and may continue to positive infinity. Additionally, sequences are enclosed with curly braces. Consider the sequence $a_n = \{2, 5, 8, 11, 14, ...\}$. The first element is designated $a_1 = 2$. The second element is $a_2 = 5$ and so on.

An *explicitly defined sequence* has an underlying function with independent variable n—the index of the term. For example, you could immediately find the 10,000[th] term of a sequence that is defined explicitly. A *recursively defined sequence* has a formula that incorporates at least one previous term to compute the current nth term. In order to find the 10,000[th] term in a recursively defined sequence, you will typically need to find the previous 9,999 terms. Most sequences could be defined with both explicit and recursive formulas.

Two trivial types of sequences include arithmetic and geometric sequences. An arithmetic sequence is developed by simply adding the same constant to consecutive terms.

Arithmetic Sequence

Explicit Syntax:　　$a_n = a_1 + (n-1)d$, where d is a common difference

Recursive Syntax:　　$\begin{cases} a_1 = ---- \text{ (typically given)} \\ a_n = a_{n-1} + d \end{cases}$

An example of an arithmetic sequence is $\{100, 105, 110, 115, 120,...\}$. The common difference d is 5. The two syntaxes are:

Explicit Syntax:　　$a_n = 100 + (n-1)5$

Recursive Syntax:　　$\begin{cases} a_1 = 100 \\ a_n = a_{n-1} + 5 \end{cases}$

Let's find the ninth term by using the two methods. The explicit formula provides $a_9 = 100 + (9-1)5 = 140$. The recursive formula requires more work: $a_6 = a_5 + 5 = 125$,

$a_7 = a_6 + 5 = 130$, $a_8 = a_7 + 5 = 135$, and $a_9 = a_8 + 5 = 140$. The recursive formula nearly always requires more work and is inefficient. If possible, attempt to convert a recursive formula into an explicit model.

A *geometric sequence* is created by multiplying consecutive elements by the same constant. Consider a rubber ball initially dropped from a height of 10 feet. On the first bounce, the ball comes back to 8.5 feet. After the second bounce, the ball reaches a height of 7.23 feet, and so on. With each successive bounce, the ball reaches a height equal to 85% of its previous height. Stated differently, the previous height is multiplied by 0.85 to get the current height. The two forms of geometric sequences are:

Geometric Sequence

Explicit Syntax: $a_n = a_1 * r^{n-1}$, where r is the common multiplier

Recursive Syntax: $\begin{cases} a_1 = ---- \text{ (typically given)} \\ a_n = a_{n-1} * r \end{cases}$

Example

A house has a value that grows 9% every year. If the house currently costs $40,000, what is the building's value 30 years from now?

Solution:
The value of the home each year creates a geometric sequence with factor r = 1.09. We are also given the first term $a_1 = \$40,000$. 30 years from now, the term subscript will be 31. Using the explicit formula,
$$a_{31} = a_1 * 1.09^{31-1} = 40,000 * 1.09^{30} = \$530,707$$

A *series* is the sum of the elements within a sequence. The symbol for a sum of terms is S_n. In summation form, $S_n = \sum_{i=1}^{n} a_i$. The general equation for an arithmetic series is:

Arithmetic Series

$$S_n = \frac{n}{2}(2a_1 + (n-1)d)$$

The basic formula for a geometric series is

Geometric Series

(1.) If $n < \infty$, then

(a.) If $|r| < 1$, then $S_n = \dfrac{a_1 * (1 - r^n)}{(1 - r)}$

(b.) If $|r| > 1$, then $S_n = \dfrac{a_1 * (r^n - 1)}{(r - 1)}$

(2.) If $n = \infty$, then

(a.) If $|r| < 1$, then $S_\infty = \dfrac{a_1}{(1 - r)}$

(b.) If $|r| > 1$, then $S_\infty = \pm\infty$

Example

Evaluate the following series:

a. The sum of all the integers from 1 to 1000, inclusive.
b. The sum of the elements in $\{5000, 4900, 4800, 4700, \ldots, 0\}$.
c. The sum of the elements in $\{4.5, 3.96, 3.4848, 3.0666, 2.6986, \ldots\}$
d. The sum of the terms generated by multiplying each previous term by 1.15, starting with 10, and ending with the 20th term.

Solutions:

a.
This sequence is arithmetic with $d = 1$.

$$S_{1000} = \frac{1000}{2}(2*1 + (1000 - 1)*1) = 500{,}500$$

b.
This sequence is arithmetic with $d = -100$, $a_1 = 5000$, and $n = \dfrac{5000}{100} + 1 = 51$.

$$S_{51} = \frac{51}{2}(2*5000 + (51 - 1)*(-100)) = 127{,}500$$

c.
This sequence is geometric with $r = \dfrac{3.96}{4.5} = 0.88$ and $n = \infty$.

$$S_\infty = \frac{4.5}{(1 - 0.88)} = \frac{4.5}{0.12} = 37.5$$

d.
This sequence is geometric with $r = 1.15$, $a_1 = 10$, and $n = 20$.

$$S_{20} = \frac{10*(1.15^{20} - 1)}{(1.15 - 1)} = 1{,}024.43583$$

Several other specific types of sequences exist. An *alternating sequence* has elements that alternate between positive and negative signs. A simple alternating sequence might have the terms {4, -2, 1, -1/2, 1/4, -1/8, 1/16, ...}, formed by multiplying the previous term by -1/2. A *harmonic sequence* is the reciprocal of an arithmetic sequence. To form a harmonic sequence, the elements of an arithmetic sequence are reciprocated. An example of a harmonic sequence is {1/6, 1/9, 1/12, 1/15, 1/18, ...}. The *Fibonacci Sequence* is {1, 1, 2, 3, 5, 8, 13, 21, ...}, where the previous two elements add together to form the next element. Explicitly, the n+1st term of the Fibonacci Sequence is $a_{n+1} = a_n + a_{n-1}$.

Section 4-2 Introduction to Limits

Limits are valuable for evaluating functions near endpoints of their domains. Limits also form the core of may proofs and definitions in mathematics. Sequences and functions may have limits.

The limit of a sequence is the value the elements approach as the subscript n approaches infinity. The sequence will appear to level-off around the limit. A *convergent* sequence has a limit, while a *divergent* sequence approaches $\pm\infty$ and never settles arbitrarily close to a certain number. Several rules for evaluating limits of sequences are displayed below:

Properties of Sequence Limits:
(1.) A constant sequence has a limit equal to that constant value.
(2.) For sequences defined explicitly with a rational function of two

polynomials $\dfrac{g}{h}$ ...

    a.   If the degree of g is greater than the degree of h, the sequence is divergent and the terms approach infinity.

    b.   If the degree of h is greater than the degree of g, the sequence is convergent with a limit of zero.

    c.   If the degrees of g and h are equal, the sequence is convergent and the limit equals the ratio of the coefficients tied to the two highest order terms.

Example

Find the limits of the following sequences:

a. $a_n = \dfrac{10n^8 + 5n^6 + 14}{15n^6 + 12n^3}$

b. $b_n = \dfrac{16n^{10} + 19n^4 + 17n^2}{20n^{13} + 5n^9 + 70}$

---

c. $c_n = \dfrac{45n^6 - 15n^3}{18n^6 - 14n}$

Solutions:

a.
The numerator has degree 8, and the denominator has degree 6. Since the degree of the numerator exceeds that of the denominator, the sequence is divergent and approaches infinity as n becomes arbitrarily large.

b.
Degree of numerator = 10 < Degree of denominator = 13
∴ Sequence b is convergent with limit zero

c.
Degree of numerator = degree of denominator = 6
∴ Sequence c is convergent with limit $\dfrac{45}{18} = 2.5$.

Limits of functions are very similar to limits for sequences. The limit notation for functions is generally in the form:

$$\lim_{x \to c} f(x)$$

The above expression reads "the limit of f(x) as x approaches c."

Another way of writing a limit is: $f(x) \to b$ as $x \to c$. This statement reads "f(x) approaches b as x approaches c." The value 'b' is the limit of f(x). The function is not evaluated precisely at c, but at a value arbitrarily close to c. For functions that include c in their domain, the limit is simply f(c). Typically, however, c is not included in the function's domain, so the limit must be computed manually.

Example

Consider the function tan(x). This function is undefined for $x = \dfrac{\pi}{2} + \pi n$, where n is any integer. When x = $\pi/2$, for example, the tangent function would return positive infinity (the slope is infinitely large for a ray pointing straight up). If x = $-\pi/2$, then the tangent function would yield negative infinity. Stated differently, the limit of the tangent function as x *increases* to $\pi/2$ is positive infinity. The limit of the tangent function as x *decreases* to $\pi/2$ is negative infinity. The function appears to have two very different limits around x = $\pi/2$, so the limit is undefined here.

There are two ways to approach c—from the right or from the left. A function may have a limit as you approach the target from the right, but not as you approach it from the left. The "right" and "left" terms assume the x-axis is the horizontal axis. When approaching a target from the left, use the '-' sign after the target. The *left-hand limit* of f is:

$$\lim_{x \to c-} f(x)$$

The above expression reads "the limit of f(x) as x approaches c from the left."

When approaching a target from the right, use the '+' sign after the target. The *right-hand limit* of f is:

$$\lim_{x \to c+} f(x)$$

If the limit of f(x) as x approaches c from the right and the left is the same value, then the limit is defined. On the other hand, if the limits from the right and left are different values, then the limit "does not exist."

Example
Evaluate the following limit by computing f(x) with x-values arbitrarily closer to 4:
$$\lim_{x \to 4} \frac{x^2 - 16}{x - 4}.$$

Solution:

The function is undefined when x = 4, since $f(4) = \dfrac{4^2 - 16}{4 - 4} = \dfrac{0}{0}$.

x < 4	f(x)
3.5	7.5
3.9	7.9
3.99	7.99
3.999	7.999
3.9999	7.9999

$$\lim_{x \to 4^-} \frac{x^2 - 16}{x - 4} = 8$$

x > 4	f(x)
4.5	8.50000
4.1	8.10000
4.01	8.01000
4.001	8.00100
4.0001	8.00010

$$\lim_{x \to 4^+} \frac{x^2 - 16}{x - 4} = 8$$

$$\lim_{x \to 4^-} \frac{x^2 - 16}{x - 4} = \lim_{x \to 4^+} \frac{x^2 - 16}{x - 4} = 8$$

$$\therefore \lim_{x \to 4} \frac{x^2 - 16}{x - 4} = 8$$

Example
Find the limit below:
$$\lim_{x \to \pi/2} \frac{x^3}{\cos(x)}.$$

Solution:
The limit of the function cannot be evaluated directly, since the denominator of the fraction, $\cos(\pi/2)$, is zero.

Let's evaluate the limit of the function as x approaches its target from the right and left.

From the left…

x < $\pi/2$	f(x)

1.4	16.14430
1.5	47.71181
1.55	179.07698
1.5705	13,072.02606
1.5707	40,228.38721

$$\lim_{x \to \pi/2^-} \frac{x^3}{\cos(x)} = \infty$$

From the right...

x > π / 2	f(x)
1.6	-140.27627
1.59	-209.33110
1.58	-428.56451
1.571	-19,036.83126
1.5708	-1,055,158.00666

$$\lim_{x \to \pi/2^+} \frac{x^3}{\cos(x)} = -\infty$$

$$\lim_{x \to \pi/2^-} \frac{x^3}{\cos(x)} \neq \lim_{x \to \pi/2^+} \frac{x^3}{\cos(x)}$$

$$\therefore \lim_{x \to \pi/2} \frac{x^3}{\cos(x)} = \text{d.n.e.} \quad \text{(does not exist)}$$

Example
Compute the following limit:

$$\lim_{x \to 0} \frac{\tan^{-1}(x)}{x}$$

From the left...

x < 0	f(x)
-0.5	0.92730
-0.1	0.99669
-0.01	0.99997
-0.001	≈ 1
-0.0001	≈ 1

$$\lim_{x \to 0^-} \frac{\tan^{-1}(x)}{x} = 1$$

From the right...

x > 0	f(x)
0.5	0.92730
0.1	0.99669
0.01	0.99997
0.001	≈ 1
0.0001	≈ 1

$$\lim_{x \to 0^+} \frac{\tan^{-1}(x)}{x} = 1$$

$$\lim_{x \to 0^-} \frac{\tan^{-1}(x)}{x} = \lim_{x \to 0^+} \frac{\tan^{-1}(x)}{x} = 1$$

$$\therefore \lim_{x \to 0} \frac{\tan^{-1}(x)}{x} = 1$$

Limit Properties:

Suppose $\lim_{x \to c} f(x)$ **and** $\lim_{x \to c} g(x)$ **both exist. Then,**

(1.) $\lim_{x \to c} (f(x) + g(x)) = \lim_{x \to c} f(x) + \lim_{x \to c} g(x)$

(2.) $\lim_{x \to c} K * f(x) = K * \lim_{x \to c} f(x)$, where K is a constant

(3.) $\lim_{x \to c} (f(x) * g(x)) = \lim_{x \to c} f(x) * \lim_{x \to c} g(x)$

(4.) $\lim_{x \to c} \frac{f(x)}{g(x)} = \frac{\lim_{x \to c} f(x)}{\lim_{x \to c} g(x)}$, assuming $\lim_{x \to c} g(x) \neq 0$

$$(5.) \quad \lim_{x \to c} (f(x))^n = \left(\lim_{x \to c} f(x) \right)^n$$

The limit of a constant is simply the constant value. That is, $\lim_{x \to c} (K) = K$, where K is a constant. For example, $\lim_{x \to 10} (25) = 25.$

Example
Calculate the following limit:

$$\lim_{x \to 7} \left(x + \frac{x^2 - 49}{x - 7} \right)$$

Solution:

$$= \lim_{x \to 7} (x) + \lim_{x \to 7} \left(\frac{x^2 - 49}{x - 7} \right)$$

$$= 7 + \lim_{x \to 7} \left(\frac{(x - 7)(x + 7)}{(x - 7)} \right)$$

$$= 7 + \lim_{x \to 7} (x + 7)$$

$$= 7 + (7 + 7) = 21$$

Example
Calculate the following limit:

$$\lim_{x \to 0} \frac{\sqrt{25 + x} - 5}{10x}$$

Solution:
Since the limit of g(x) (the denominator) is zero, we cannot use the limit property for the quotient of two expressions.

$$\frac{\sqrt{25 + x} - 5}{10x} = \frac{\sqrt{25 + x} - 5}{10x} * \left(\frac{\sqrt{25 + x} + 5}{\sqrt{25 + x} + 5} \right) = \frac{\left(\sqrt{25 + x} \right)^2 - 25}{10x(\sqrt{25 + x} + 5)}$$

$$= \frac{25 + x - 25}{10x(\sqrt{25+x}+5)} = \frac{x}{10x(\sqrt{25+x}+5)} = \frac{1}{10(\sqrt{25+x}+5)}$$

$$\lim_{x \to 0} \frac{\sqrt{25+x}-5}{10x} = \lim_{x \to 0} \frac{1}{10(\sqrt{25+x}+5)} = \frac{1}{10(\sqrt{25+0}+5)} = 0.01$$

Example

Calculate the following limit:

$$\lim_{x \to -2} \frac{x^6 - 4x^4}{x+2}$$

Solution:

$$\frac{x^6 - 4x^4}{x+2} = \frac{x^4 * (x^2 - 4)}{x+2} = x^4 * \frac{(x^2 - 4)}{x+2}$$

$$\lim_{x \to -2} \frac{x^6 - 4x^4}{x+2} = \lim_{x \to -2} x^4 * \frac{(x^2 - 4)}{x+2}$$

$$= \lim_{x \to -2} x^4 \ * \ \lim_{x \to -2} \frac{(x^2 - 4)}{x+2}$$

$$= 16 \ * \ \lim_{x \to -2} \frac{(x^2 - 4)}{x+2}$$

$$= 16 \ * \ \lim_{x \to -2} \frac{(x-2)(x+2)}{x+2}$$

$$= 16 \ * \ \lim_{x \to -2} (x-2)$$

$$= 16 * (-4) = -64$$

Example

Compute the following limit:

$$\lim_{x \to 8} \left(\sqrt[5]{x+10} \right)^9$$

Solution:

$$\left(\sqrt[5]{x+10} \right)^9 = (x+10)^{(1/5)*9} = (x+10)^{9/5}$$

$$\lim_{x \to 8} \left(\sqrt[5]{x+10} \right)^9 = \left(\lim_{x \to 8} (x+10) \right)^{9/5} = 18^{9/5} \approx 181.7567$$

Section 4-3 Evaluating Infinite Limits

Infinite limits describe the behavior of functions as they become very large in absolute value in their dependent and independent variables. As x approaches positive or negative infinity, the function might level-off around a certain y-value or the function could continue climbing to infinity. A function might also encounter an x-value that it simply cannot cross; the function splits to $\pm\infty$ around a particular x-value.

Consider a hyperbola defined as $f(x) = \dfrac{1}{x}$. Find the limit of f as x approaches 0.

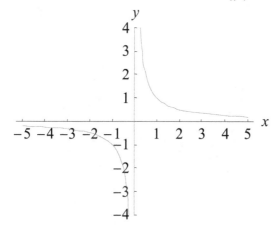

Solution:
The quantity we must find is
$$\lim_{x \to 0} \frac{1}{x}$$

The function is clearly undefined at x = 0; plugging 0 into the function will result in a divide-by-zero error. What is the function's behavior shortly before and shortly after x = 0? We should find the limit of f as x approaches zero from both the right and left. A simple way to evaluate a troublesome limit involves using t-tables. The tables below show the values of f for small x-values:

x	f(x)
-1	-1
-0.1	-10
-0.01	-100

| -0.001 | -1,000 |
| -0.0001 | -10,000 |

x	f(x)
1	1
0.1	10
0.01	100
0.001	1,000
0.0001	10,000

The function's output values will continue to decrease towards negative infinity as x becomes closer and closer to zero but remains below zero. The opposite is true for very small positive x-values, where the function is approaching positive infinity.

The hyperbola appears to graze the vertical line x = 0 but never cross it. x = 0 is a line that the original function becomes infinitely closer to. For the hyperbola, the line x = 0 is a vertical asymptote. A *vertical asymptote* exists at x = a if the function's limit as $x \to a$ from the right or left is $\pm\infty$. Stated differently, x = a is a vertical asymptote iff

$$\lim_{x \to a^+} f(x) = \pm\infty \quad \text{and} \quad \lim_{x \to a^-} f(x) = \pm\infty .$$

Instead of using t-tables, you could evaluate the limits using implicit logic.

From the left...

$$\lim_{x \to 0^-} \frac{1}{x} = \frac{1}{\text{very small negative number}} = \frac{1}{-0.000001} = -\infty$$

From the right...

$$\lim_{x \to 0^+} \frac{1}{x} = \frac{1}{\text{very small positive number}} = \frac{1}{0.000001} = \infty$$

$$\lim_{x \to 0^-} \frac{1}{x} = -\infty \neq \lim_{x \to 0^+} \frac{1}{x} = \infty$$

∴ limit d.n.e.

Example

Find $\lim_{x \to 3\pi/2} \tan(x)$

Solution:

The tangent function is undefined when $x = \dfrac{\pi}{2} + \pi n$ $\forall$ integers n. The slope in the unit circle will approach positive or negative infinity for these x-values.

$$\lim_{x \to 3\pi/2^-} \left(\frac{\sin(x)}{\cos(x)} \right) = \frac{-1}{\text{small negative}} = \text{positive large number} = \infty$$

$$\lim_{x \to 3\pi/2^+} \left(\frac{\sin(x)}{\cos(x)} \right) = \frac{-1}{\text{small positive}} = \text{negative large number} = -\infty$$

$$\lim_{x \to 3\pi/2^-} f(x) \quad \ne \quad \lim_{x \to 3\pi/2^+} f(x)$$

$$\therefore \quad \lim_{x \to 3\pi/2} f(x) = \text{d.n.e.}$$

Computing an infinite limit often requires some simplifying logic. Suppose the function for which you are trying to find a limit is essentially a fraction. If the numerator becomes infinitely large relative to the denominator, then the limit must be $\pm\infty$.

That is, $\dfrac{<\text{a positive constant}>}{0.000....01} = \infty$ and $\dfrac{<\text{a positive constant}>}{-0.000....01} = -\infty$ and

$\dfrac{<\text{a negative constant}>}{0.000....01} = -\infty$ and $\dfrac{<\text{a negative constant}>}{-0.000....01} = \infty$

A function can also have one or two horizontal asymptotes. The horizontal line y = c is a *horizontal asymptote* of function f(x) iff $f(x) \to c$ as $x \to \pm\infty$. That is, $\lim_{x \to \pm\infty} f(x) = c$.

A function can cross its horizontal asymptote many times, honing in to a constant y-value. Typically, however, the function will just become very close to the horizontal asymptote without crossing it.

Example
The inverse tangent function has two horizontal asymptotes—one at $y = \pi/2$ and another at $y = -\pi/2$.

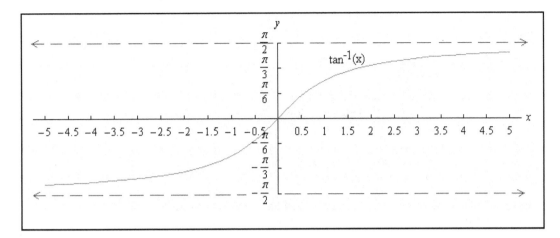

The two basic types of discontinuity—removable and essential—may be defined in terms of limits. Refer to section 1-13 for details on the discontinuities.

The function f(x) has a removable discontinuity at x = a iff $\lim\limits_{x \to a} f(x)$ exists and is finite, and f is undefined at x = a.

The function f(x) has a jump/essential discontinuity at x = a iff $\lim\limits_{x \to a} f(x)$ does not exist, and f is undefined at x = a. A jump/essential discontinuity is synonymous with a vertical asymptote. If a graph has a vertical asymptote at x = a, then it also has an essential discontinuity at x = a.

Example

Find the discontinuities of $f(x) = \dfrac{x+5}{x^2 - 25}$.

Solution:

$$f(x) = \frac{x+5}{(x+5)(x-5)} = \frac{1}{x-5}$$

The function has two discontinuities—one with x = 5 and another at x = -5.

x = 5:

$$\lim_{x \to 5^+} f(x) = \lim_{x \to 5^+} \left(\frac{1}{x-5} \right) = \frac{1}{\text{small positive}} = \infty$$

$$\lim_{x \to 5^-} f(x) = \lim_{x \to 5^-} \left(\frac{1}{x-5} \right) = \frac{1}{\text{small negative}} = -\infty$$

$$\lim_{x \to 5^+} f(x) \neq \lim_{x \to 5^-} f(x) \text{ , and f(5) is undefined}$$

∴ f has a jump/essential discontinuity at x = 5.

Since $\lim_{x \to 5^+} f(x)$ and $\lim_{x \to 5^-} f(x)$ equal $\pm\infty$, f has a vertical asymptote at x = 5.

x = -5:

$$\lim_{x \to -5^+} f(x) = \lim_{x \to -5^+} \left(\frac{1}{x-5} \right) = \frac{1}{-10} = \text{-0.1}$$

$$\lim_{x \to -5^-} f(x) = \lim_{x \to -5^-} \left(\frac{1}{x-5} \right) = \frac{1}{-10} = \text{-0.1}$$

$$\lim_{x \to -5} f(x) = -0.1 \text{ , and f is undefined at x = -5.}$$

∴ f has a removable discontinuity at x = -5.

Example

Repair the removable discontinuity in $f(x) = \dfrac{0.75x^2 - 3x}{x}$.

Solution:
The function is undefined when x = 0.

To simplify, $f(x) = 0.75 \left(\dfrac{x^2}{x} \right) - 3 \left(\dfrac{x}{x} \right) = 0.75x - 3$, a line

When x = 0, the above expression equals -3. The point (0, -3) would fill the removable discontinuity.

Rewriting f as a piecewise function,

$$f(x) = \begin{cases} \dfrac{0.75x^2 - 3x}{x}, & \text{if } x \neq 0 \\ -3, & \text{if } x = 0 \end{cases}$$

Example

Find the vertical asymptotes of $f(x) = \dfrac{6x + 2}{x^2 - 3}$.

Solution:

The function is undefined for $x = \pm\sqrt{3}$.

$x = \sqrt{3}$:

x^-	f(x)
1.6	-26.36
1.7	-110.91
1.73	-1,743.66
1.731	-3,403.68
1.732	-70,409.09

x^+	f(x)
1.75	200
1.74	450.72
1.735	1,213.69
1.733	3,769.53
1.7325	7,964.66

$$\lim_{x \to \sqrt{3}^-} f(x) = -\infty \quad \neq \quad \lim_{x \to \sqrt{3}^+} f(x) = \infty$$

$\therefore x = \sqrt{3}$ is a vertical asymptote.

$x = -\sqrt{3}$:

x^-	f(x)
-1.75	-136
-1.74	-306
-1.735	-822
-1.733	-2,553
-1.7325	-5,394

x^+	f(x)

-1.6	17
-1.7	75
-1.73	1,180
-1.731	2,304
-1.732	47,682

$$\lim_{x \to -\sqrt{3}^-} f(x) = -\infty \qquad \neq \qquad \lim_{x \to -\sqrt{3}^+} f(x) = \infty$$

$\therefore \; x = -\sqrt{3}$ is a vertical asymptote.

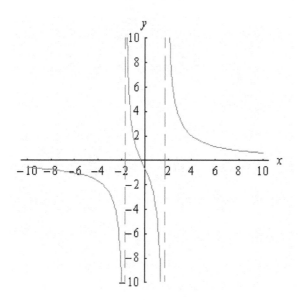

Section 4-4 Evaluating Limits of Rational Functions

In section 4-2, we explored the limits of sequences defined by rational functions. We found that some sequences approach a constant as the subscript grows very large, while other sequences rise to infinity. The same rules that applied for sequences also apply for polynomials as their independent variables approach positive or negative infinity. If a rational function has a limit as x approaches $\pm\infty$, that limit is likely a horizontal asymptote. Use the guide below for quickly determining the horizontal asymptotes for a rational function:

Horizontal Asymptotes for Rational Functions
(1.) When the numerator degree equals the denominator degree, the horizontal asymptote is found by dividing the coefficients of the largest degrees.

(2.) When the numerator degree exceeds the denominator degree, the function has no horizontal asymptotes.

(3.) When the numerator degree is below the denominator degree, the horizontal asymptote is y = 0.

Finding the limits of a rational function is very simple. First, divide the numerator and denominator separately by the greatest term of x within the denominator. For example, if the largest power of x in the denominator is 5, then you should divide the top and bottom of the fraction by x^5. This division creates negative exponents in the denominator, which are easier to evaluate with limits. Remember that the limit of $\dfrac{c}{x^n}$ as x approaches infinity (where n ≥ 1 and c is a constant) is simply $\dfrac{c}{\infty} = 0$. If we can convert all the terms in the denominator to the form $\dfrac{c}{x^n}$, then the limit calculation becomes quite easy.

Example

Determine the limit using simplification algebra: $\lim_{x \to \infty} \left(\dfrac{6x+2}{x^2-3} \right)$

Solution:
(a.) You could use the previous three properties of rational functions and horizontal asymptotes. Since the numerator degree is smaller than the denominator degree, a horizontal asymptote is y = 0. So, the limit of the function as $x \to \infty$ is likely 0.

(b.) Using simplification algebra,

$$\lim_{x \to \infty} \left(\dfrac{6x+2}{x^2-3} \right)\left(\dfrac{\frac{1}{x^2}}{\frac{1}{x^2}}\right) = \lim_{x \to \infty} \left(\dfrac{\frac{6}{x}+\frac{2}{x^2}}{1-\frac{3}{x^2}} \right) = \dfrac{\frac{6}{\infty}+\frac{2}{\infty}}{1-\frac{3}{\infty}} = \dfrac{0+0}{1-0} = 0$$

Example

Find the following limit: $\lim_{x \to \infty} \left(\dfrac{10x^4+6x^2+17}{2x^4+18x^3+40x} \right)$

Solution:
(a.) Using the horizontal asymptote-rational function properties, since the degrees of the numerator and denominator (4) are equal, the horizontal asymptote equals the quotient of

the coefficients for x^4. That is, the asymptote is $y = \dfrac{10}{2} = 5$. The limit as $x \to \infty$ is also likely 5.

(b.) Using simplifying algebra,

$$\lim_{x \to \infty} \left(\frac{10x^4 + 6x^2 + 17}{2x^4 + 18x^3 + 40x} \right)\frac{\left(\frac{1}{x^4}\right)}{\left(\frac{1}{x^4}\right)} = \lim_{x \to \infty} \left(\frac{10 + \dfrac{6}{x^2} + \dfrac{17}{x^4}}{2 + \dfrac{18}{x} + \dfrac{40}{x^3}} \right)$$

$$= \frac{10 + \dfrac{6}{\infty} + \dfrac{17}{\infty}}{2 + \dfrac{18}{\infty} + \dfrac{40}{\infty}} = \frac{10 + 0 + 0}{2 + 0 + 0} = 5$$

Example

Find the limit: $\displaystyle\lim_{x \to \infty} \left(\frac{15x^6 + 4x^3 + 20x}{5x^3 + 65x + 3} \right)$

Solution:
(a.) Using the horizontal asymptote-rational function properties…
    (numerator degree = 6) > (denominator degree = 3)
    $\therefore$ the function has no horizontal asymptotes and an infinite limit as $x \to \infty$.

(b.) Using simplifying algebra,

$$\lim_{x \to \infty} \left(\frac{15x^6 + 4x^3 + 20x}{5x^3 + 65x + 3} \right)\frac{\left(\frac{1}{x^3}\right)}{\left(\frac{1}{x^3}\right)} = \lim_{x \to \infty} \left(\frac{15x^3 + 4 + \dfrac{20}{x^2}}{5 + \dfrac{65}{x^2} + \dfrac{3}{x^3}} \right)$$

$$\frac{15*\infty + 4 + \dfrac{20}{\infty}}{5 + \dfrac{65}{\infty} + \dfrac{3}{\infty}} = \frac{\infty + 4 + 0}{5 + 0 + 0} = \frac{\infty}{5} = \infty$$

Example

Find the limit: $\displaystyle\lim_{x \to \infty} \frac{\sqrt[3]{8x^3 + 6x}}{5x + 11}$

Solution:

$$\lim_{x \to \infty} \frac{\sqrt[3]{8x^3 + 6x}}{5x + 11} \frac{\left(\frac{1}{\sqrt[3]{x^3}}\right)}{\left(\frac{1}{x}\right)} = \lim_{x \to \infty} \left(\frac{\dfrac{\sqrt[3]{8x^3 + 6x}}{\sqrt[3]{x^3}}}{5 + \dfrac{11}{x}} \right)$$

$$\text{Numerator} = \sqrt[3]{\frac{8x^3 + 6x}{x^3}} = \sqrt[3]{8 + \frac{6}{x^2}}$$

$$\text{Limit} = \lim_{x \to \infty} \left(\frac{\sqrt[3]{8 + \dfrac{6}{x^2}}}{5 + \dfrac{11}{x}} \right) = \frac{\sqrt[3]{8 + \dfrac{6}{\infty}}}{5 + \dfrac{11}{\infty}} = \frac{\sqrt[3]{8 + 0}}{5 + 0} = \frac{\sqrt[3]{8}}{5} = \frac{2}{5}$$

Section 4-5 Development of the Derivative

Two types of lines are used to describe the slope of a function around a certain point in the function. A *secant line* is used to approximate the slope of a function over a wider section of the domain. The secant line will cross the graph at two points. The secant slope does not represent instantaneous change but provides an average of the change over a part of the domain.

A *tangent line* will cross the graph once at the targeted point. The slope of the tangent line will have the same slope as the base function at the point of interest. In other words, the slope of the tangent line will provide the instantaneous rate of change in the base function at precisely the tangent point. It is still possible for the tangent line to cross the graph in more than one point somewhere farther down the graph. A tangent line is a more specific type of secant line that measures the rate of change over an infinitely small interval.

Example
Consider the function $f(x) = 0.6x^3$.
     a. Find the secant line through (2, 4.8) and (3, 16.2).
     b. Find the secant line through (2, 4.8) and (2.5, 9.375)
     c. Find the approximate tangent line through (2, 4.8).

Solutions:
     a. $slope = m = \dfrac{16.2 - 4.8}{3 - 2} = 11.4$

       Using point-slope formula...

$$y - y_1 = m(x - x_1)$$
$$y - 4.8 = 11.4(x - 2)$$
$$y - 4.8 = 11.4x - 22.8$$
$$y = 11.4x - 18$$

b. $slope = m = \dfrac{9.375 - 4.8}{2.5 - 2} = 9.15$

$$y - y_1 = m(x - x_1)$$
$$y - 4.8 = 9.15(x - 2)$$
$$y - 4.8 = 9.15x - 18.3$$
$$y = 9.15x - 13.5$$

c. The slope of the tangent line is the limit of the slope for the secant line as the x-difference approaches zero. We can pick an x-value slightly greater than 2 to approximate the tangent line.

Use the points (2, 4.8) and (2.001, 4.8072)

$$slope = m = \dfrac{4.8072 - 4.8}{2.001 - 2} = 7.2$$

$$y - y_1 = m(x - x_1)$$
$$y - 4.8 = 7.2(x - 2)$$
$$y - 4.8 = 7.2x - 14.4$$
$$y = 7.2x - 9.6$$

Example

Consider the function $f(x) = 3x^2$. Find the tangent line to the parabola at x=3 by averaging two secant lines. One secant line crosses the function at x=2 and x=3, and the other secant line intersects f at x=3 and x=4.

Solution:
First, we need several points from function f.
f(2) = 12, f(3) = 27, f(4) = 48

The secant line through (2, 12) and (3, 27):
$$m_1 = \dfrac{27 - 12}{3 - 2} = 15$$

The secant line through (3, 27) and (4, 48):

$$m_2 = \frac{48 - 27}{4 - 3} = 21$$

Average the slopes for the two secant lines:
$$m = \frac{m_1 + m_2}{2} = 18$$

Use the point-slope formula for a line:
$$y - y_1 = m(x - x_1)$$
$$y - 27 = 18(x - 3)$$
$$y - 27 = 18x - 54$$
$$y = 18x - 27$$

In mathematics, a derivative is used to measure the change in one variable with respect to another variable. In other words, the derivative provides the instantaneous rate of change in a function at a single point on the function. Since a tangent line has a slope equal to the instantaneous change of the function at one point on the graph, the creation of the derivative starts with the tangent line. Recall that the slope of a line equals rise over run. We need two points along the graph to determine slope. Let one point be (x, f(x)), and allow the second point to be (x+h, f(x+h)), where 'h' is a constant difference. Currently, the slope of the graph over these two points is:

$$\text{slope} = \frac{y_2 - y_1}{x_2 - x_1} = \frac{f(x + h) - f(x)}{(x + h) - x} = \frac{f(x + h) - f(x)}{h}$$

We need to find the slope at a single point, so the difference 'h' must be infinitely close to zero. Now, the slope at (x, f(x)) becomes:

$$\text{slope} = \lim_{h \to 0} \frac{f(x + h) - f(x)}{h}$$

Simplifying the above limit for any function f will provide the instantaneous change in f precisely at point (x, f(x)). You should use the previous properties of limits, along with algebra, to simplify the limit. Evaluating the limit directly at h = 0 will produce an error, since you will have a fraction with zero in the denominator. You must force 'h' out of the denominator.

Definition of the First Derivative

Since the first derivative corresponds exactly with instantaneous slope, the limit involving slope becomes:

$$f'(x) = \lim_{h \to 0} \frac{f(x+h) - f(x)}{h}$$

This equation states that the derivative of function f precisely at x equals the limit of the slope formula as the horizontal change approaches zero. Again, the derivative represents the instantaneous change at a single point (x, f(x)) on a graph.

Example

Develop the tangent line for $f(x) = 2x^2 + 3$ at x = 1.

Solution:

When x = 1, the function yields 5. We must find the tangent line to f at the point (1, 5).

$$\text{slope} = \lim_{h \to 0} \frac{f(x+h) - f(x)}{h} = \lim_{h \to 0} \frac{(2(x+h)^2 + 3) - (2x^2 + 3)}{h}$$

$$= \lim_{h \to 0} \frac{(2x^2 + 4xh + 2h^2 + 3) - (2x^2 + 3)}{h}$$

$$= \lim_{h \to 0} \frac{4xh + 2h^2}{h} = \lim_{h \to 0} \frac{h(4x + 2h)}{h} = \lim_{h \to 0} (4x + 2h)$$

$$= 4x + 2*0 = 4x$$

slope of the tangent line at (1, 5) = 4 * 1 = 4

Using the point-slope formula for a line...

$$y - y_1 = m(x - x_1)$$
$$y - 5 = 4(x - 1)$$
$$y - 5 = 4x - 4$$
$$y = 4x + 1 \qquad \leftarrow \text{ the tangent line to f(x) at the point (1, 5)}$$

Example

Develop the tangent line to $f(x) = 9x^3 + 7x^2 + x$ for x = 6.

Solution:

f(6) = 2,202 → We need to find the tangent line at point (6, 2202)

$$f'(x) = \lim_{h \to 0} \frac{f(x+h) - f(x)}{h}$$

$$= \lim_{h \to 0} \frac{(9(x+h)^3 + 7(x+h)^2 + (x+h)) - (9x^3 + 7x^2 + x)}{h}$$

$$= \lim_{h \to 0} \frac{(9(x+h)(x^2 + 2xh + h^2) + 7(x^2 + 2xh + h^2) + (x+h)) - (9x^3 + 7x^2 + x)}{h}$$

$$= \lim_{h \to 0}$$
$$\frac{(9(x^3 + 2x^2h + xh^2 + x^2h + 2xh^2 + h^3) + 7x^2 + 14xh + 7h^2 + x + h) - 9x^3 - 7x^2 - x}{h}$$

$$= \lim_{h \to 0}$$
$$\frac{9x^3 + 18x^2h + 9xh^2 + 9x^2h + 18xh^2 + 9h^3 + 7x^2 + 14xh + 7h^2 + x + h - 9x^3 - 7x^2 - x}{h}$$

$$= \lim_{h \to 0} \frac{27x^2h + 27xh^2 + 9h^3 + 14xh + 7h^2 + h}{h}$$

$$= \lim_{h \to 0} \frac{h(27x^2 + 27xh + 9h^2 + 14x + 7h + 1)}{h}$$

$$= \lim_{h \to 0} (27x^2 + 27xh + 9h^2 + 14x + 7h + 1)$$

$$= (27x^2 + 27x*0 + 9*0^2 + 14x + 7*0 + 1)$$

$$= (27x^2 + 14x + 1)$$

$$f'(6) = (27*6^2 + 14*6 + 1) = 1{,}057$$

Using the point-slope formula for a line…

$$y - y_1 = m(x - x_1)$$
$$y - 2202 = 1057(x - 6)$$
$$y - 2202 = 1057x - 6342$$
$$y = 1057x - 4140 \qquad \leftarrow \text{the tangent line to f(x) at the point (6, 2202)}$$

Symbolic Forms of Derivatives

The derivative of the variable y with respect to the variable x has the following expression:

$$\frac{dy}{dx}$$

Note that when a derivative is shown in "fractional" form with the bar, the function you are differentiating is in the numerator, and the independent variable is in the denominator.

Similarly, the derivative of the function f with respect to its independent variable x is in the format (with square brackets around the function name):

$$\frac{d}{dx}[f(x)]$$

Another way of writing derivatives is with apostrophes. The first derivative of f is written f '(x), with the apostrophe after the function name. The expression $f'(x)$ reads "f prime x." The number of apostrophes corresponds to the order of the derivative. The second derivative of f is: $f''(x)$, read "f double prime x." The second derivative equals the derivative of the first derivative. Usually the apostrophes are only used up to the third derivative. For the fourth derivative and beyond, the number of derivatives is enclosed within parentheses above the function name. For example, $f^{(n)}(x)$ represents the nth derivative of f. The nth derivative equals the derivative of all the previous (n – 1) derivatives.

Section 4-6 Behavior of the First Derivative

A function is not differentiable at sharp, un-rounded corners. The derivative does not exist…
(1.) at an angle

(2.) at a cusp

The slope is simply undefined at these corners. The graphs do not flow smoothly. The slope is one value to the right of the corner and another value immediately to the left of the corner. In other words, the graph of the first derivative has a jump discontinuity at a cusp or corner.

A function is also not differentiable if the limit at x = a is infinite (a vertical asymptote exists). The derivative is also undefined at the endpoints of the function, assuming the domain for the function contains an interval.

If function f(x) is *differentiable* at x = a, then the function is continuous at x = a. In other words, if $f'(a)$ exists, then f(x) is defined at x = a and $\lim_{x \to a} f(x) = f(a)$.

Several other corollaries include:
(1.) If f(x) is discontinuous at x = a, then f'(a) does not exist.
(2.) A point (a, f(a)) could exist where f is continuous but not differentiable.

Section 4-7 First Derivatives of Polynomials

The derivatives of polynomials are the easiest derivatives to evaluate. Recall that a polynomial is the sum of the independent variable raised to various integer powers, with coefficients often bonded to each element of the function. An example of a polynomial is $f(x) = 7x^{10} + 30x^8 + 12x^5 + 53x + 200$. The highest power is 10, so the function is a tenth degree polynomial.

Consider polynomials to the zero[th] degree. These functions are single numbers without the use of the independent variable. The polynomials are in the format $f(x) = a$, where 'a' is a constant. The graphs of these functions are straight, horizontal lines. Since the graph is not changing vertical-wise, the slope is zero and thus the first derivative is zero. That is, the derivative of a constant is 0.

The next level of polynomials is the first degree polynomial in the format $f(x) = ax + b$. Since 'a' represents the slope, and the first derivative of a function gives the instantaneous slope at a certain point along the function, the first derivative of the line must be 'a' at all possible points. The derivative of a first degree polynomial simply equals the coefficient for x, which is the constant 'a.' The development of the derivative is as follows:

$$f'(x) = \frac{d}{dx}[f(x)] = \frac{d}{dx}[ax + b] = \frac{d}{dx}[ax] + \frac{d}{dx}[b] = a + 0 = a$$

Note especially that $\frac{d}{dx}[ax] = a$.

Consider an expression of the form ax^n, where 'a' and 'n' are real numbers (positive or negative). The first derivative of the expression is:

$$\frac{d}{dx}[ax^n] = anx^{n-1}$$

Note that we simply bring the original exponent down and multiply it by the independent variable (and its original coefficient 'a'). The new exponent for the independent variable is (n − 1).

Example
Find the derivatives of the following functions:
  a. $f(x) = 17$
  b. $g(x) = 40x$
  c. $h(x) = 520x + 85$
  d. $m(x) = 6x^2$
  e. $f(x) = 11x^2 + 72$
  f. $h(x) = 34x^5 + 8x^3 + x + 45$
  g. $w(x) = 62x^3 + 57x^2 + 3x + 75$

Solutions:
  a. $f'(x) = 0$; the derivative of a constant is zero
  b. $g'(x) = 40$; the derivative of a line is its slope
  c. $h'(x) = \frac{d}{dx}[520x + 85] = \frac{d}{dx}[520x] + \frac{d}{dx}[85] = 520 + 0 = 520$
  d. $m'(x) = 6 * 2 * x^{2-1} = 12x$
  e. $f'(x) = \frac{d}{dx}[11x^2 + 72] = \frac{d}{dx}[11x^2] + \frac{d}{dx}[72] = 11 * 2 * x^{2-1} + 0 = 22x$
  f. $h'(x) = \frac{d}{dx}[34x^5 + 8x^3 + x + 45]$

$$= \frac{d}{dx}[34x^5] + \frac{d}{dx}[8x^3] + \frac{d}{dx}[x] + \frac{d}{dx}[45]$$
$$= (34 * 5 * x^4) + (8 * 3 * x^2) + 1 + 0$$
$$= 170x^4 + 24x^2 + 1$$

  g. $w'(x) = \frac{d}{dx}[62x^3 + 57x^2 + 3x + 75]$

$$= \frac{d}{dx}[62x^3] + \frac{d}{dx}[57x^2] + \frac{d}{dx}[3x] + \frac{d}{dx}[75]$$
$$= (62 * 3 * x^2) + (57 * 2 * x^1) + 3 + 0$$

$$= 186x^2 + 114x + 3$$

Notice that the derivative of the polynomial reduces the overall order of the function by 1. In example g, the original function was a cubic polynomial. The derivative of the function creates a parabola or second-order function.

Section 4-8 Properties of Derivatives

Most functions contain a variety of terms with a range of operators. Expressions may be added together, multiplied, or raised to exponents. Calculating the derivative of a complicated function could be difficult. The derivative rules provide ways to break apart complicated functions and differentiate each component separately. Most of the rules in this section pertain to the basic math operations that can lie between expressions.

The *coefficient rule* for derivatives states that the coefficient in a term to which the derivative is being applied may be taken outside the derivative expression. Suppose g(x) is an expression using x, and 'a' is a constant. Then,

Suppose $f(x) = a * g(x)$
The derivative of f is then:
$$f'(x) = a * g'(x)$$

Example
Compute the first derivatives for the following functions:
    a. $f(x) = 5\cos(x)$
    b. $g(x) = 17(8 + 4x)$

Solutions:
    a. $f'(x) = 5 * \dfrac{d}{dx}[\cos(x)] = 5 * (-\sin(x)) = -5\sin(x)$
    b. $g'(x) = 17 * \dfrac{d}{dx}[8 + 4x] = 17 * (0 + 4) = 68$

One of the key properties of derivatives is the *summation rule*. The derivative of a sum of expressions is the sum of the derivatives of the individual expressions. In other words, the derivative can be "distributed" to all the terms within a sum of mathematical

---

expressions. Shown below is the formalization of the summation rule, where each $g_i(x)$ function is an expression within the primary function f:

Suppose $f(x) = g_1(x) + g_2(x) + g_3(x) + ... + g_n(x)$

The derivative of f is then:

$$f'(x) = g_1'(x) + g_2'(x) + g_3'(x) + ... + g_n'(x)$$

Example

If $f(x) = x^5 + x^3$, find...

(a.) f'(x)

(b.) $\dfrac{d}{dx}[9 * f(x)]$

Solution:

(a.) $f'(x) = 5x^4 + 3x^2$

(b.) $\dfrac{d}{dx}[9 * f(x)] = 9 * f'(x) = 45x^4 + 27x^2$

The *difference rule* is very similar to the summation rule except for the use of minus signs:

Suppose $f(x) = g_1(x) - g_2(x) - g_3(x) - .... - g_n(x)$

The derivative of f is then:

$$f'(x) = g_1'(x) - g_2'(x) - g_3'(x) - .... - g_n'(x)$$

Example

Calculate the first derivatives for these functions:

  a. $f(x) = \sin(x) + 6x^3$

  b. $g(x) = 4e^x + \cos(x) - 10x$

Solutions:

  a. $f'(x) = \dfrac{d}{dx}[\sin(x)] + \dfrac{d}{dx}[6x^3] = \cos(x) + 18x^2$

  b. $g'(x) = \dfrac{d}{dx}[4e^x] + \dfrac{d}{dx}[\cos(x)] - \dfrac{d}{dx}[10x] = 4e^x - \sin(x) - 10$

Another important property for derivatives is the *product rule*. The rule is formally stated as:

Suppose $f(x) = g(x) * h(x)$, where g and h are expressions featuring x.
The derivative of f is then:
$$f'(x) = g(x) * h'(x) + g'(x) * h(x)$$

In other words, the derivative of f(x) will be the first function times the derivative of the second function, plus the derivative of the first function times the second function.

Example

Find the first derivatives for the following functions using the Product Rule:

a. $f(x) = x^5 * \sin(x)$

b. $g(x) = \ln(x) * 2x^{-8}$

Solutions:

a. $f'(x) = x^5 * \cos(x) + 5x^4 * \sin(x)$

b. $g'(x) = \ln(x) * 2(-8)x^{-9} + \dfrac{1}{x} * 2x^{-8} = -16 * \ln(x) * x^{-9} + 2x^{-9}$

The *quotient rule* is effective when computing the derivative of the quotient of two expressions.

$$\frac{d}{dx}\left[\frac{f(x)}{g(x)}\right] = \frac{g(x) * f'(x) - f(x) * g'(x)}{(g(x))^2}$$

Example

Find the derivative of $w(x) = \dfrac{\sin(x)}{\sqrt[3]{x}}$.

Solution:

$f(x) = \sin(x)$, $f'(x) = \cos(x)$

$g(x) = \sqrt[3]{x}$, $g'(x) = \dfrac{1}{3}x^{-2/3}$

$$w'(x) = \frac{\sqrt[3]{x} * \cos(x) - \sin(x) * \dfrac{1}{3}x^{-2/3}}{x^{2/3}}$$

Power Chain Rule

Often, you will find an expression involving the independent variable raised to the power of some number.

Suppose $f(x) = g(x)^n$, where g(x) is an expression featuring x, and n is any

real number.

The derivative of f is then:

$$f'(x) = n * g(x)^{n-1} * g'(x)$$

Stated differently, the exponent must drop down and multiply with g(x), the original exponent is decremented by 1, and you must find the derivative of g(x) and multiply it by the rest of the expression. This method of differentiation is stated more formally as the *Chain Rule* in a later section.

Example

Differentiate $f(x) = (x^5 + 4x^2)^7$

Solution:
One method of computing the derivative of f would be to undo the factorization and obtain a very large polynomial without the 7th power operation.

A shorter method involves differentiating the outside expression first, followed by differentiating the inner expression. Function f can be viewed as the composite of two functions: x^7 as the outer function and $(x^5 + 4x^2)$ as the inner function.

$$f'(x) = 7 * (x^5 + 4x^2)^6 + \frac{d}{dx}\left[x^5 + 4x^2\right]$$
$$f'(x) = 7(x^5 + 4x^2)^6 + 5x^4 + 8x$$

Example

Differentiate $g(x) = \left(\sin(x)\right)^5$

Solution:
Bring the exponent, 5, down next to the base, sin(x), and decrease the current exponent by 1. Then, differentiate the base:

$$g'(x) = 5\left(\sin(x)\right)^4 * \frac{d}{dx}\left[\sin(x)\right] = 5\left(\sin(x)\right)^4 * \cos(x)$$

Example

Find the first derivative of this function: $f(x) = \left(\cos(x^2)\right)^4$

Solution:

$$f'(x) = 4\left(\cos(x^2)\right)^3 * \frac{d}{dx}\left[\cos(x^2)\right]$$

$$\frac{d}{dx}\left[\cos(x^2)\right] = -\sin(x^2) * \frac{d}{dx}\left[x^2\right] = -\sin(x^2) * 2x$$

$$f'(x) = -4\left(\cos(x^2)\right)^3 * \sin(x^2) * 2x$$

Example

Find the first derivative of: $h(x) = \sqrt{\ln(x)}$

Solution:

$$h'(x) = \frac{1}{2} * (\ln(x))^{-1/2} * \frac{d}{dx}\left[\ln(x)\right] = \frac{1}{2} * (\ln(x))^{-1/2} * \frac{1}{x} = \frac{1}{2x\sqrt{\ln(x)}}$$

According to the Mean Value Theorem, if the secant line connecting points (a, f(a)) and (b, f(b)) has slope m, there must be at least one value c within the interval with the function's instantaneous slope equal to m.

Mean Value Theorem:

Suppose function f is differentiable for all values in [a, b]. $\exists$ a value c with $a < c < b$ so that $f'(c) = \dfrac{f(b) - f(a)}{b - a}$.

Section 4-9 The Chain Rule

The *Chain Rule* provides a method to differentiate any number of nested expressions.

If $f(x) = g(h(x))$, then the first derivative of f using the Chain Rule is $f'(x) = g'(h(x)) * h'(x)$.

To use the Chain Rule, first take the derivative of the outer function, using the inner function h as the independent variable. Then, multiply the result by the derivative of the inner function.

Example

Compute the derivative of the following functions using the Chain Rule:

    a. $f(x) = \sqrt{6x^{-4} + 3x^{-2} + 80}$

    b. $g(x) = \cos(x^3)$

Solutions:

a. $f'(x) = \frac{1}{2}\left(6x^{-4} + 3x^{-2} + 80\right)^{-1/2} * \frac{d}{dx}\left[6x^{-4} + 3x^{-2} + 80\right]$

$= \frac{1}{2}\left(6x^{-4} + 3x^{-2} + 80\right)^{-1/2} * (6(-4)x^{-5} + 3(-2)x^{-3})$

$= \frac{1}{2}\left(6x^{-4} + 3x^{-2} + 80\right)^{-1/2} * (-24x^{-5} - 6x^{-3})$

b. $g'(x) = -\sin(x^3) * \frac{d}{dx}\left[x^3\right] = -\sin(x^3) * 3x^2$

Example

If $f(x) = \frac{1}{4}\cos(x^2)$, find the slope of the tangent line to f when x = 8.

Solution:

$f'(x) = \frac{1}{4}(-\sin(x^2)) * 2x$

$f'(8) = \frac{1}{4}(-\sin(8^2)) * 16 \approx -3.6801$

Section 4-10 Second Derivatives

The second derivative of function f will monitor the slope of f'(x). Just as the original function changes its slope countless times, the slope of the first derivative function will change over its course. When f'(x) is increasing, f''(x) > 0, and when f'(x) is decreasing, f''(x) < 0. When f'(x) changes from increasing to decreasing (or vice versa), the second derivative of f must shift from positive to negative and intersect the x-axis. The points on function f where f''(x) = 0 are called *inflection points*. In other words, to find the inflection points for f, simply find the roots of f''(x) and calculate the corresponding points on f.

The term *concavity* describes the value of the second derivative. The parent function f is *concave up* when f''(x) > 0. In other words, the slope of f must be increasing in a concave up region. The parent function f is *concave down* when f''(x) < 0. The slope of f will be decreasing over a concave down region. At the inflection points, when f''(x) = 0, the original function is changing concavity from up to down (or vice versa). The sketch of a function with its concavity in each region is shown below. The inflection points are the large dots:

A few points:
> *The concave up regions are facing up like a cup.
> *The concave down regions face down and appear like mounds.
> *The original function f can be increasing and/or decreasing in a concave up region.
> *The original function can be increasing and/or decreasing in a concave down region.

In a concave up interval, the slope of f may be negative but rising toward zero, or the slope is positive and continuing to grow. Either way, f'(x) has a positive slope in a concave up area.

In a concave down interval, the slope of f could be positive but falling to zero, or the slope is negative and becoming more negative. f'(x) must have a negative slope in a concave down interval.

To find the inflection points and regions of concavity for f, find the second derivative of f, f''(x). Then, compute the roots of f''(x), which will provide the inflection points. Test f''(x) between each root. For example, if c_1 and c_2 are two roots of f''(x), then calculate f''(x) for $x \in (c_1, c_2)$. If f''(x) is positive in (c_1, c_2), then f is concave up over the interval. On the other hand, if f''(x) is negative in the interval, then f is concave down.

Example
Find the inflection points and regions of concavity for $f(x) = 0.2x^3 - x + 4$.

Solution:
$f'(x) = 0.6x^2 - 1$
$f''(x) = 1.2x$

Find the roots of f''(x)...
$$1.2x = 0 \quad \rightarrow \quad x = 0$$

The original function f has one inflection point, which is (0, 4).

To the left of x = 0,
$$f''(-1) = -1.2 \quad \rightarrow \quad \text{f is concave down}$$

To the right of x = 0,

$$f''(1) = 1.2 \quad \rightarrow \quad \text{f is concave up}$$

f is concave down in the interval $(-\infty, 0)$ and concave up in the interval $(0, \infty)$.

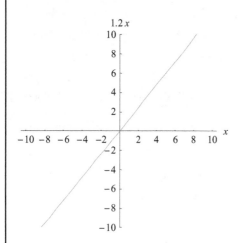

From the graph above, notice that f''(x) is below the x-axis in the region of downward concavity and above the x-axis in the region of upward concavity.

Example

Find the regions of concavity for $f(x) = \dfrac{1}{2}x^4 - 0.8x^2$.

Solution:

$$f'(x) = 2x^3 - 1.6x$$
$$f''(x) = 6x^2 - 1.6 = 0$$
$$\downarrow$$
$$6x^2 = 1.6 \quad \rightarrow \quad x^2 = 0.26667 \quad \rightarrow \quad x = \pm\sqrt{0.26667} \approx \pm 0.5164$$

$$f''(-1) = 4.4$$
$$f''(0) = -1.6$$
$$f''(1) = 4.4$$

f is concave up in $(-\infty, -0.5164)$, concave down in $(-0.5164, 0.5164)$, and concave up in $(0.5164, \infty)$.

Example

Find the second order derivatives for the polynomials below:

    a. $f(x) = 65x$

    b. $g(x) = 80x^3 + 43x + 90$

---

c. $h(x) = 24x^5 + 89x^4$

d. $m(x) = 78x^{10} + 4x^3$

Solutions:

For each of these examples, you must first find the first derivative of each function, and then find the derivative of the initial derivative.

a. $f'(x) = 65$

$f''(x) = 0$

b. $g'(x) = 80 * 3 * x^2 + 43 + 0 = 240x^2 + 43$

$g''(x) = 240 * 2 * x + 0 = 480x$

c. $h'(x) = 24 * 5 * x^4 + 89 * 4 * x^3 = 120x^4 + 356x^3$

$h''(x) = 120 * 4 * x^3 + 356 * 3 * x^2 = 480x^3 + 1,068x^2$

d. $m'(x) = 78 * 10 * x^9 + 4 * 3 * x^2 = 780x^9 + 12x^2$

$m''(x) = 780 * 9 * x^8 + 12 * 2 * x = 7,020x^8 + 24x$

Example

Find the second derivatives of these functions:

a. $f(x) = \sin(x)$

b. $g(x) = \cos(5x^3)$

c. $h(x) = \ln(x^6)$

Solutions:

a. $f'(x) = \cos(x)$

$f''(x) = \frac{d}{dx}[\cos(x)] = -\sin(x)$

b. $g'(x) = -\sin(5x^3) * \frac{d}{dx}[5x^3] = -\sin(5x^3) * (5 * 3 * x^2) = -15\sin(5x^3) * x^2$

To find the second derivative, we must apply the product rule.

$g''(x) = -15\sin(5x^3) * 2x - 15\sin(5x^3) * 15x^2 * x^2$

$= -30\sin(5x^3) * x - 225\sin(5x^3) * x^4$

c. $h'(x) = \frac{1}{x^6} * \frac{d}{dx}[x^6] = \frac{1}{x^6} * 6x^5 = \frac{6}{x}$

$h''(x) = \frac{d}{dx}[6x^{-1}] = 6 * (-1)x^{-2} = \frac{-6}{x^2}$

If the order of a derivative of a polynomial is higher than the degree of the polynomial, the result must be zero. For instance, suppose we are working with the function $h(t) = t^2 + 3t - 8$. The degree of h is 2. Taking the first derivative of h reduces the function's degree to 1: $h'(t) = 2t + 3$. Differentiating again will lower the degree to zero: $h''(t) = 2$. When the order of the derivative matches the degree of the initial polynomial, a constant value results. In this case, taking the second derivative of a second-degree polynomial yields a constant. Evaluating the third, fourth, fifth, and higher derivatives of h will just produce zero. Again, if we differentiate beyond the polynomial's degree, the value zero results.

Example

Find the 45th derivative of $f(x) = 287x^{42} + 91x^{35} + 12x^{20}$

Solution:
Solving this derivative manually would require several pages of work. To find the nth derivative, you would need all the previous (n – 1) derivatives. Since the order of the derivative (45) is greater than the degree of the polynomial (42), the solution to the derivative is zero.

Example

Evaluate the following higher order derivatives:

a. Find the second derivative of: $f(x) = 4x^6 + \sin(x)$

b. Find the second derivative of: $g(x) = \sqrt{x^7 + 1}$

c. Find the third derivative of: $h(x) = \cos(x) + \sqrt{x} + 8x^4$

Solutions:

a.

$$f'(x) = 4*6*x^5 + \cos(x)$$

$$f''(x) = 24*5*x^4 - \sin(x) = 120x^4 - \sin(x)$$

b.

$$g'(x) = \frac{1}{2}(x^7 + 1)^{-1/2} * \frac{d}{dx}[x^7 + 1] = \frac{1}{2}(x^7 + 1)^{-1/2} * 7x^6$$

$$g''(x) = \frac{1}{2}(x^7 + 1)^{-1/2} * 42x^5 + \left(\frac{1}{2}\right)\left(\frac{-1}{2}\right)(x^7 + 1)^{-3/2} * \frac{d}{dx}[x^7 + 1] * 7x^6$$

$$\downarrow$$

$$g''(x) = 21x^5(x^7 + 1)^{-1/2} - \frac{1}{4}(x^7 + 1)^{-3/2} * 7x^6 * 7x^6$$

$$g''(x) = 21x^5(x^7 + 1)^{-1/2} - \frac{49}{4}x^{12}(x^7 + 1)^{-3/2}$$

---

c.

$$h'(x) = -\sin(x) + \frac{1}{2}x^{-1/2} + 32x^3$$

$$h''(x) = -\cos(x) + \left(\frac{1}{2}\right)\left(\frac{-1}{2}\right)x^{-3/2} + 96x^2$$

$$h'''(x) = \sin(x) - \left(\frac{1}{4}\right)\left(\frac{-3}{2}\right)x^{-5/2} + 192x$$

$$\downarrow$$

$$h'''(x) = \sin(x) + \left(\frac{3}{8}\right)x^{-5/2} + 192x$$

Section 4-11 Derivatives of Trigonometric Functions

The basic trigonometric functions, along with their inverses, have derivatives that are important to remember. The basic trig functions produce another trig function when differentiated, while the inverse trig functions yield ratios. All the previous derivative rules, such as the chain rule, apply to trigonometric functions.

$$\frac{d}{dx}\left[\sin(x)\right] = \cos(x)$$

$$\frac{d}{dx}\left[\cos(x)\right] = -\sin(x)$$

$$\frac{d}{dx}\left[\tan(x)\right] = \sec^2(x)$$

Example

Find the second derivatives of these functions:

a. $m(x) = \cos(15x)$ **b.** $p(x) = \sin(x)^4$

Solutions:

a. $m'(x) = -\sin(15x) * \dfrac{d}{dx}[15x] = -15\sin(15x)$

     $m''(x) = -15 * \cos(15x) * \dfrac{d}{dx}[15x] = -225\cos(15x)$

b. $p'(x) = 4 * \sin(x)^3 * \dfrac{d}{dx}[\sin(x)] = 4\sin(x)^3 * \cos(x)$

$$p''(x) = 4\sin(x)^3 * \frac{d}{dx}[\cos(x)] + \frac{d}{dx}[4\sin(x)^3] * \cos(x)$$

$$= 4\sin(x)^3 * (-\sin(x)) + 4*3*\sin(x)^2 * \frac{d}{dx}[\sin(x)] * \cos(x)$$

$$= -4\sin(x)^4 + 12\sin(x)^2 * \cos(x)^2$$

$$\frac{d}{dx}\left[\sin^{-1}(x)\right] = \frac{1}{\sqrt{1-x^2}}$$

$$\frac{d}{dx}\left[\cos^{-1}(x)\right] = -\frac{1}{\sqrt{1-x^2}}$$

$$\frac{d}{dx}\left[\tan^{-1}(x)\right] = \frac{1}{1+x^2}$$

Example

Differentiate the given functions

a. $f(x) = \sin^{-1}(x^2)$

b. $g(x) = \tan^{-1}(\sqrt{x^4 + 7x})$

Solutions:

a.

$$f'(x) = \frac{1}{\sqrt{1-\left(x^2\right)^2}} * \frac{d}{dx}\left[x^2\right] = \frac{2x}{\sqrt{1-x^4}}$$

b.

$$g'(x) = \frac{1}{1+\left(\sqrt{x^4+7x}\right)^2} * \frac{d}{dx}\left[\sqrt{x^4+7x}\right]$$

$$= \frac{1}{1+x^4+7x} * \frac{1}{2}\left(x^4+7x\right)^{-1/2} * \frac{d}{dx}\left[x^4+7x\right]$$

$$= \frac{4x^3+7}{2(1+x^4+7x)\sqrt{x^4+7x}}$$

Example

Differentiate $f(x) = \cos^{-1}(12x^6) * \sqrt[3]{25x^5}$

Solution:

$$f'(x) = \frac{d}{dx}\left[\cos^{-1}(12x^6)\right] * \sqrt[3]{25x^5} + \cos^{-1}(12x^6) * \frac{d}{dx}\left[\sqrt[3]{25x^5}\right]$$

$$\downarrow$$

$$= \frac{-1}{\sqrt{1-(12x^6)^2}} * \frac{d}{dx}\left[12x^6\right] * \sqrt[3]{25x^5} + \cos^{-1}(12x^6) * \frac{1}{3} * \left(25x^5\right)^{-2/3} * \frac{d}{dx}\left[25x^5\right]$$

$$= \frac{-72x^5 * \sqrt[3]{25x^5}}{\sqrt{1-144x^{12}}} + \cos^{-1}(12x^6) * \frac{1}{3} * \left(25x^5\right)^{-2/3} * 125x^4$$

$$\frac{d}{dx}\left[\csc(x)\right] = -\csc(x) * \cot(x)$$

$$\frac{d}{dx}\left[\sec(x)\right] = \sec(x) * \tan(x)$$

$$\frac{d}{dx}\left[\cot(x)\right] = -\csc^2(x)$$

Section 4-12 Derivatives of the Exponential Function

Exponential functions take the form $f(x) = a^x$, where 'a' is a constant. Remember that all exponential functions pass through the point (0, 1), since any base to the power of zero is 1. The slope of the exponential function at point (0, 1) is an essential component in the function's derivative. The derivative of an exponential function is: $f'(x) = a^x * f'(0)$. This is a preliminary formula as we will later derive a simplified expression for f '(0). This derivative is difficult to build since you need the first derivative at zero to find the general first derivative. The first step in constructing the derivative is to compute f '(0). You could estimate f '(0) with a table that has one column of x-values approaching zero and another column containing the approximated slopes.

Example

If $f(x) = 6.5^x$, find

    (a.) f'(0)

    (b.) f'(4)

Solutions:

(a.)

$$f\,'(0) = \frac{\lim}{h \to 0} \frac{f(x+h) - f(x)}{h} = \frac{\lim}{h \to 0} \frac{f(h) - f(0)}{h} = \frac{\lim}{h \to 0} \frac{6.5^h - 1}{h}$$

h	lim
0.1	2.0584
0.01	1.8894
0.001	1.8736
0.0001	1.8720
0.00001	1.8718

$\lim \approx 1.8718 \approx f\,'(0)$

(b.)

$f\,'(4) = a^4 * f\,'(0) = 6.5^4 * 1.8718 \approx 3{,}341.28$

The most common exponential function has base 'e.' 'e' is the base in $f(x) = a^x$ for which f'(0) = 1. The slope at point (0, 1) is exactly 1. The derivative of the base-e exponential function becomes $f\,'(x) = a^x * f\,'(0) = e^x * 1 = e^x$.

$$\frac{d}{dx}\left[e^x\right] = e^x$$

$$\frac{d}{dx}\left[e^{g(x)}\right] = e^{g(x)} * g'(x)$$

Example0
Find the first derivatives of the following expressions:

    a. e^{4x}

    b. $e^{6x^2 + 7x + 30}$

    c. e^1

    d. $\left(e^{5x}\right)^3$

Solutions:

    a. $\dfrac{d}{dx}\left[e^{4x}\right] = e^{4x} * \dfrac{d}{dx}[4x] = e^{4x} * 4$

    b. $\dfrac{d}{dx}\left[e^{6x^2+7x+30}\right] = e^{6x^2+7x+30} * \dfrac{d}{dx}\left[6x^2 + 7x + 30\right] = (12x + 7) * e^{6x^2+7x+30}$

    c. The derivative of a constant is zero; or $\dfrac{d}{dx}\left[e^1\right] = e^1 * \dfrac{d}{dx}[1] = e^1 * 0 = 0$

d. $\dfrac{d}{dx}\left[\left(e^{5x}\right)^{3}\right]=3*\left(e^{5x}\right)^{2}*\dfrac{d}{dx}\left[e^{5x}\right]=3*e^{10x}*e^{5x}*\dfrac{d}{dx}[5x]=3*e^{15x}*5=15e^{15x}$

While we have a simple formula for computing derivatives for exponential functions of base e, we still need a precise and elegant equation for the first derivative of a general exponential function with base 'a.' The example below shows how $f\,'(0)$ may be calculated exactly for an exponential function with any base. This procedure makes use of the fact that $e^{\wedge}\ln(x)=x$, and the derivative of e^{x} is the original function.

Example
Find the derivative precisely of $f(x)=20.5^{x}$.

Solution:
$$20.5^{x}=\left(e^{\ln(20.5)}\right)^{x}=e^{\ln(20.5)*x}$$

$$\dfrac{d}{dx}\left[e^{\ln(20.5)*x}\right]=e^{\ln(20.5)*x}*\ln(20.5)=\left(e^{\ln(20.5)}\right)^{x}*\ln(20.5)=20.5^{x}*\ln(20.5)$$
$$\text{(using chain rule)}$$

Now we have a general formula for the derivative of $f(x)=a^{x}$, where $f\,'(0)=\ln(a)$.

Derivative of a General Exponential Function
If $f(x)=a^{x}$, then $f\,'(x)=a^{x}*\ln(a)$.

Section 4-13 Derivatives of Logarithms

Logarithms have two simple derivative formulas depending on the base of the log. For natural logs, the derivative is the reciprocal of the logarithm's argument. If the base is any value other than 'e,' then you must include the natural log of the base in the denominator:

$$\dfrac{d}{dx}\left[\log_{a}(x)\right]=\dfrac{1}{x*\ln(a)}$$

$$\dfrac{d}{dx}\left[\ln(x)\right]=\dfrac{1}{x}$$

Example

Compute the first derivatives of the following logs:

    a. $f(x) = \log_{10}(x)$

    b. $g(x) = \log_2(x)$

Solutions:

    a. $f'(x) = \dfrac{1}{x * \ln(10)} \approx \dfrac{1}{x * 2.30259}$

    b. $g'(x) = \dfrac{1}{x * \ln(2)} \approx \dfrac{1}{x * 0.69315}$

Section 4-14 Implicit Differentiation

Implicit differentiation can be applied to an equation containing two or more variables. In addition, both sides of the equation may contain a mix of constants and the variables.

Suppose an equation contains variables x and y, and you wish to find the derivative of y with respect to x. We must assume that y is a function of x. Then, differentiate both sides of the equation separately. Since each term involving y theoretically contains x-terms, each y-term must be differentiated as though it were a function of x. The differentiation will likely produce at least one $\dfrac{dy}{dx}$ term, which you must then solve for to obtain an expression for $\dfrac{dy}{dx}$ that contains x- and y-terms.

Example

Find the derivative of y with respect to x from the equation: $x^2 y^3 + 5xy^2 = 9x$

Solution:

$$x^2 y^3 + 5xy^2 = 9x$$

$$\downarrow$$

$$\left(\frac{d}{dx}\left[x^2\right] * y^3 + x^2 * \frac{d}{dx}\left[y^3\right] \right) + \left(\frac{d}{dx}\left[5x\right] * y^2 + 5x * \frac{d}{dx}\left[y^2\right] \right) = 9$$

$$\left(2x * y^3 + x^2 * 3y^2 * \frac{dy}{dx} \right) + \left(5 * y^2 + 5x * 2y * \frac{dy}{dx} \right) = 9$$

$$2xy^3 + 3x^2 y^2 * \frac{dy}{dx} + 5y^2 + 10xy * \frac{dy}{dx} = 9$$

$$\frac{-2xy^3 - 5y^2 \qquad\qquad -2xy^3 - 5y^2}{3x^2y^2 * \frac{dy}{dx} + 10xy * \frac{dy}{dx} = 9 - 2xy^3 - 5y^2}$$

$$\frac{dy}{dx}\left(3x^2y^2 + 10xy\right) = 9 - 2xy^3 - 5y^2$$

$$\frac{dy}{dx} = \frac{9 - 2xy^3 - 5y^2}{3x^2y^2 + 10xy}$$

Example

Find the derivative of y with respect to x from the equation: $5y^2 + 6x^2 = 20$

Solution:

$$5 * 2y * \frac{dy}{dx} + 6 * 2 * x = 0$$

$$10y * \frac{dy}{dx} + 12x = 0$$

$$10y * \frac{dy}{dx} = -12x$$

$$\frac{dy}{dx} = \frac{-12x}{10y} = \frac{-6x}{5y}$$

Example

Find the derivative of y with respect to x from the equation: $8x^2y - 10x = 15xy^3$

Solution:

$$\left(\frac{d}{dx}\left[8x^2\right] * y + 8x^2 * \frac{dy}{dx}\right) - 10 = \left(\frac{d}{dx}\left[15x\right] * y^3 + 5x * \frac{d}{dx}\left[y^3\right]\right)$$

$$\downarrow$$

$$16xy + 8x^2 * \frac{dy}{dx} - 10 = 15y^3 + 5x * 3y^2 * \frac{dy}{dx}$$

$$\frac{-15y^3 - 8x^2 * \frac{dy}{dx} \qquad\qquad -15y^3 - 8x^2 * \frac{dy}{dx}}{16xy - 15y^3 - 10 = 15xy^2 * \frac{dy}{dx} - 8x^2 * \frac{dy}{dx}}$$

$$16xy - 15y^3 - 10 = \frac{dy}{dx}\left(15xy^2 - 8x^2\right)$$

$$\frac{dy}{dx} = \frac{16xy - 15y^3 - 10}{15xy^2 - 8x^2}$$

Section 4-15 Logarithmic Differentiation

Logarithmic differentiation is a powerful tool for computing difficult derivatives. Logarithmic differentiation works well with functions composed of a fraction with expressions on the top and bottom, such as a rational function. To use logarithmic differentiation, first take the natural log of both sides. You will probably need to use the laws of logarithms to make the expressions more readable. Then, use implicit differentiation, solving for $\dfrac{dy}{dx}$ in the end.

Example
Differentiate the following function by employing logarithmic differentiation:

$$y = \frac{2x^7}{\sqrt{22x^4 + 6}}$$

Solution:
First, take the natural log of both sides...

$$\ln(y) = \ln(2x^7) - \ln(\sqrt{22x^4 + 6})$$

$$\ln(y) = \ln(2) + 7 * \ln(x) - \frac{1}{2} * \ln(22x^4 + 6)$$

Second, take the derivative of both sides with respect to x (implicitly differentiate)...

$$\frac{1}{y} * \frac{dy}{dx} = 0 + 7 * \frac{1}{x} - \frac{1}{2} * \frac{1}{22x^4 + 6} * (22 * 4x^3 + 0)$$

$$\downarrow$$

$$\frac{1}{y} * \frac{dy}{dx} = \frac{7}{x} - \frac{88x^3}{44x^4 + 12}$$

$$\frac{dy}{dx} = y \left(\frac{7}{x} - \frac{88x^3}{44x^4 + 12} \right)$$

$$\frac{dy}{dx} = \left(\frac{2x^7}{\sqrt{22x^4 + 6}} \right)\left(\frac{7}{x} - \frac{88x^3}{44x^4 + 12} \right)$$

Example
Differentiate the following function by using logarithmic differentiation:

$$y = \left(18x^5\right)^{\sqrt[3]{x}}$$

Solution:

$\ln(y) = \sqrt[3]{x} * \ln(18x^5)$

$\downarrow$

$\dfrac{1}{y} * \dfrac{dy}{dx} = \dfrac{d}{dx}\left[\sqrt[3]{x}\right] * \ln(18x^5) + \sqrt[3]{x} * \dfrac{d}{dx}\left[\ln(18x^5)\right]$

$\downarrow$

$\dfrac{1}{y} * \dfrac{dy}{dx} = \dfrac{1}{3}x^{-2/3} * \ln(18x^5) + \sqrt[3]{x} * \dfrac{1}{18x^5} * 90x^4$

$\downarrow$

$\dfrac{dy}{dx} = y * \left(\dfrac{\ln(18x^5)}{3x^{2/3}} + \dfrac{\sqrt[3]{x} * 90x^4}{18x^5}\right)$

$\downarrow$

$\dfrac{dy}{dx} = \left(18x^5\right)^{\sqrt[3]{x}} * \left(\dfrac{\ln(18x^5)}{3x^{2/3}} + \dfrac{90}{18x^{2/3}}\right)$

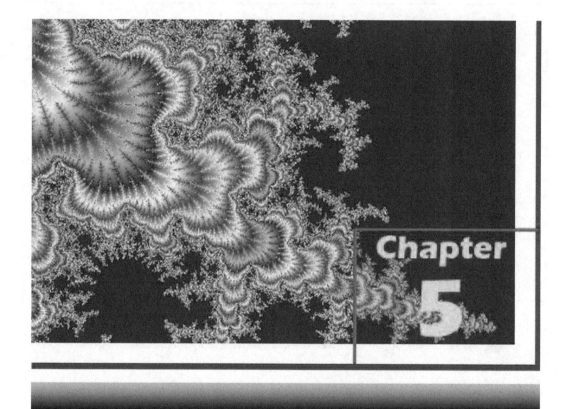

Chapter 5
Applications of Derivatives

Derivatives have countless uses in higher math and engineering. They provide quantitative ways to describe the behavior of functions. Using derivatives, we can find high and low points in a function, or we could develop a spline to fit data points. They also aid greatly in the development of proofs and new theorems. Since derivatives specialize in modeling change, they help to describe changes in a system over time.

Section 5-1 Simplifying Limits by Using Derivatives

L'Hospital's Rule enables you to simplify a limit through differentiation. The rule is useful when evaluating the limit of a rational expression. The limit must be indeterminate, such as $\dfrac{0}{0}$ or $\dfrac{\pm\infty}{\pm\infty}$. In other words, the numerator and denominator must both approach zero, or they must both near positive or negative infinity, while calculating the limit.

L'Hospital's Rule

Consider the limit expression: $\displaystyle \lim_{x \to c} \frac{g(x)}{h(x)}$.

To use the rule, one of two cases must be met:
  (1.) The numerator and denominator both approach zero.
$$\lim_{x \to c} \frac{g(x) \to 0}{h(x) \to 0}$$

  (2.) The numerator and denominator approach positive or negative infinity.
$$\lim_{x \to c} \frac{g(x) \to \pm\infty}{h(x) \to \pm\infty}$$

The rule states:
$$\lim_{x \to c} \frac{g(x)}{h(x)} \overset{L'H}{=} \lim_{x \to c} \frac{g'(x)}{h'(x)}$$

When applying L'Hospital's Rule, place the "L'H" over the equal sign.

Example
Evaluate the following limits using L'Hospital's Rule:

  a. $\displaystyle \lim_{x \to 1} \frac{5x - 5}{\ln(x)}$

  b. $\displaystyle \lim_{x \to \infty} \frac{6x^2 + 7x}{50x^2 + 40}$

  c. $\displaystyle \lim_{x \to 0} \frac{10x}{\sin(x)}$

$$\textbf{d.} \quad \lim_{x \to 0} \frac{\sin^{-1}(4x)}{0.2x^3 + x}$$

Solutions:

a. As x → 1, the numerator, 5x – 5, approaches 0.
As x → 1, the denominator, ln(x), approaches 0.
Since the numerator and denominator both have a limit of zero, as x approaches its target, we can apply L'Hospital's Rule.

$$\lim_{x \to 1} \frac{5x - 5}{\ln(x)} \overset{L'H}{=} \lim_{x \to 1} \frac{5}{\left(\dfrac{1}{x}\right)} = \lim_{x \to 1} 5x = 5$$

b. As x → ∞, the numerator and the denominator both approach +∞.
Therefore, we can use L'Hospital's Rule.

$$\lim_{x \to \infty} \frac{6x^2 + 7x}{50x^2 + 40} \overset{L'H}{=} \lim_{x \to \infty} \frac{12x + 7}{100x} \overset{L'H}{=} \lim_{x \to \infty} \frac{12}{100} = 0.12$$

You can apply the rule multiple times if necessary, as long as the numerator and denominator both approach zero or both approach $\pm \infty$.

c. Since the numerator and denominator both approach zero as $x \to 0$, we can apply L'Hospital's Rule.

$$\lim_{x \to 0} \frac{10x}{\sin(x)} \overset{L'H}{=} \lim_{x \to 0} \frac{10}{\cos(x)} = \frac{10}{\cos(0)} = \frac{10}{1} = 10$$

d. The numerator and denominator both equal zero when x = 0, so we can apply L'Hospital's Rule.

$$\lim_{x \to 0} \frac{\sin^{-1}(4x)}{0.2x^3 + x} \overset{L'H}{=} \lim_{x \to 0} \frac{\dfrac{1}{\sqrt{1 - (4x)^2}} * 4}{0.6x^2 + 1} = \frac{\dfrac{1}{\sqrt{1 - 0}} * 4}{0 + 1} = \frac{\dfrac{1}{\sqrt{1}} * 4}{1} = 4$$

Section 5-2 Extrema

The extrema for a function refer to the set of high and low points that the function generates. A graph may have localized extrema where the function is simply higher or lower at a point relative to its neighbors, or it can have one point that is greater than all other points in the function. Some graphs do not have an absolute minimum or maximum but grow to infinity. First and second derivatives are powerful tools for quickly determining which points on a function are high or low relative to the other points on the graph.

Local Extrema

The graph of a function can dip and rise many times over its course. The peaks are referred to as *local maxima*, while the lower points are called *local minima*. In a sine wave, for example, each crest of the wave is a local maximum, and each trough is a local minimum.

The point (x1, f(x1)) is a local maximum of function f iff $f(x_1) \geq f(x)$ for all x surrounding x1.

The point (x1, f(x1)) is a local minimum of function f iff $f(x_1) \leq f(x)$ for all x surrounding x1.

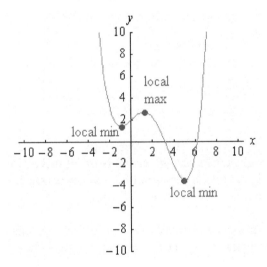

Absolute Extrema
A function can only have one absolute maximum and one absolute minimum.

The point (x1, f(x1)) is an *absolute maximum* for function f iff $f(x_1) \geq f(x)$ for all $x \in$ Domain(f).

The point (x2, f(x2)) is an *absolute minimum* for function f iff $f(x_1) \leq f(x)$ for all $x \in$ Domain(f).

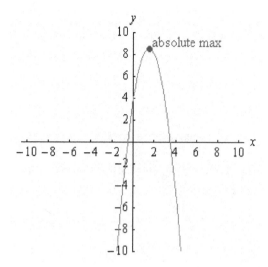

The first derivative of a function gives a wealth of information about the locations of extrema within the function. Assume f'(x) is the first derivative of f. When f'(x) = 0, the parent graph levels off and there is no change in f(x) at that point. A *critical point* of function f is a point (c, f(c)) where f'(c) = 0 or f'(c) does not exist. In other words, critical points occur at the roots of f'(x). Each critical point could yield a local or absolute extreme. The extrema can also transpire at a function's endpoints. Therefore, to find all the extrema for a function, you must examine the graph's behavior around the critical points and also at the endpoints.

A local maximum will occur at point (c, f(c)) when f is increasing to the left of c and decreasing to the right of c. The increasing and decreasing behaviors of f translate to a derivative that is positive to the left of c and negative to the right of c. As the derivative changes from positive to negative, it must cross the x-axis at one of its roots.

A local minimum occurs at point (c, f(c)) when f is decreasing to the left of c and increasing to the right of c. The derivative will change from negative to positive as the derivative function passes over x = c.

Fermat's Theorem:
If function f has a relative maximum or minimum at x = c, then $f'(c) = 0$ or f'(c) does not exist.

The converse of Fermat's Theorem is not true. A function's derivative could have a root at x = c, but point (c, f(c)) is not a relative maximum/minimum. An example of the converse failing is $f(x) = x^3$ at x = 0. For this function, $f'(x) = 3x^2$ and $f'(0) = 0$. However, point (0, 0) is not a local maximum/minimum for f.

Example

Consider the function $f(x) = 0.2x^3 - x + 4$. Find the local extrema of f by examining the function's first derivative.

Solution:

$f'(x) = 0.2 * 3 * x^2 - 1 + 0 = 0.6x^2 - 1$

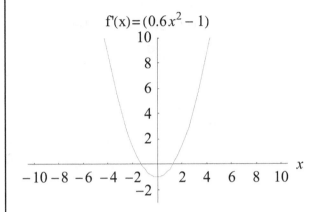

$f'(x) = (0.6x^2 - 1)$

Find the roots of f'(x)...

$f'(x) = 0 = 0.6x^2 - 1$

$\downarrow$

$1 = 0.6x^2$

$\frac{5}{3} = x^2 \quad \rightarrow \quad x = \pm\sqrt{\frac{5}{3}}$

$x = \sqrt{5/3} \approx 1.29099$:

to the left of $x = \sqrt{5/3}$,

$\qquad f'(1.28) = -0.01696 \quad \rightarrow$ f is decreasing

to the right of $x = \sqrt{5/3}$,

$\qquad f'(1.30) = 0.014 \quad \rightarrow$ f is increasing

f(x) decreases before $x = \sqrt{5/3}$ and increases thereafter.

$\therefore \ (\sqrt{5/3}, \ 3.13934)$ is a local minimum.

$x = -\sqrt{5/3} \approx -1.29099$:

to the left of $x = -\sqrt{5/3}$,

$\qquad f'(-1.30) = 0.014 \quad \rightarrow$ f is increasing

to the right of $x = -\sqrt{5/3}$,

$f'(-1.28) = -0.01696 \quad \rightarrow \quad$ f is decreasing

f(x) increases before x = $-\sqrt{5/3}$ and decreases thereafter.
$\therefore (-\sqrt{5/3}, \ 4.86066)$ is a local maximum.

Example

Find the local extrema for $f(x) = \dfrac{1}{2}x^4 - 0.8x^2$ by utilizing only the first derivative.

Solution:
$f'(x) = 2x^3 - 1.6x$

$\downarrow$

$2x^3 - 1.6x = 0$

$x(2x^2 - 1.6) = 0$

$\downarrow \qquad\qquad \downarrow$

$x = 0 \qquad \downarrow$

$\qquad\qquad 2x^2 - 1.6 = 0 \quad \rightarrow \quad 2x^2 = 1.6 \quad \rightarrow \quad x^2 = 0.8 \quad \rightarrow \quad x = \pm\sqrt{0.8}$

Roots of f'(x): $x = 0, \ x = \sqrt{0.8}, \ x = -\sqrt{0.8}$

Critical points of f(x): $(0, 0), \ (\sqrt{0.8}, -0.32), \ (-\sqrt{0.8}, -0.32)$

critical point (0, 0):
to the left of x = 0,
$\qquad f'(-0.5) = 0.55 \quad \rightarrow \quad$ f is increasing

to the right of x = 0,
$\qquad f'(0.5) = -0.55 \quad \rightarrow \quad$ f is decreasing

(0, 0) is a local maximum of f.

critical point ($\sqrt{0.8}$, -0.32):
to the left of x = $\sqrt{0.8}$,
$\qquad f'(0.5) = -0.55 \quad \rightarrow \quad$ f is decreasing

to the right of x = $\sqrt{0.8}$,
$\qquad f'(1) = 0.4 \quad \rightarrow \quad$ f is increasing

($\sqrt{0.8}$, -0.32) is a local minimum of f.

---

critical point $(-\sqrt{0.8}, -0.32)$:

to the left of $x = -\sqrt{0.8}$,

$\qquad f'(-1) = -0.4 \quad \rightarrow \quad$ f is decreasing

to the right of $x = -\sqrt{0.8}$,

$\qquad f'(-0.5) = 0.55 \quad \rightarrow \quad$ f is increasing

$(-\sqrt{0.8}, -0.32)$ is a local minimum of f.

The second derivative gives immediate information about whether a critical point is a minimum or maximum. When a graph dips downwards and forms a local minimum, the graph is concave up and the second derivative must be positive. Correspondingly, when a graph forms a hill at a local maximum, the graph will be concave down with a second derivative that is negative. So, examining the second derivatives at critical points should quickly reveal whether the point is a minimum or maximum. Use the guide below for deciphering critical points with the aid of second derivatives:

(1.) If f'(c) = 0 and f''(c) > 0, then (c, f(c)) is a local minimum.
(2.) If f'(c) = 0 and f''(c) < 0, then (c, f(c)) is a local maximum.
(3.) If f'(c) = 0 and f''(c) = 0, then (c, f(c)) is neither a local minimum nor maximum.

Example

Find the relative extrema of $f(x) = \dfrac{1}{8}x^5 + 5x^2$ by examining the second derivative at the critical points.

Solution:

$$f'(x) = \frac{5}{8}x^4 + 10x = 0$$

$$\downarrow$$

$$\frac{5}{8}x^4 = -10x$$

$$\frac{5}{8}x^3 = -10 \quad \rightarrow \quad x^3 = -16 \quad \rightarrow \quad x = \sqrt[3]{-16} \approx -2.5198$$

$x = 0$ is the second trivial solution

Critical Points: $(0, 0)$, $(-2.5198, 19.0488)$

$$f''(x) = \frac{20}{8}x^3 + 10$$

    Comprehensive Math Review for Actuarial Exams

$f''(0) = 10 > 0$

$f''(-2.5198) = -30 < 0$

$\therefore$ (0, 0) is a local minimum, and (-2.5198, 19.0488) is a local maximum.

The previous few examples show how to find the relative extrema in a function. We still need to find the absolute extrema of a function over a certain interval. Absolute extrema (but not relative extrema) can occur at a graph's endpoints. To calculate the absolute maximum and minimum, you must compute the function at its endpoints and critical points and choose the largest and smallest values of f.

Steps for finding the absolute extrema for function f on [a, b]:
- (1.) Find the critical points of f in the interval (a, b).
- (2.) Compute f at the endpoints of [a, b] (i.e., obtain the points (a, f(a)) and (b, f(b))).
- (3.) Select the absolute maximum and minimum from among the critical points and endpoints.

Example

Find the absolute extrema of f over the interval [-1, 2], where $f(x) = -3x^2 + 4x + 6$.

Solution:

$f'(x) = -6x + 4 = 0$

$\downarrow$

$-6x = -4 \quad \rightarrow \quad x = 2/3$

Critical Points: (2 / 3, 22 / 3)
Endpoints: (-1, -1), (2, 2)
Absolute Maximum: (2 / 3, 22 / 3)
Absolute Minimum: (-1, -1)

Example

Find the absolute extrema of f over [-10, 10], where $f(x) = \dfrac{1}{2}x^3 - 4x^2$.

Solution:

$f'(x) = \dfrac{3}{2}x^2 - 8x = 0$

$\downarrow$

$\dfrac{3}{2}x^2 = 8x \quad \rightarrow \quad \dfrac{3}{2}x = 8 \quad \rightarrow \quad x = 16/3$

Critical Points: (16 / 3, -37.9259)
Endpoints: (-10, -900), (10, 100)
Absolute Maximum: (10, 100)
Absolute Minimum: (-10, -900)

Extreme Value Theorem
Suppose function f is continuous over [a, b]. The function must have an absolute minimum and an absolute maximum over [a, b].

Section 5-3 Connected Rates of Change

The method of "connected rates of change" is used to describe changes in a system that has several variables, such as volume, radius, and other dimensions. Geometric figures and their associated equations are very common in this class of problems. In addition, time is typically the underlying variable. The problems usually measure each dimension with respect to time. Suppose that we are describing a growing sphere. The sphere grows in terms of volume, and it also grows in terms of radius.

The procedure for solving "connected rates of change" problems is very straightforward. We first need to find an equation that fits the problem at hand. Then, take the derivative of both sides with respect to time. Treat every unknown variable as a potential function of time. We are actually employing implicit differentiation as this stage. Finally, solve for the requested rate (such as $\frac{dr}{dt}$) or dimension.

As an example, suppose we have a cylindrical storage tank filling with oil. The radius of the tank is fixed at 40 feet. The height of the oil is rising by 1 foot per hour. At what rate is the volume of the oil changing (in cubic feet per hour)?

First of all, we need to find an equation that describes the problem. Since we are dealing with a cylinder, along with height and volume, the equation for the volume of a cylinder is appropriate:

$$V = \pi r^2 h$$

Then, let's fill in the known quantities. From the description of the problem, the radius is 40:

$$V = \pi * 1600 \text{ ft.}^2 * h \quad \rightarrow \quad V = 5,026.55 \text{ ft.}^2 * h$$

Next, implicitly differentiate both sides of the equation:

$$\frac{dV}{dt} = 5{,}026.55 \text{ ft.}^2 * \frac{dh}{dt}$$

We also know from the problem description that the height is increasing by 1 foot per hour. That is, $\frac{dh}{dt} = 1 \text{ ft./hr.}$.

$$\frac{dV}{dt} = 5{,}026.55 \text{ ft.}^2 * 1 \text{ ft./hr.} \qquad \rightarrow \qquad \frac{dV}{dt} = 5{,}026.55 \text{ ft.}^3 \text{/hr.}$$

Our final answer is shown above. The volume of the oil is growing by 5,026.55 cubic feet per hour. For these problems, it is wise to keep the units throughout the math work. Your final solution should have units that match the requested quantity in the problem.

Example

A circle of bacteria is expanding rapidly. It's radius is changing at 0.02 cm./s. What is the rate of change in the area of the circle, when its radius is 3 cm.?

Solution:

$$A = \pi r^2$$

↓   Take the derivative of both sides with respect to time.

$$\frac{dA}{dt} = \pi * 2r * \frac{dr}{dt}$$

↓

$$\frac{dA}{dt} = \pi * 2 * (3 \text{ cm.}) * \left(0.02 \frac{\text{cm.}}{\text{s.}} \right)$$

↓

$$\frac{dA}{dt} = 0.37699 \text{ cm.}^2\text{/s.}$$

Example

Consider a star that is collapsing to a white dwarf. It's volume is shrinking at a constant rate of $7*10^{15}$ m.^{3}/s. What is the change in the star's radius per second, when the radius is 10^6 m.?

Solution:

$$V = \frac{4}{3} \pi r^3 \qquad \text{(volume of a sphere)}$$

↓

$$\frac{dV}{dt} = \frac{4}{3} \pi * 3r^2 * \frac{dr}{dt}$$

↓

$$-7*10^{15} \text{ m.}^3/\text{s.} = \frac{4}{3}\pi*3(10^6 \text{ m.})^2 * \frac{dr}{dt}$$

$$-7*10^{15} \text{ m.}^3/\text{s.} = 1.25664*10^{13} \text{ m.}^2 * \frac{dr}{dt}$$

$$\frac{dr}{dt} = \frac{-7*10^{15} \text{ m.}^3/\text{s.}}{1.25664*10^{13} \text{ m.}^2}$$

$$\frac{dr}{dt} = -557.04233 \text{ m./s.}$$

Example

An airplane has a ground speed of 550 miles/hour. It is currently 60 miles from the airport (ground distance), and is 4 miles above the ground. How fast is the plane approaching the airport?

Solution:

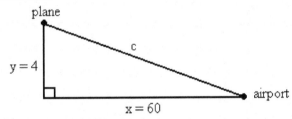

$$x^2 + y^2 = c^2$$
$$x^2 + 16 = c^2$$
$$2x * \frac{dx}{dt} + 0 = 2c * \frac{dc}{dt}$$
$$\downarrow$$
$$120 * 550 = 2c * \frac{dc}{dt}$$

$$60^2 + 4^2 = c^2 \quad \rightarrow \quad c^2 = 3,616 \quad \rightarrow \quad c = 60.1332 \text{ miles}$$

$$66,000 = 120.2664 * \frac{dc}{dt}$$

$$\frac{dc}{dt} = 548.7817 \text{ miles/hour}$$

Example

A jet fighter is 2 miles from a radar station (the actual distance from station to jet). From the perspective of the station, the angle between the ground and the airplane is 0.3 radians. The station also calculates that at the current moment, the angle is changing at 0.05 radians/s. What is the fighter's ground speed?

Solution:

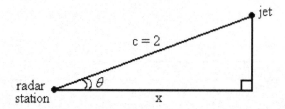

$$\cos(\theta) = \frac{x}{2}$$

$$\downarrow$$

$$-\sin(\theta) * \frac{d\theta}{dt} = \frac{1}{2} * \frac{dx}{dt}$$

$$-\sin(0.3) * (0.05 \text{ radians/s.}) = \frac{1}{2} * \frac{dx}{dt}$$

$$\frac{dx}{dt} = -0.02955 \text{ miles/s.}$$

The plane is approaching the radar station at 0.02955 miles/s.

Example
A box-shaped pool is filling with water at a rate of 0.22 m.³/min. What is the change in height of the pool per minute, if the length is 5 m. and the width is 3 m.?

Solution:
$$V = l * w * h$$
$$V = (15 \ m.^2) * h$$
$$\downarrow$$
$$\frac{dV}{dt} = (15 \ m.^2) * \frac{dh}{dt}$$
$$0.22 \ m.^3 /\text{min.} = (15 \ m.^2) * \frac{dh}{dt}$$
$$\frac{dh}{dt} = \frac{0.22 \ m.^3 /\text{min.}}{15 \ m.^2}$$

$$\frac{dh}{dt} \approx 0.01467 \text{ m./min.}$$

Section 5-4 Approximating Transcendental Functions with Polynomials

You can approximate nearly any function over a finite interval with a polynomial. Polynomial approximations are easier for a computer to evaluate. At a processor level, most computers can handle only the four primitive math operations—addition, subtraction, multiplication, and division. Floating point math is very time-consuming for machines, too. Polynomials are the simplest class of functions. They require only the four basic operators. Additionally, integer exponents can be treated as repeated multiplication.

The process of finding an approximating polynomial relies heavily on differentiation. First of all, you need to choose a point of tangency in the original function. The initial and new functions will both pass through this point. Usually the approximating function does not match the original function over all x-values; the two functions are very close over a small x-interval. The second stage involves matching the derivatives of the original function with those of the new function. For an approximating polynomial of degree n, you need to match the zero through n^{th} derivatives of the initial function at the point of tangency. The zeroth derivative simply means that $f(x_1) = g(x_1)$, where f is the original function and g is the estimated function. You must also match the first, second, third, and all higher derivatives until you reach n: $f'(x_1) = g'(x_1)$, $f''(x_1) = g''(x_1)$, $f'''(x_1) = g'''(x_1)$, ..., $f^{(n)}(x_1) = g^{(n)}(x_1)$. For instance, if you want to approximate a function f(x) with a first-degree line g(x) around x = 1, the following must be true: $f(1) = g(1)$ and $f'(1) = g'(1)$.

Example

Suppose we have the function $f(x) = \sqrt{6+x^3}$ and wish to estimate the function with a parabola around x = 3. A graph of the function is shown here:

The tangent point is (3, 5.74456). Since the approximating parabola is of degree 2, we must match the first two derivatives of f with those from g (the estimating polynomial).

$$f'(x) = \frac{1}{2} * \left(6 + x^3\right)^{-1/2} * 3x^2$$

$$f''(x) = \frac{1}{2} * \left(6 + x^3\right)^{-1/2} * 6x + \frac{1}{2} * \left(-\frac{1}{2}\right) * \left(6 + x^3\right)^{-3/2} * 3x^2 * 3x^2$$

$$f'(3) = 2.35005$$
$$f''(3) = 0.60532$$

The approximating quadratic, along with its derivatives, are:

$$\begin{cases} g(x) = ax^2 + bx + c \\ g'(x) = 2ax + b \\ g''(x) = 2a \end{cases}$$

We create a system by setting the three previous equations equal to their counterparts from function f:

$$\begin{cases} 9a + 3b + c = 5.74456 \\ 6a + b = 2.35005 \\ 2a = 0.60532 \end{cases}$$

Then, use back substitution to solve for the coefficients a, b, and c.

$$2a = 0.60532 \quad \rightarrow \quad a = 0.30266$$

$$6a + b = 2.35005$$
$$1.81596 + b = 2.35005 \quad \rightarrow \quad b = 0.53409$$

$$9a + 3b + c = 5.74456$$
$$2.72394 + 1.60227 + c = 5.74456 \quad \rightarrow \quad c = 1.41835$$

$$g(x) = 0.30266x^2 + 0.53409x + 1.41835$$

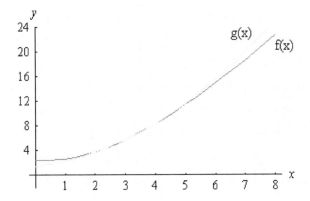

The graph of f(x) and its approximation are shown above. As you can see, the approximating quadratic does an excellent job of following the course of f(x).

Example

Consider the function $f(x) = \cos(x)$.

Approximate the function around x = ½ with…

a. a constant

b. a line

c. a parabola

Solutions:

a. You must match only the y-value, so the approximate function is $g(x) = 0.87758$.

b. You must match the y-value and the slope, so

$$y - y_1 = m(x - x_1)$$
$$\downarrow$$
$$y - 0.87758 = (-\sin(0.5))(x - 0.5)$$
$$y - 0.87758 = -0.47943(x - 0.5)$$
$$y - 0.87758 = -0.47943x + 0.23971$$
$$g(x) = -0.47943x + 1.11729$$

c. You must match the y-value, f '(x), and f ''(x),…

$$\begin{cases} g(x) = ax^2 + bx + c \\ g'(x) = 2ax + b \\ g''(x) = 2a \end{cases} \qquad \begin{cases} f(x) = \cos(x) \\ f'(x) = -\sin(x) \\ f''(x) = -\cos(x) \end{cases}$$

At x = 0.5,

$$\begin{cases} f(0.5) = 0.87758 = a * \dfrac{1}{4} + b * \dfrac{1}{2} + c \\[2mm] f'(0.5) = -0.47943 = 2a * \dfrac{1}{2} + b \\[2mm] f''(0.5) = -0.87758 = 2a \end{cases}$$

$-0.87758 = 2a \;\;\rightarrow\;\; a = -0.43879$

$-0.47943 = -0.43879 + b \;\;\rightarrow\;\; b = -0.04064$

$0.87758 = -0.43879 * \dfrac{1}{4} - 0.04064 * \dfrac{1}{2} + c \;\;\rightarrow\;\; c = 1.0076$

$g(x) = -0.43879x^2 - 0.04064x + 1.0076$

Example

Approximate the following function at $(0, 1)$ with a parabola: $f(x) = e^x$

Solution:
We must match f(0), f'(0), and f''(0) with the new approximation function.

$f(0) = 1$

$f'(0) = e^0 = 1$

$f''(0) = e^0 = 1$

$g(0) = ax^2 + bx + c = c$ $\qquad\qquad$ $\begin{cases} c = f(0) = 1 \\ b = f'(0) = 1 \\ 2a = f''(0) = 1 \;\;\rightarrow\;\; a = 1/2 \end{cases}$

$g'(0) = 2ax + b = b \qquad\qquad \rightarrow$

$g''(0) = 2a$

$g(x) = \dfrac{1}{2}x^2 + x + 1$

Example

Approximate the following function at x = 3 with a cubic function: $f(x) = \ln(5x)$

Solution:
Again, we must match f(3), f'(3), f''(3), and f'''(3).

$f(3) = 2.70805$

$f'(3) = \dfrac{1}{5x} * 5 = \dfrac{1}{x} = 1/3$

$$f''(3) = -x^{-2} = -1/9$$
$$f'''(3) = -(-2)x^{-3} = 2/27$$

$$g(x) = ax^3 + bx^2 + cx + d$$
$$g'(x) = 3ax^2 + 2bx + c$$
$$g''(x) = 6ax + 2b$$
$$g'''(x) = 6a$$
$$\downarrow$$
$$g(3) = a*27 + b*9 + c*3 + d = 2.70805$$
$$g'(3) = 3a*9 + 2b*3 + c = 1/3$$
$$g''(3) = 6a*3 + 2b = -1/9$$
$$g'''(3) = 6a = 2/27$$

$$a \approx 0.01235 = 1/81$$
b = -1/6
c = 1
$$d \approx 0.87472$$

$$g(x) \approx \frac{1}{81}x^3 - \frac{1}{6}x^2 + x + 0.87472$$

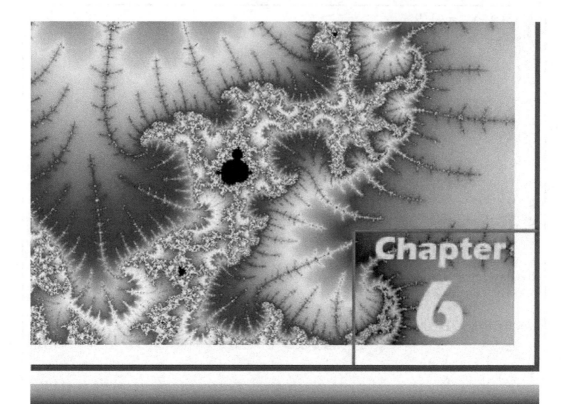

Chapter 6
Single Integration

The derivative and the integral are the two primary tools of calculus. These two functions are complementary. This chapter introduces the integral. Integrals are used to find precise areas under functions. Double integrals find the volume below a surface.

Prior to starting a calculus class, you probably learned how to compute the areas of simple geometric figures, such as rectangles, triangles, and circles. These area formulas are very limited and cannot be applied when calculating the areas of more complex regions. Integrals allow you to precisely compute the area of a region that does not ascribe to a geometric shape. If you can define the border of a region with a function or several functions, you can compute the area of the region with integrals.

Section 6-1 Riemann Sums

Consider the function $f(x) = x^2 + 3$. Suppose we wish to find the area below the function and above the x-axis in the interval [0, 4].

Unfortunately, a common formula does not exist for the area we are trying to find. You could approximate the area with several geometric shapes, such as a rectangle for the bottom region and a right triangle for the top. A more straightforward approach is to approximate the area with several vertical rectangles. You could choose rectangles that match the general flow of the function as shown in the plot below, calculate the area of each rectangle, and then sum the areas to obtain an approximation to the true area below f(x).

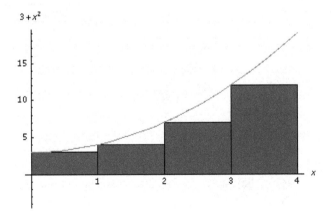

The rectangles above each have a width of 1 unit, and their height equals the value of f(x) at the left endpoint. The rectangles clearly underestimate the actual area. The table below describes the four rectangles:

Rectangle Index (i)	Width	x_i	$f(x_i)$	Area
1	1	0	3	3
2	1	1	4	4
3	1	2	7	7
4	1	3	12	12

Total Area = 26

We could also approximate the area with the rectangles below:

These rectangles again have a width of 1 unit, but the height is determined by the value of the function at the right endpoint. These rectangles overestimate the area. The following table gives information on the approximating rectangles:

Rectangle Index (i)	Width	x_i	$f(x_i)$	Area
1	1	1	4	4
2	1	2	7	7
3	1	3	12	12
4	1	4	19	19

Total Area = 42

In this example, the left-endpoint rectangles understate the area, while the right-endpoint rectangles overstate the area. Perhaps rectangles exist that provide a more moderate estimate of the area. Since we have already tried left- and right-endpoint rectangles, we could try mid-point rectangles. The rectangles below have a height equal to the value of the function at the mid-point of each interval.

Rectangle Index (i)	Width	x_i	$f(x_i)$	Area
1	1	0.5	3.25	3.25
2	1	1.5	5.25	5.25
3	1	2.5	9.25	9.25
4	1	3.5	15.25	15.25

Total Area = 33

The mid-point rectangles produced a total area of 33 square units. The true area of the region of interest is 33.33333 square units (this exact answer was determined using integrals, which will be introduced later). In this example, the mid-point rectangles clearly provided the best estimate of the area.

Multiple methods exist for estimating an area with rectangles. A *Riemann Sum* uses the areas of vertical rectangles to approximate the total area under a graph. You may choose rectangles according to three rules: the left-hand endpoint rule, right-hand endpoint rule, and midpoint rule. The estimation starts with an interval [a, b] and the decision to use n equal-length subintervals, each of size $\Delta x = \dfrac{b-a}{n}$. You then need to determine the endpoints for each subinterval. The chart below provides the left-most endpoint for the first rectangle:

Left-hand endpoint rule	$x_1 = a$
Right-hand endpoint rule	$x_1 = a + \Delta x$
Midpoint rule	$x_1 = a + \dfrac{\Delta x}{2}$

The next endpoint equals the previous endpoint plus Δx. Rather than calculating the endpoints recursively, you can use an explicit formula for x_i that makes use of the index i:

Left-hand endpoint rule	$x_i = a + \Delta x * (i-1)$
Right-hand endpoint rule	$x_i = a + \Delta x * i$
Midpoint rule	$x_i = a + \dfrac{\Delta x}{2} + \Delta x * (i-1)$

The subscript i on the endpoint x_i will start at 1 and end with n. The finishing step is to find the area of each rectangle and sum the areas to produce your estimate for the total region under the graph of interest. Remember that the area of a rectangle is its width times height. All these rectangles have the identical width of Δx and varying height equal to $f(x_i)$. The area formula, regardless of which rule you use, is:

Total Area of Approximating Rectangles

$$Area = \sum_{i=1}^{n} f(x_i) * \Delta x$$

You should create a table containing all the endpoints, rectangle widths, rectangle heights, and rectangle areas. The area of a function above the x-axis is positive area, while the region below the x-axis has negative area.

Example
Estimate the area under $f(x) = e^{0.5x}$ for the interval [2, 8]. You should use the left-hand endpoint rule and 5 rectangles.

Solution:
a = 2, b = 8, n = 5

$$\Delta x = \frac{b-a}{n} = \frac{8-2}{5} = 1.2$$

Rectangle Index (i)	Width	x_i	$f(x_i)$	Area
1	1.2	2	2.71828	3.26194
2	1.2	3.2	4.95303	5.94364
3	1.2	4.4	9.02501	10.83001
4	1.2	5.6	16.44465	19.73358
5	1.2	6.8	29.9641	35.95692

Total Area = 75.72609

2.71828$^{0.5x}$

Estimated Area = 75.7259
Actual Area = 103.76

Example

Approximate the area under $f(x) = 0.2x^2 + x - 4$ over the interval [0, 6]. You should use the midpoint rule and 4 rectangles.

Solution:
a = 0, b = 6, n = 4

$$\Delta x = \frac{b-a}{n} = \frac{6-0}{4} = 1.5$$

Rectangle Index (i)	Width	x_i	$f(x_i)$	Area
1	1.5	0.75	-3.1375	-4.70625
2	1.5	2.25	-0.7375	-1.10625
3	1.5	3.75	2.5625	3.84375
4	1.5	5.25	6.7625	10.14375

Total Area = 8.175

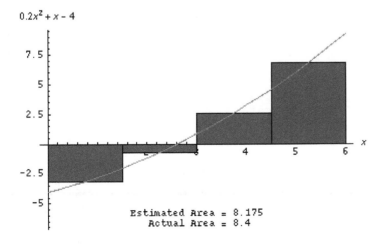

$0.2x^2 + x - 4$

Estimated Area = 8.175
Actual Area = 8.4

Choosing a smaller width for the rectangles results in a more accurate approximation for the area below a function. Narrower rectangles also mean that you need more rectangles to estimate a region. In fact, using infinitely many rectangles will result in a perfectly precise calculation of the area.

The Riemann Sums Theory uses an infinite number of approximating rectangles to find an area. This theory states that as $n \to \infty$ and the rectangle width, Δx, approaches zero, the sum of the areas of the approximating rectangles equals the true area under the function. The theory is true for all three endpoint rules.

Riemann Sums Theory

$$\text{Actual Area} = \lim_{n \to \infty} \sum_{i=1}^{n} f(x_i) * \Delta x$$

When calculating Riemann Sums, the following list of properties for the summation operation can be quite helpful:

Properties of the Summation Operation

(1.) $\sum_{i=1}^{n} c = nc$, where c is a constant

(2.) $\sum_{i=1}^{n} cx_i = c * \sum_{i=1}^{n} x_i$, where c is a constant

(3.) $\sum_{i=1}^{n} x_i + y_i = \sum_{i=1}^{n} x_i + \sum_{i=1}^{n} y_i$

(4.) $\sum_{i=1}^{n} x_i - y_i = \sum_{i=1}^{n} x_i - \sum_{i=1}^{n} y_i$

(5.) $\sum_{i=1}^{n} i = \frac{n(n+1)}{2}$

(6.) $\sum_{i=1}^{n} i^2 = \frac{n(n+1)(2n+1)}{6}$

(7.) $\sum_{i=1}^{n} i^3 = \left(\frac{n(n+1)}{2} \right)^2$

Section 6-2 The Anti-derivative

An *anti-derivative* is the opposite of a derivative. A capital letter, such as F, denotes the anti-derivative of a function. When creating an anti-derivative, you need to ask, "What function, when differentiated, will yield the original function?"

We now have several different functions:
  f = original function
  f' = first derivative of the original function
  F = anti-derivative
  F' = first derivative of the anti-derivative

You must think of derivatives in reverse. The derivative of the anti-derivative results in the original function: $F'(x) = f(x)$. Similarly, the anti-derivative of the derivative creates the initial function: $F(f'(x)) = f(x)$.

Computing anti-derivatives may require trial and error at first. You can choose a function for the anti-derivative that you think produces the original function when differentiated and check that your hypothesis is true. In a scientific method-like manner, you might continue tweaking your anti-derivative until its first derivative equals f.

Consider the horizontal line $f(x) = 5$. To find the antiderivative of f, we must uncover the function that when differentiated generates the initial function, 5. What functions produce only a constant when differentiated? All lines have a constant slope and thus a constant derivative. So, the anti-derivative must have a first-degree term with x. Does $F(x) = 5x$ work? The derivative is $F'(x) = 5 = f(x)$. As a result, we know the antiderivative is 5x. However, several other possibilities exist for F(x). Does $F(x) = 5x + 10$ work? The derivative is also 5, the original function. The same is true for $F(x) = 5x + 1$, $F(x) = 5x + 2$, and $F(x) = 5x + 3$. Adding any constant to the proposed antiderivative appears to create another valid antiderivative.

Every function has infinitely many antiderivatives. Suppose we have found the antiderivative of function f, which is F. We know that $F'(x) = \dfrac{d}{dx}[F(x)] = f(x)$. What happens if we add a constant 'c' onto the antiderivative? After all, the derivative of a constant is zero. The derivative now becomes $\dfrac{d}{dx}[F(x) + c] = F'(x) + 0 = f(x)$, the original function. So, $F(x) + c$ is also an antiderivative of function f. When computing most anti-derivatives, add a constant 'c' onto the anti-derivative, where c is any real number.

The most common antiderivatives are those involving polynomials. Suppose we need to find the anti-derivative of $f(x) = 8x^2$. The first derivative of F must produce the original f. For polynomials, the derivation process reduces all the exponents by 1. In anticipation of this reduction in exponents, we need to add 1 onto all the powers in f. Our proposed anti-derivative is then $F(x) = 8x^3$. The derivative of F would be $F'(x) = 3*8x^2 = 24x^2 \neq f(x)$. The exponent of 3 comes down next to the term and inflates the coefficient. To counter the 3, we could multiply the term by 1 / 3. Does $F(x) = \frac{1}{3}*8x^3$ work? Check the derivative: $F'(x) = 3*\frac{1}{3}*8x^2 = 8x^2 = f(x)$. To determine the anti-derivative of a single term in a polynomial, add 1 to the original exponent, and multiply x by the inverse of the new exponent. The original coefficient does not change and is still multiplied by the new term.

Power Rule for Antidifferentiation
If $f(x) = x^n$, where n is a real number not equal to -1, then

$$F(x) = \frac{1}{n+1}*x^{n+1} + C$$

Example
Find the anti-derivatives of the following expressions:

    a. x^3

    b. $5x^2 + 67x^{10}$

    c. $\cos(x)$

Solutions:

    a. The derivative of what expression will yield the original function, x^3? Recall that the derivative of a polynomial reduces the exponent of each term by 1. So, the anti-derivative must have the term x^4. However, the derivative of x^4 is $4x^3$—similar to the original function above but with the extra '4' coefficient. To eliminate the coefficient, we must divide the proposed anti-derivative by 4. The original expression can also be written $x^3 + 0$. We need to find a term in the anti-derivative for the '0.' Since the derivative of any constant is zero, we need to add the constant c to the anti-derivative.

    Final anti-derivative: $\frac{1}{4}x^4 + c$

    Check:

        The derivative of the anti-derivative should result in the original function.

$$\frac{d}{dx}\left[\frac{1}{4}x^4 + c\right] = \frac{1}{4} * 4 * x^3 + 0 = x^3$$

b. The derivative of some expression—the anti-derivative—will result in $5x^2 + 67x^{10}$. For this polynomial, we must increase the exponent of each term by 1, and divide the associated coefficient by the new power. We also need to add the constant c again.

Final anti-derivative: $\dfrac{1}{3} * 5x^3 + \dfrac{1}{11} * 67x^{11} + c = \dfrac{5}{3}x^3 + \dfrac{67}{11}x^{11} + c$

Check:

$$\frac{d}{dx}\left[\frac{5}{3}x^3 + \frac{67}{11}x^{11} + c\right] = 3 * \frac{5}{3}x^2 + 11 * \frac{67}{11}x^{10} + 0 = 5x^2 + 67x^{10} = \text{original func}$$

c. The derivative of which trigonometric function will produce $\cos(x)$?

Final anti-derivative: $\sin(x) + c$

Check: $\dfrac{d}{dx}[\sin(x) + c] = \cos(x) + 0 = \text{original func}$

Example

What are the antiderivatives of these expressions?

a. e^x

b. $\dfrac{1}{1 + x^2}$

c. $-\dfrac{1}{\sqrt{1 - x^2}}$

d. $\dfrac{1}{x}$

Solutions:

a. $e^x + c$

b. $\tan^{-1}(x) + c$

c. $\cos^{-1}(x) + c$

d. $\ln(x) + c$

Each application of antidifferentiation reduces the order of the derivative by 1. f''(x) becomes f'(x) after antidifferentiating. You can start with a high-order derivative and calculate the original, base function with repeated applications of antidifferentiation.

Example

What is the antiderivative of $g(x) = \sin(5x) + 6x^4 + 20x^2 + \dfrac{1}{8x}$, if it is known that $G(1) = 5$?

Solution:

$$G(x) = -\cos(5x) * \frac{1}{5} + 6 * \frac{1}{5} * x^5 + 20 * \frac{1}{3} * x^3 + \ln(8x) * \frac{1}{8} + C$$

$$G(1) = 5 = -\cos(5) * \frac{1}{5} + 6 * \frac{1}{5} + 20 * \frac{1}{3} + \ln(8) * \frac{1}{8} + C$$

$$5 = -0.05673 + 1.2 + 6.66667 + 0.25993 + C$$

$$C = -3.06987$$

$$G(x) = \frac{-\cos(5x)}{5} + \frac{6}{5}x^5 + \frac{20}{3}x^3 + \frac{\ln(8x)}{8} - 3.06987$$

Example

You are given that $g'(x) = e^{4x} + \dfrac{1}{\sqrt{1-9x^2}}$ and $g(0.25) = 8$. Find function g.

Solution:

$$g(x) = e^{4x} * \frac{1}{4} + \sin^{-1}(3x) + C$$

$$g(0.25) = 8 = e^1 * \frac{1}{4} + \sin^{-1}(0.75) + C$$

$$8 = 0.67957 + 0.84806 + C \quad \rightarrow \quad C = 6.47237$$

$$g(x) = e^{4x} * \frac{1}{4} + \sin^{-1}(3x) + 6.47237$$

Example

Suppose $g''(x) = 7x^4 + 25x^2 + 70 - \sin(2x)$. What is function g, if you are also given that $g(0.1) = 2$ and $g(0.3) = 3.5$?

Solution:

$$g'(x) = 7 * \frac{1}{5} * x^5 + 25 * \frac{1}{3} * x^3 + 70x + \cos(2x) * \frac{1}{2} + C$$

$$g(x) = \frac{7}{5} * \frac{1}{6} * x^6 + \frac{25}{3} * \frac{1}{4} * x^4 + 70 * \frac{1}{2} * x^2 + \sin(2x) * \frac{1}{2} * \frac{1}{2} + Cx + D$$

$$g(x) = \frac{7}{30} x^6 + \frac{25}{12} x^4 + 35x^2 + \sin(2x) * \frac{1}{4} + Cx + D$$

$$g(0.1) = 2 = \frac{7}{30} * 0.1^6 + \frac{25}{12} * 0.1^4 + 35 * 0.1^2 + \sin(0.2) * \frac{1}{4} + C * 0.1 + D$$

$$2 = 0.3998759 + C * 0.1 + D$$

$$1.6001241 = C * 0.1 + D$$

$$g(0.3) = 3.5 = \frac{7}{30} * 0.3^6 + \frac{25}{12} * 0.3^4 + 35 * 0.3^2 + \sin(0.6) * \frac{1}{4} + C * 0.3 + D$$

$$3.5 = 3.30821 + C * 0.3 + D$$

$$0.19179 = C * 0.3 + D$$

$$\begin{cases} 1.6001241 = 0.1C + D \\ 0.19179 = 0.3C + D \end{cases}$$

$$D = 1.6001241 - 0.1C$$

$$0.19179 = 0.3C + 1.6001241 - 0.1C$$

$$-1.40833 = 0.2C \quad \rightarrow \quad C = -7.04165$$

$$1.6001241 = 0.1 * (-7.04165) + D \quad \rightarrow \quad D = 2.30429$$

Section 6-3 Indefinite Integrals

An *integral* gives the area between the function of interest and the horizontal axis. The integral equals an infinite Riemann Sum with rectangles of zero width. The region above the horizontal axis but below the function has positive area, while any sections below the horizontal axis and above the function have negative area. That is, whenever the function drops below zero, negative area results.

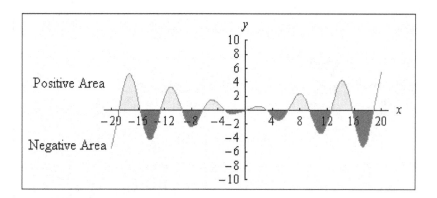

The symbol for integration is the stretched $\int$. An *indefinite integral* has the following syntax: $\int f(x)\ dx$. It does not have integration bounds. The function or expression to be integrated, which is called the *integrand*, is placed to the right of the integration symbol. The "dx" indicates the function will be integrated with respect to x. A function could have multiple independent variables, so the integration must specify which variable to integrate with respect to.

Computing an indefinite integral simply requires finding the anti-derivative of the inner function. Formally stated, $\int f(x)\ dx = F(x)$. Rather than providing a number, evaluating an indefinite integral generates a function. The constant term 'c' should be added to the anti-derivative produced when computing an indefinite integral.

The derivative and indefinite integral cancel each other out in the properties below:

$$\int f'(x)\ dx = f(x)$$

The integral of a function's derivative equals the original function.

$$\frac{d}{dx}\left[\int f(x)\ dx\right] = f(x)$$

The derivative of a function's integral equals the original function.

Example
Solve the following indefinite integrals:

    a. $\int \sqrt{x}\ dx$

    b. $\int \sec^2(x)\ dx$

Solutions:

a. $\int \sqrt{x} \ dx = F(x) = \dfrac{2}{3} x^{3/2} + C$

b. $\int = \tan(x) + C$

Example

Evaluate these indefinite integrals:

    a. $\int e^{3x} + \dfrac{1}{12x} \ dx$

    b. $\int \sqrt{10x^3} \ dx$

    c. $\int 8x^6 + \sec(x) * \tan(x) \ dx$

Solutions:

    a. $\int = e^{3x} * \dfrac{1}{3} + \ln(12x) * \dfrac{1}{12} + C$

    b. $\sqrt{10x^3} = 10^{1/2} * x^{3/2}$

        $\int = \sqrt{10} * x^{5/2} * \dfrac{2}{5} + C$

    c. $\int 8x^6 \ dx + \int \sec(x) * \tan(x) \ dx$

        $\dfrac{8}{7} x^7 + \sec(x) + C$

Section 6-4 Definite Integrals

    A *definite integral* is the area between a function f(x) and the x-axis from x = a to x = b. Definite integrals have bounds of integration, as exhibited in $\int_a^b f(x) \ dx$. This expression reads "the integral of f(x) as x goes from a to b." The lower bound for the integral—'a'—is placed below the integration symbol, and the upper bound—'b'—is situated above the symbol. The Riemann Sums Theory provides the definition of a definite integral:

$$\lim_{n \to \infty} \sum_{i=1}^{n} f(x_i) * \Delta x = \int_a^b f(x) \ dx$$

Example

Evaluate $\int_0^6 \frac{1}{20}x^3 + 0.15x^2 \; dx$ with the help of an infinite Riemann Sum.

Solution:

$$\Delta x = \frac{b-a}{n} = \frac{6-0}{n} = \frac{6}{n}$$

Start the indexing at 0 rather than 1.

$$x_0 = 0, \; x_1 = \frac{6}{n}, \; x_2 = \frac{12}{n}, \; ..., x_i = \frac{6i}{n}$$

$$\int_0^6 \frac{1}{20}x^3 + 0.15x^2 \; dx = \lim_{n \to \infty} \sum_{i=1}^{n} f(x_i) * \Delta x = \lim_{n \to \infty} \sum_{i=1}^{n} f\left(\frac{6i}{n}\right) * \frac{6}{n}$$

$$= \lim_{n \to \infty} \frac{6}{n} * \sum_{i=1}^{n} \frac{1}{20}\left(\frac{6i}{n}\right)^3 + 0.15\left(\frac{6i}{n}\right)^2$$

$$= \lim_{n \to \infty} \frac{6}{n} * \sum_{i=1}^{n} \frac{1}{20}\left(\frac{216i^3}{n^3}\right) + 0.15\left(\frac{36i^2}{n^2}\right)$$

$$= \lim_{n \to \infty} \frac{6}{n} * \sum_{i=1}^{n} \frac{10.8i^3}{n^3} + \frac{5.4i^2}{n^2}$$

$$= \lim_{n \to \infty} \sum_{i=1}^{n} \frac{64.8i^3}{n^4} + \frac{32.4i^2}{n^3}$$

$$= \lim_{n \to \infty} \frac{64.8}{n^4} * \sum_{i=1}^{n} i^3 + \frac{32.4}{n^3} * \sum_{i=1}^{n} i^2$$

$$= \lim_{n \to \infty} \frac{64.8}{n^4} * \left(\frac{n(n+1)}{2}\right)^2 + \frac{32.4}{n^3} * \left(\frac{n(n+1)(2n+1)}{6}\right)$$

$$= \lim_{n \to \infty} 32.4 * \left(\frac{n(n+1)}{n^2}\right)^2 + 5.4 * \left(\frac{n(n+1)(2n+1)}{n^3}\right)$$

$$\lim_{n \to \infty} \left(\frac{n(n+1)}{n^2}\right)^2 = 1, \text{ since the numerator and denominator have the same degree and}$$

same coefficients for the highest power

$$\lim_{n \to \infty} \frac{n(n+1)(2n+1)}{n^3} = 2, \text{ since the numerator and denominator have the same degree}$$

and the ratio of the coefficients for the highest power is 2

$$\int = 32.4*1 + 5.4*2$$
$$= 43.2$$

Computing a definite integral provides an actual value for the area below the function. Function f must be continuous on [a, b]. In addition, let F(x) be the antiderivative of f(x). The definite integral equals:

$$\int_a^b f(x) \ dx = \left[F(x)\right]_{x=a}^{x=b} = F(b) - F(a)$$

The antiderivative function F(x) returns the area under the base function f over the interval $(-\infty, x)$. F(b) is the total area under function f from $x = -\infty$ up to $x = b$. Likewise, F(a) is the area under f(x) from $-\infty$ to a. So, the expression $F(b) - F(a)$ equals the difference of areas under the function and provides only the area within the x-interval (a, b).

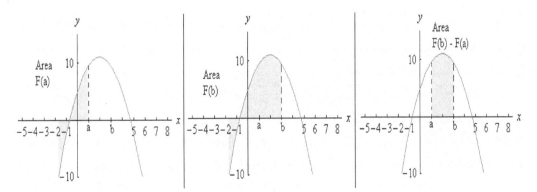

To process a definite integral, first find the antiderivative of the integrand. You should place square brackets around the antiderivative and list the bounds for x on the right side. Then, calculate the antiderivative at the two endpoints—a and b. Finally, compute the difference between the two antiderivatives, which is $F(b) - F(a)$. The constant term 'c' that appeared after most indefinite integrals is excluded from definite integrals.

Since the area is zero under a function at a single x-value, the integral could include or exclude the endpoints. Symbolically,

$$\int_a^a f(x)\ dx = 0$$

For instance, evaluating the integral of f(x) for $5 < x < 8$ is identical to evaluating the integral for $5 \le x \le 8$. Likewise, the interval of integral could have open or closed endpoints, such as [-5, 5] versus (-5, 5). Simply calculate the integral given the minimum and maximum values without considering whether the endpoints are included in the area of interest.

Example
Find the area under $f(x) = 2x$ for $0 < x < 4$.

Solution:

The area is equal to the following integral: $\int_0^4 2x\ dx$

The lower bound 'a' is replaced with x = 0, and the upper bound is x = 4. This is an example of a definite integral, since the bounds are defined.

The first task is to find the anti-derivative of f(x). What function, when differentiated, produces 2x? When the function $F(x) = x^2$ is differentiated, the result is 2x, the original function. So, the anti-derivative is $F(x) = x^2$.

$$\int_0^4 2x\ dx = \left[F(x)\right]_a^b = \left[x^2\right]_0^4 = 4^2 - 0^2 = 16$$

Properties of Integrals:

(1.) $\int_a^b f(x)\ dx = -\int_b^a f(x)\ dx$

If the bounds on the integral flip, the integral must be negated. In other terms, if you compute an integral in reverse from x = b to x = a, you must negate the area.

(2.) $\int_a^b f(x) + g(x)\ dx = \int_a^b f(x)\ dx + \int_a^b g(x)\ dx$

The integral of two expressions summed together equals the integral of the first expression plus the integral of the second expression.

(3.) $\int_a^b f(x) - g(x)\ dx = \int_a^b f(x)\ dx - \int_a^b g(x)\ dx$

(4.) $\int_a^b c\ dx = c(b-a)$, where c is a constant

(5.) $\int_a^b c * f(x)\ dx = c * \int_a^b f(x)\ dx$

(6.) $\int_a^b f(x)\ dx + \int_b^c f(x)\ dx = \int_a^c f(x)\ dx$

(7.) $\int_a^c f(x)\ dx - \int_a^b f(x)\ dx = \int_b^c f(x)\ dx$, where c > b

Example

Find the integrals of the following polynomials from x = 2 to x = 4:

    a. $f(x) = 0.2x + 3$

    b. $g(x) = 0.5x^2 + 0.75$

    c. $h(x) = 0.15x^3$

Solutions:

    a.

$$\int_2^4 0.2x + 3\ dx = \left[\frac{0.2}{2}x^2 + 3x\right]_2^4 = \left(\frac{0.2}{2}*4^2 + 3*4\right) - \left(\frac{0.2}{2}*2^2 + 3*2\right)$$
$$= (1.6 + 12) - (0.4 + 6) = 7.2$$

    b.

$$\int_2^4 0.5x^2 + 0.75\ dx = \left[\frac{0.5}{3}x^3 + 0.75x\right]_2^4$$
$$= \left(\frac{0.5}{3}*4^3 + 0.75*4\right) - \left(\frac{0.5}{3}*2^3 + 0.75*2\right)$$
$$= 10.83333$$

    c.

$$\int_{2}^{4} 0.15x^3 \ dx = \left[\frac{0.15}{4} x^4 \right]_{2}^{4} = 0.0375 * 4^4 - 0.0375 * 2^4 = 9$$

Example

Evaluate the integral of $f(x) = \sin(x)$ for $\pi/4 < x < \pi/2$.

Solution:

$$\int_{\pi/4}^{\pi/2} \sin(x) \ dx = \left[-\cos(x) \right]_{\pi/4}^{\pi/2} = -\cos(\pi/2) - (-\cos(\pi/4)) = -0 - (-\sqrt{2}/2) = \sqrt{2}/2$$

Miscellaneous Definite Integral Theorems

(1.) If $f(x) \le g(x) \ \forall \ x \in [a, b]$, then $\int_{a}^{b} f(x) \ dx \le \int_{a}^{b} g(x) \ dx$

(2.) If $c \le f(x) \le C$ on [a, b], then $c(b-a) \le \int_{a}^{b} f(x) \ dx \le C(b-a)$.

(3.) $\dfrac{d}{dx}\left[\int_{a}^{x} f(t) \ dt \right] = f(x)$

Example

Calculate the following:

a. $\dfrac{d}{dx}\left[\int_{50}^{x} \cos(t^4) + \sqrt[3]{8t^3 + 17t} \ dt \right]$

b. $\dfrac{d}{dx}\left[\int_{0}^{x} 9t^5 + \sec^3(t) \ dt \right]$

Solutions:

a. $= f(x) = \cos(x^4) + \sqrt[3]{8x^3 + 17x}$

b. $= f(x) = 9x^5 + \sec^3(x)$

Section 6-5 Integration by Parts

Integration by parts is helpful when the function inside the integral is the product of two expressions. The contents of the original function are replaced with the symbols 'u' and "dv," which are multiplied together. We also need to find the derivative of u, called "du," and the anti-derivative of dv, which is 'v.' Integration by parts entails reversing the product rule for derivatives. Recall that the product rule is:

$$(uv)' = u'v + uv'$$

Integrating the product rule with indefinite integrals yields:

$$\int (uv)' = \int u'v + uv' = \int u'v + \int uv'$$

Consider the very first integral on the left side. Remember that the integral of a derivative is the inner function (the function being differentiated). Therefore, we can set the above integrals equal to uv :

$$\int u'v + \int uv' = uv$$

Rearranging produces:

$$\int uv' = uv - \int u'v$$

The integration by parts formulas are slightly different for definite and indefinite integrals:

Integration by Parts Formula for Indefinite Integrals

$$\int u * dv = uv - \int du * v$$

Integration by Parts Formula for Definite Integrals

$$\int_a^b u * dv = [uv]_a^b - \int_a^b du * v$$

As an example, consider the definite integral below:

$$\int_0^1 15x * e^{2x} \; dx$$

To evaluate the integral by conventional means, we need to find the anti-derivative for the function in the integral. What function, when differentiated, would produce $15x*e^{2x}$? Finding this anti-derivative is most difficult. We could, however, break the function into two pieces. One part will be labeled 'u,' and the other component is "dv." Suppose we choose u and dv as follows:

let $u = 15x$
let $dv = e^{2x} \ dx$

The expression for dv will always contain "dx," where x is the initial independent variable. The formula for by-parts integration becomes:

$$\int_0^1 15x*e^{2x} \ dx = [uv]_0^1 - \int_0^1 du * v$$

To complete the formula, we need expressions for du and v.

$$du = 15 \ dx$$
$$v = \frac{1}{2}e^{2x}$$

du is the derivative of u, and v is the anti-derivative of dv.

$$\int_0^1 15x*e^{2x} \ dx = \left[15x * \frac{1}{2}e^{2x}\right]_0^1 - \int_0^1 15 * \frac{1}{2}e^{2x} \ dx$$

Calculating the anti-derivative and the integral separately...

$$\left[15x*\frac{1}{2}e^{2x}\right]_0^1 = 7.5(1*e^{2*1} - 0*e^{2*0}) = 7.5e^2$$

$$\int_0^1 15*\frac{1}{2}e^{2x} \ dx = 7.5\int_0^1 e^{2x} \ dx = 7.5 * \left[\frac{1}{2}e^{2x}\right]_0^1 = 3.75*(e^{2*1} - e^{2*0}) = 3.75e^2 - 3.75$$

$$\int_0^1 15x*e^{2x} \ dx = 7.5e^2 - (3.75e^2 - 3.75) = 3.75e^2 + 3.75$$

The next example shows the high importance of choosing the correct expression for u.

Example
Calculate the following integral using integration by parts:

$$\int_4^7 x * \sin(x) \ dx$$

Solution:

(a.)

The first step in integrating by parts is to choose the expressions for u and dv. Suppose we let $u = \sin(x)$ and $dv = x \ dx$. Now,

let $u = \sin(x)$ $\rightarrow$ $du = \cos(x) \ dx$

let $dv = x \ dx$ $\rightarrow$ $v = \frac{1}{2}x^2$

Note that the "dx" symbol must be included in the expressions for du and dv.

$$\int_4^7 x * \sin(x) \ dx = \left[\sin(x) * \frac{1}{2}x^2 \right]_4^7 - \int_4^7 \cos(x) * \frac{1}{2}x^2 \ dx$$

The first anti-derivative can be evaluated by placing 7 and 4 in the expression. The integral on the right side will require another round of integration by parts. Let's set $u = \cos(x)$ and $dv = \frac{1}{2}x^2 \ dx$. Now,

let $u = \cos(x)$ $\rightarrow$ $du = -\sin(x) \ dx$

let $dv = \frac{1}{2}x^2 \ dx$ $\rightarrow$ $v = \frac{1}{6}x^3$

$$\int_4^7 \cos(x) * \frac{1}{2}x^2 \ dx = \left[\cos(x) * \frac{1}{6}x^3 \right]_4^7 - \int_4^7 -\sin(x) * \frac{1}{6}x^3 \ dx$$

This integral has become increasingly more complicated. We can evaluate the anti-derivative on the left side, but the integral on the right side would require another round of integration by parts. This cycle of integration by parts appears to be continuing indefinitely. Did we choose the wrong value for 'u' at the start?

(b.)

Suppose we let $u = x$ and $dv = \sin(x) \ dx$. The integration by parts process becomes:

let $u = x$ $\rightarrow$ $du = 1 \ dx$

let $dv = \sin(x) \ dx$ $\rightarrow$ $v = -\cos(x)$

$$\int_4^7 x * \sin(x) \ dx = \left[-x * \cos(x) \right]_4^7 - \int_4^7 -\cos(x) \ dx$$

$$= \left((-7*\cos(7)) - (-4*\cos(4))\right) + \int_4^7 \cos(x) \ dx$$

$$= (-5.27729) - (2.61456) + \left[\sin(x)\right]_4^7$$

$$= -7.89185 + (\sin(7) - \sin(4))$$

$$= -7.89185 + 0.65699 - (-0.7568)$$

$$= -6.47626$$

If you become stuck in a repetitive cycle of integration by parts, start the problem over with a different value of 'u.'

Use the key below when choosing the expression for u. The first choice for u should be logarithmic functions, such as natural logs. If the original function does not contain logs, then search for inverse trigonometric functions. Work down the list until you find an expression that exists within your original integral, and assign it to u. If you choose an expression for dv that is higher on the list than the expression type for u, you might become caught in the integration by parts loop. You should try to find a value for u that is easy to differentiate, and a value for dv that is easy to anti-differentiate. The new integral that results from by-parts holds $du * v$, which must also be easy to integrate.

Optimal Choice for u:
L -- Logs
I -- Inverse Trig Functions
A -- Algebraic Functions
T -- Trig Functions
E -- Exponential Functions

Example
Solve the following integral:

$$\int_0^{10} 4e^x * x^2 \ dx$$

Solution:
Using the LIATE key, u must be $4x^2$, the algebraic expression.

let $u = 4x^2$ → $du = 8x \ dx$

let $dv = e^x \ dx$ → $v = e^x$

$$\int_0^{10} 4e^x * x^2 \ dx = \left[4x^2 * e^x\right]_0^{10} - \int_0^{10} 8xe^x \ dx$$

$$\left[4x^2 * e^x\right]_0^{10} = 4*10^2 * e^{10} - 4*0^2 * e^0 = 400e^{10}$$

Solving $\int_0^{10} 8xe^x \; dx$ will require more integration by parts.

let $u = 8x$ $\qquad \rightarrow \qquad du = 8 \; dx$

let $dv = e^x \; dx$ $\qquad \rightarrow \qquad v = e^x$

$$\int_0^{10} 8xe^x \; dx = \left[8x * e^x\right]_0^{10} - \int_0^{10} 8e^x \; dx$$

$$= (8*10*e^{10} - 8*0*e^0) - \left[8e^x\right]_0^{10}$$

$$= 80e^{10} - (8e^{10} - 8e^0) = 72e^{10} + 8$$

$$\int_0^{10} 4e^x * x^2 \; dx = \left[4x^2 * e^x\right]_0^{10} - \int_0^{10} 8xe^x \; dx = 400e^{10} - (72e^{10} + 8) = 328e^{10} - 8$$

Example

Find the indefinite integral for $f(x) = \ln(x)$.

Solution:

Must Find: $\int \ln(x) \; dx$

let $u = \ln(x)$ $\qquad \rightarrow \qquad du = \dfrac{1}{x} \; dx$

let $dv = 1 \; dx$ $\qquad \rightarrow \qquad v = x$

$$\int \ln(x) \; dx = \ln(x) * x - \int \frac{1}{x} * x \; dx = \ln(x) * x - \int 1 \; dx = \ln(x) * x - (x + c)$$

$$= \ln(x) * x - x + c$$

Example

Evaluate this integral: $\int_0^1 \cos(x) * 8x^2 \; dx$

Solution:

let $u = 8x^2$ $\qquad \rightarrow \qquad du = 16x \; dx$

let $dv = \cos(x) \; dx$ $\qquad \rightarrow \qquad v = \sin(x)$

$$\int = \left[\sin(x)*8x^2\right]_0^1 - \int_0^1 16x*\sin(x)\,dx$$

$$= 6.73177 - \int_0^1 16x*\sin(x)\,dx$$

let $u = 16x$ $\rightarrow$ $du = 16\ dx$

let $dv = \sin(x)$ $\rightarrow$ $v = -\cos(x)$

$$\int_0^1 16x*\sin(x)\,dx = \left[-16x*\cos(x)\right]_0^1 - \int_0^1 -16\cos(x)\,dx$$

$$= -8.64484 + \int_0^1 16\cos(x)\,dx$$

$$= -8.64484 + \left[16\sin(x)\right]_0^1 = -8.64484 + 13.46354 = 4.8187$$

original integral $= 6.73177 - 4.8187 = 1.91307$

Example

Evaluate this integral: $\displaystyle\int_2^5 \ln(x^2)*(x^7 + 13x^2)\,dx$

Solution:

let $u = \ln(x^2)$ $\rightarrow$ $du = \dfrac{1}{x^2}*2x\ dx = \dfrac{2}{x}\,dx$

let $dv = x^7 + 13x^2\ dx \rightarrow$ $v = \dfrac{1}{8}x^8 + \dfrac{13}{3}x^3$

$$\int = \left[\ln(x^2)*\left(\frac{1}{8}x^8 + \frac{13}{3}x^3\right)\right]_2^5 - \int_2^5 \frac{2\left(\frac{1}{8}x^8 + \frac{13}{3}x^3\right)}{x}\,dx$$

$$= 158{,}823 - \int_2^5 \frac{1}{4}x^7 + \frac{26}{3}x^2\,dx$$

$$= 158{,}823 - \left[\frac{1}{32}x^8 + \frac{26}{9}x^3\right]_2^5 = 158{,}823 - (12{,}568 - 31) = 146{,}286$$

Section 6-6 Simplifying Integrals by Substitution

The functions within many integrals are too difficult to anti-differentiate directly. Suppose you need to integrate the function $f(x) = \dfrac{x^2}{9 + x^3}$ over $5 < x < 10$. The first step in performing the integration is to find the anti-derivative of f, which is nearly impossible to find without the aid of a computer. The function contains x^2 in the numerator, which is very close to the derivative of the denominator. We can simplify the function by setting the new variable 'u' to $u = 9 + x^3$. The integral has become:

$$\int_5^{10} \frac{x^2}{9 + x^3}\ dx = \int_5^{10} \frac{x^2}{u}\ dx$$

The integral on the right still contains x. To completely eliminate x, we need a new expression for the remainder of the function-- $x^2\ dx$ --that uses only u and du. The derivative of u is:

$$du = 3x^2\ dx$$

To get $x^2\ dx$, divide both sides of the function above by 3:

$$\frac{1}{3} du = x^2\ dx$$

Now, we can write the integral as:

$$\int_5^{10} \frac{x^2}{9 + x^3}\ dx = \int_5^{10} \frac{1}{u} * \frac{1}{3}\ du$$

The original integration bounds need to change since we are integrating with respect to u rather than x. The lower bound was x = 5, which now corresponds to $u = 9 + 5^3 = 134$. Similarly, the upper bound will change from x = 10 to $u = 9 + 10^3 = 1,009$. The correct integral is:

$$\int_{134}^{1009} \frac{1}{u} * \frac{1}{3}\ du$$

Calculating the integral produces

$$= \frac{1}{3}\left[\ln(u)\right]_{134}^{1009} = \frac{1}{3}*(\ln(1009) - \ln(134)) = 0.67296$$

In the above example, we substituted the contents of the original function with expressions featuring u and du. Integration by substitution is effective when the original function contains one expression which is the derivative or near-derivative of another expression in the function. After choosing 'u,' you need to replace the remainder of the original function with an expression containing "du."

Example

Evaluate this integral: $\int_{1}^{2}\ln(x^6)*6x^5\ dx$

Solution:

let $u = x^6$

$\quad du = 6x^5\ dx$

When x = 1, u = 1.
When x = 2, u = 64.

$$\int_{1}^{2}\ln(x^6)*6x^5\ dx = \int_{1}^{64}\ln(u)\ du$$

From a previous example, we found that $\int\ln(x)\ dx = \ln(x)*x - x + c$

$$\int_{1}^{64}\ln(u)\ du = \left[\ln(x)*x - x\right]_{1}^{64} = (\ln(64)*64 - 64) - (\ln(1)*1 - 1)$$

$$\approx 202.16852 + 1 \approx 203.16852$$

Example

Evaluate: $\int_{3}^{4}8x\sqrt{4x^2}\ dx$

Solution:

let $u = 4x^2$

$\quad du = 8x\ dx$

When x = 3, u = 36
When x = 4, u = 64

$$\int_{3}^{4} 8x\sqrt{4x^2}\ dx = \int_{36}^{64}\sqrt{u}\ du = \left[\frac{2}{3}u^{3/2}\right]_{36}^{64} = \frac{2}{3}\left(64^{3/2} - 36^{3/2}\right) = 197.33333$$

Example

Compute: $\displaystyle\int_{5}^{6} \sin(0.2x^2 + 4) * 10x\ dx$

Solution:

let $u = 0.2x^2 + 4$

$$du = 0.4x\ dx\ \rightarrow\ \frac{du}{0.4} = x\ dx\ \rightarrow\ 10*\frac{du}{0.4} = 10x\ dx\ \rightarrow\ 10x\ dx = 25\ du$$

When x = 5, u = 9
When x = 6, u = 11.2

$$\int_{5}^{6} \sin(0.2x^2 + 4) * 10x\ dx = \int_{9}^{11.2} \sin(u) * 25\ du$$

$$= 25 \int_{9}^{11.2} \sin(u)\ du$$

$$= 25\left[-\cos(u)\right]_{9}^{11.2} = -25(\cos(11.2) - \cos(9))$$

$$= -25(0.20301 - (-0.91113))$$

$$= -27.8535$$

Example

Compute: $\displaystyle\int \sin(x) * \cos(x)\ dx$

Solution:

let $u = \sin(x)$

$du = \cos(x)\ dx$

$$\int = \int u\ du = \frac{1}{2}u^2 + c = \frac{1}{2}\sin^2(x) + c$$

Example

Evaluate: $\displaystyle\int \cos^{-1}(x)\ dx$

Solution:

The function contains two components-- $\cos^{-1}(x)$ and $(1\ dx)$. Since inverse trig functions have priority over algebraic functions, u should be $\cos^{-1}(x)$.

let $u = \cos^{-1}(x)$ $\rightarrow$ $du = -\dfrac{1}{\sqrt{1-x^2}}\ dx$

let $dv = 1\ dx$ $\rightarrow$ $v = x$

$$\int \cos^{-1}(x)\ dx = \cos^{-1}(x) * x + \int \frac{x}{\sqrt{1-x^2}}\ dx$$

The integral requires substitution.

let $u = 1 - x^2$

$du = -2x\ dx$ $\rightarrow$ $x\ dx = -\dfrac{1}{2} du$

$$\int \frac{x}{\sqrt{1-x^2}}\ dx = \int \frac{1}{\sqrt{u}} * \left(\frac{-1}{2}\right)\ du = \frac{-1}{2} \int \frac{1}{\sqrt{u}}\ du = \frac{-1}{2} * \left(2u^{1/2} + c\right)$$

$$= -u^{1/2} + c = -(1 - x^2)^{1/2} + c$$

$$\int \cos^{-1}(x)\ dx = \cos^{-1}(x) * x - (1 - x^2)^{1/2} + c$$

Section 6-7 Improper Integrals

Up to this point, we have only evaluated integrals with reasonable traits. All the integrals have been over finite intervals of their independent variables, and the functions have never remained within finite bounds. How do we deal with functions that have vertical asymptotes? Since the function approaches positive or negative infinity around a vertical asymptote, is the area infinitely large in these regions? Functions may also extend forever in both directions of the x variable. If a function remains greater than zero as x nears infinity, does the integral equal infinity, too? In some cases, these theoretical areas are infinitely large, but often the area is a finite value. *Improper integrals* involve functions that extend to positive or negative infinity horizontally or which have discontinuities.

Improper Integral of Type 1
-These integrals feature infinite x intervals.

(1.) If $\int\limits_{a}^{t} f(x)\, dx$ exists $\forall\ t \geq a$, then $\int\limits_{a}^{\infty} f(x)\, dx = \lim\limits_{t \to \infty} \int\limits_{a}^{t} f(x)\, dx$, assuming the limit is finite and the integral is convergent.

(2.) If $\int\limits_{t}^{a} f(x)\, dx$ exists $\forall\ t \leq a$, then $\int\limits_{-\infty}^{a} f(x)\, dx = \lim\limits_{t \to -\infty} \int\limits_{t}^{a} f(x)\, dx$, assuming the limit is finite and the integral is convergent.

(3.) If $\int\limits_{a}^{\infty} f(x)\, dx$ and $\int\limits_{-\infty}^{a} f(x)\, dx$ are convergent, then

$$\int\limits_{-\infty}^{\infty} f(x)\, dx = \int\limits_{-\infty}^{a} f(x)\, dx + \int\limits_{a}^{\infty} f(x)\, dx\,.$$

Evaluating a type 1 improper integral requires computing the limit of an integral as one of the bounds goes to $\pm\infty$. You may need to employ L'Hospital's Rule when computing the limits or use other simplifying methods. The series of steps for a type 1 improper integral are displayed below. At the third stage, you determine the antiderivative of the integrand. Then, you calculate the limit of F(b) – F(a). You can take a shortcut in the limit calculation by plugging $\pm\infty$ directly into the expression for F(a) or F(b). For instance, if $F(x) = 1/x$, we know the function runs to zero as x becomes very large positive or negative.

$$\int\limits_{a}^{b} f(x)\, dx = \lim\limits_{t \to \pm\infty} \int\limits_{a}^{b} f(x)\, dx = \lim\limits_{t \to \pm\infty} \left[F(x)\right]_{a}^{b} = \lim\limits_{t \to \pm\infty} F(b) - F(a) = F(b) - F(a)$$

Example

Is $\int\limits_{-\infty}^{0} e^{x}\, dx$ convergent or divergent?

Solution:
$$\int\limits_{-\infty}^{0} e^{x}\, dx = \lim\limits_{t \to -\infty} \int\limits_{t}^{0} e^{x}\, dx = \lim\limits_{t \to -\infty} \left[e^{x}\right]_{t}^{0} = \lim\limits_{t \to -\infty} (e^{0} - e^{t}) = \lim\limits_{t \to -\infty} (1 - e^{t})$$
$$= 1 - e^{-\infty} = 1$$

The integral is convergent.

Example

Is $\int\limits_{2}^{\infty} \dfrac{1}{1+x^{2}}\, dx$ convergent or divergent?

Solution:

$$\int_{2}^{\infty}\frac{1}{1+x^2}\,dx = \lim_{t \to \infty} \int_{2}^{t}\frac{1}{1+x^2}\,dx = \lim_{t \to \infty} \left[\tan^{-1}(x)\right]_{2}^{t} = \lim_{t \to \infty} \tan^{-1}(t) - \tan^{-1}(2)$$

$$= \tan^{-1}(\infty) - \tan^{-1}(2) = \frac{\pi}{2} - 1.10715 \approx 0.46365$$

The integral is convergent.

Example

Evaluate $\int_{-\infty}^{0} 3xe^x\,dx$

Solution:

$$\int_{-\infty}^{0} 3xe^x\,dx = \lim_{t \to -\infty} \int_{t}^{0} 3xe^x\,dx$$

let $u = 3x \qquad \rightarrow \qquad du = 3\,dx$

let $dv = e^x\,dx \rightarrow \qquad v = e^x$

$$\int_{t}^{0} 3xe^x\,dx = \left[3xe^x\right]_{t}^{0} - \int_{t}^{0} 3e^x\,dx = -3te^t - \left[3e^x\right]_{t}^{0} = -3te^t - (3 - 3e^t) = -3te^t - 3 + 3e^t$$

$$\lim_{t \to -\infty} \int_{t}^{0} 3xe^x\,dx = \lim_{t \to -\infty} -3te^t - 3 + 3e^t = 0 - 3 + 0 = \text{-3}$$

Improper Integral of Type 2
-These integrals deal with discontinuous functions (including vertical asymptotes, jump discontinuities, and removable discontinuities).

(1.) If f is continuous on [a, b) with a discontinuity at b, then
$$\int_{a}^{b} f(x)\,dx = \lim_{t \to b^-} \int_{a}^{t} f(x)\,dx \text{, assuming the limit is finite (and convergent).}$$

(2.) If f is continuous on (a, b] with a discontinuity at a, then
$$\int_{a}^{b} f(x)\,dx = \lim_{t \to a^+} \int_{t}^{b} f(x)\,dx \text{, assuming the limit is finite (and convergent).}$$

(3.) If f is discontinuous at c with $a < c < b$, and $\int_a^c f(x)\ dx$ and $\int_c^b f(x)\ dx$ are

convergent, then

$$\int_a^b f(x)\ dx = \int_a^c f(x)\ dx + \int_c^b f(x)\ dx$$

Example

Calculate $\int_3^4 \dfrac{x^2 - 16}{x - 4}\ dx$

Solution:
The function has a removable discontinuity at $x = 4$ (the 'b' bound). We need to use equation 1 from type 2 improper integrals.

$$\lim_{t \to 4^-} \int_3^t \frac{x^2 - 16}{x - 4}\ dx = \lim_{t \to 4^-} \int_3^t (x + 4)\ dx = \lim_{t \to 4^-} \left[\frac{1}{2}x^2 + 4x \right]_3^t$$

$$= \lim_{t \to 4^-} \frac{1}{2}t^2 + 4t - \left(\frac{1}{2}3^2 + 4*3 \right) = \lim_{t \to 4^-} \frac{1}{2}t^2 + 4t - 16.5$$

$$= \frac{1}{2}4^2 + 4*4 - 16.5 = 7.5$$

Example

Calculate $\int_0^5 \ln(x)\ dx$

Solution:
The function has a vertical asymptote at $x = 0$.

$$\int_0^5 \ln(x)\ dx = \lim_{t \to 0^+} \int_t^5 \ln(x)\ dx$$

let $u = \ln(x) \quad \rightarrow \quad du = \dfrac{1}{x}\ dx$

let $dv = 1\ dx \quad \rightarrow \quad v = x$

$$\int_t^5 \ln(x)\ dx = \left[x*\ln(x)\right]_t^5 - \int_t^5 1\ dx = 5*\ln(5) - t*\ln(t) - \left[x\right]_t^5 = 5\ln(5) - t*\ln(t) - 5 + t$$

$$\lim_{t \to 0^+} t*\ln(t) = \lim_{t \to 0^+} \frac{\ln(t)}{1/t} \underset{L'H}{=\!=\!=} \lim_{t \to 0^+} \frac{1/t}{-(1/t^2)} = \lim_{t \to 0^+} -t = 0$$

$$\int_0^5 \ln(x)\ dx = \lim_{t \to 0^+} 5\ln(5) - t*\ln(t) - 5 + t = 5\ln(5) - 0 - 5 + 0 = 5\ln(5) - 5 \approx 3.04719$$

Example

Calculate $\int_3^6 \sqrt{x-3} + 2\ dx$

Solution:
The integrand is discontinuous at x = 3.

$$\int_3^6 \sqrt{x-3} + 2\ dx = \lim_{t \to 3^+} \int_t^6 \sqrt{x-3} + 2\ dx = \lim_{t \to 3^+} \left[\frac{2}{3}(x-3)^{3/2} + 2x\right]_t^6$$

$$= \lim_{t \to 3^+} \frac{2}{3}(6-3)^{3/2} + 2*6 - \left(\frac{2}{3}(t-3)^{3/2} + 2t\right)$$

$$= \lim_{t \to 3^+} 15.4641 - \frac{2}{3}(t-3)^{3/2} - 2t$$

$$= 15.4641 - \frac{2}{3}(3-3)^{3/2} - 2*3 = 15.4641 - 0 - 6 = 9.4641$$

Section 6-8 Calculating Areas between Functions

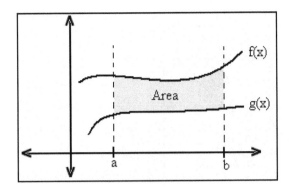

　　　　To compute the area between two functions, you must subtract the integrals of each function. This method allows you to calculate "squiggly" areas which might lie far from the x-axis. The theorem is formally stated as

---

Area between Functions Theorem
Suppose that $f(x) \geq g(x)$ $\forall$ $x \in (a, b)$. Then the area between the two functions is:

$$Area = \int_a^b f(x) - g(x)\ dx = \int_a^b f(x)\ dx - \int_a^b g(x)\ dx$$

You must use a new integral whenever f surpasses g or g surpasses f. That is, you need separate integrals for each interval when $f > g$ or $g > f$.
　　　　The theorem applies to areas above and below the x-axis. The theorem still holds when one or both functions lie below the x-axis and would presumably have negative area. Additionally, the functions may cross the x-axis arbitrarily many times without needed more than one integral. A proof that negative areas when subtracted still produce a positive net area is shown below. Suppose functions f and g are negative at $x = 0$, with $g(0) = -C$.

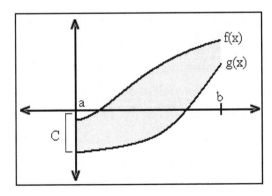

We can correct the negative functions by shifting both functions up by C units. The graph then becomes

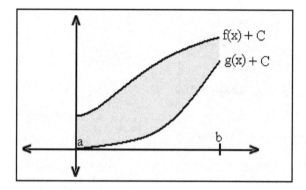

Applying the area theorem, we find that

$$Area = \int_a^b (f(x)+C)-(g(x)+C) \; dx = \int_a^b f(x)+C-g(x)-C \; dx = \int_a^b f(x)-g(x) \; dx$$

Therefore, translating both graphs into positive territory results in an area between the functions equal to the original (positive and negative) area in the middle of the functions.

Example
Find the shaded area between the two parabolas in the diagram below:

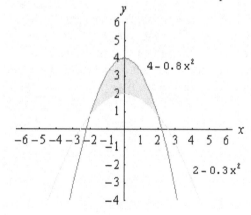

Solution:

$4 - 0.8x^2 = 2 - 0.3x^2$

$2 = 0.5x^2$

$x^2 = 4 \quad \rightarrow \quad x = \pm 2$

$$\int_{-2}^{2} f(x) - g(x) \ dx = \int_{-2}^{2} (4 - 0.8x^2) - (2 - 0.3x^2) \ dx = \int_{-2}^{2} (2 - 0.5x^2) \ dx$$

$$= \left[2x - 0.5 * \frac{1}{3} * x^3 \right]_{-2}^{2} = \left(2*2 - (1/6)*(2^3) \right) - \left(2*(-2) - (1/6)*(-2^3) \right)$$

$$= 8/3 - (-8/3) = 16/3$$

Example

Find the shaded area between the two functions:

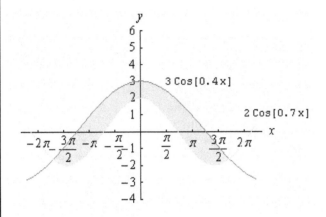

Solution:

With the help of a graphing calculator, the two functions intersect at
x = -5.3665 and x = 5.3665

$$\int_{-5.3665}^{5.3665} f(x) - g(x) \ dx = \int_{-5.3665}^{5.3665} 3\cos(0.4x) - 2\cos(0.7x) \ dx$$

$$= \int_{-5.3665}^{5.3665} 3\cos(0.4x) \ dx - \int_{-5.3665}^{5.3665} 2\cos(0.7x) \ dx$$

$$= \left[3*\sin(0.4x)*\frac{1}{0.4} \right]_{-5.3665}^{5.3665} - \left[2*\sin(0.7x)*\frac{1}{0.7} \right]_{-5.3665}^{5.3665}$$

$$= (6.29067 + 6.29066) - (-1.64835 - 1.64835)$$
$$= 15.87804$$

Example

Find the highlighted area between the two functions:

Solution:
Since the cubic function and the line are greater than each other at different points in the plot, we cannot simply subtract the two functions in the same integral. We need to use two integrals separated at x = 0.

Points of Intersection:
$$0.8x = -x + 0.2x^3$$
$$0.8 = -1 + 0.2x^2$$
$$1.8 = 0.2x^2 \quad \rightarrow \quad 9 = x^2 \quad \rightarrow \quad x = \pm3$$

$$\int_{-3}^{0}(-x+0.2x^3)-0.8x \ dx \ + \ \int_{0}^{3}0.8x-(-x+0.2x^3) \ dx$$

$$\int_{-3}^{0}-1.8x+0.2x^3 \ dx \ + \ \int_{0}^{3}1.8x-0.2x^3 \ dx$$

$$\left[\frac{-1.8}{2}x^2+\frac{0.2}{4}x^4\right]_{-3}^{0} + \left[\frac{1.8}{2}x^2-\frac{0.2}{4}x^4\right]_{0}^{3}$$

$$-\left(\frac{-1.8}{2}(-3)^2+\frac{0.2}{4}(-3)^4\right) + \left(\frac{1.8}{2}3^2-\frac{0.2}{4}3^4\right)$$

$$-(-8.1+4.05)+(8.1-4.05) = 4.05+4.05 = 8.1$$

Section 6-9 Partial Fraction Integration

Integration by partial fractions is vital when calculating integrals of rational functions. Assume that the integrand is the fraction of two polynomials. That is, we are trying to find $\int \frac{f(x)}{g(x)} \, dx$. Also assume that the numerator has a smaller degree than the denominator. We need to decompose the rational function into the sum of many simpler fractions. When creating the partial fractions, focus on the denominator. The first step involves factoring the denominator. If the denominator is already factored, you can skip this step. The denominator can contain arbitrarily many sets of parentheses, each of which is raised to a positive integer (the power could be greater than 1). For each factor in the denominator, you will need a separate fraction for the final decomposition. We must solve for the numerators that make the entire sum of smaller fractions equal the original rational function. Assume that each numerator in the decomposition is an unknown polynomial of the form $A + Bx + Cx^2 + Dx^3 + \ldots$. The numerator will have a degree 1 less than the degree of the denominator's factor. Next, we need to solve for all the unknown letters A, B, C, and so on. To add all the smaller fractions, they must have a common denominator. A quick common denominator is achieved by multiplying the numerator and denominator of the other fractions by the denominator of the current fraction. Finally, set the original numerator equal to the unknown numerator, and solve for the letters. This process is best explained with an example.

Suppose we must compute the partial fraction decomposition for $\dfrac{x-5}{6x^2 - 8x + 2}$.

The denominator might be factored as $\dfrac{x-5}{(3x-1)(2x-2)}$. The denominator holds two factors, each to the power of 1 and each of degree 1. So, the partial fraction decomposition will contain two fractions. Since both factors in the denominator have degree 1, the numerators for the new fractions will have degree 0 (one less). The decomposition is:

$$\frac{x-5}{(3x-1)(2x-2)} = \frac{A}{(3x-1)} + \frac{B}{(2x-2)}$$

In the next stage, we find a common denominator. Using the cheap method, the common denominator is $(3x-1)(2x-2)$. The decomposition is now

$$\frac{x-5}{(3x-1)(2x-2)} = \frac{A(2x-2)}{(3x-1)(2x-2)} + \frac{B(3x-1)}{(2x-2)(3x-1)}$$

We needed to multiply the top and bottom of each fraction by the factor that was missing from the original fraction. For example, we multiplied the top and bottom of the first fraction by (2x – 2), which is the term in the denominator of the second fraction. Solving for the unknowns A and B is simple. The following equality holds for all real numbers x:

$$x - 5 = A(2x - 2) + B(3x - 1)$$

We could give x any value we desire. For simplicity, let's use x = 0 and x = 1.

$$0 - 5 = A(2*0 - 2) + B(3*0 - 1)$$
$$-5 = A(-2) + B(-1)$$
$$-5 = -2A - B$$
$$5 = 2A + B$$

$$1 - 5 = A(2*1 - 2) + B(3*1 - 1)$$
$$-4 = A(2 - 2) + B(3 - 1)$$
$$-4 = 2B$$

We now have a simple system to solve featuring variables A and B.

$$B = -2 \quad \text{and} \quad A = 3.5$$

The final partial fraction decomposition is:

$$\frac{x - 5}{6x^2 - 8x + 2} = \frac{3.5}{(3x - 1)} + \frac{-2}{(2x - 2)}$$

Example
Find the partial fraction decomposition for:
$$\frac{x + 6}{(x + 7)^2(x - 2)}$$

Solution:
$$\frac{x + 6}{(x + 7)^2(x - 2)} = \frac{A}{(x + 7)} + \frac{B}{(x + 7)^2} + \frac{C}{x - 2}$$

$$\frac{x + 6}{(x + 7)^2(x - 2)} = \frac{A(x + 7)(x - 2)}{(x + 7)(x + 7)(x - 2)} + \frac{B(x - 2)}{(x + 7)^2(x - 2)} + \frac{C(x + 7)^2}{(x - 2)(x + 7)^2}$$

Numerator = $A(x + 7)(x - 2) + B(x - 2) + C(x + 7)^2 = x + 6$

Let x = 0:
$$A(7)(-2) + B(-2) + C(7)^2 = 6$$
$$-14A - 2B + 49C = 6$$

Let x = 1:
$$A(8)(-1) + B(-1) + C(8)^2 = 7$$
$$-8A - B + 64C = 7$$

Let x = 2:
$$A(9)(0) + B(0) + C(9)^2 = 8$$
$$C*81 = 8$$

Solve the system…
$$C = 8/81$$

$$\begin{cases} -14A - 2B + 392/81 = 6 \\ -8A - B + 512/81 = 7 \end{cases}$$

$$-14A - 2B + 392/81 = 6$$
$$-14A - 2B = 94/81$$
$$-14A = (94/81) + 2B$$
$$A = \frac{(94/81) + 2B}{-14}$$

$$-8\left(\frac{(94/81) + 2B}{-14}\right) - B + 512/81 = 7$$
$$0.66314 + 1.14286B - B + 512/81 = 7$$
$$B = 1/9$$

$$A = \frac{(94/81) + 2(1/9)}{-14} = -8/81$$

$$\frac{x+6}{(x+7)^2(x-2)} = \frac{-8/81}{(x+7)} + \frac{1/9}{(x+7)^2} + \frac{8/81}{x-2}$$

To integrate a rational function that has been decomposed, simply integrate the decomposition. The rational function now consists of several smaller fractions, each with a simple polynomial in the denominator. Integrate these smaller fractions and sum the results.

Example

Evaluate $\displaystyle\int_{7}^{8} \frac{2x^2 - x + 4}{3x(x^2 - 25)}\, dx$

Solution:

First, compute the partial fraction decomposition…

$$\frac{2x^2-x+4}{3x(x^2-25)}=\frac{2x^2-x+4}{3x(x-5)(x+5)}=\frac{A}{3x}+\frac{B}{x-5}+\frac{C}{x+5}$$

$$\frac{2x^2-x+4}{3x(x^2-25)}=\frac{A(x-5)(x+5)}{3x(x-5)(x+5)}+\frac{B*3x*(x+5)}{(x-5)*3x*(x+5)}+\frac{C*3x*(x-5)}{(x+5)*3x*(x-5)}$$

$$2x^2-x+4=A(x-5)(x+5)+B*3x*(x+5)+C*3x*(x-5)$$

Let x = 0:
$$4=A(-5)(5)$$
$$4=-25A \quad \rightarrow \quad A=-0.16$$

Let x = 5:
$$49=B*3*5*10$$
$$49=B*150 \quad \rightarrow \quad B=0.32667$$

Let x = -5:
$$59=C*3(-5)*(-5-5)$$
$$59=C*150 \quad \rightarrow \quad C=0.39333$$

$$\frac{2x^2-x+4}{3x(x^2-25)}=\frac{-0.16}{3x}+\frac{0.32667}{x-5}+\frac{0.39333}{x+5}$$

$$\int_7^8 \frac{2x^2-x+4}{3x(x^2-25)}\,dx=\int_7^8 \frac{-0.16}{3x}+\frac{0.32667}{x-5}+\frac{0.39333}{x+5}\,dx$$

$$=\left[-0.16*\ln(3x)*(1/3)+0.32667*\ln(x-5)+0.39333*\ln(x+5)\right]_7^8$$
$$=1.19826-1.04144$$
$$=0.15682$$

Example

Evaluate $\int_0^1 \frac{2x^2-x+4}{(x^3-8)(x^2-49)}\,dx$

Solution:
$$\frac{2x^2-x+4}{(x^3-8)(x-7)(x+7)}=\frac{Ax^2+Bx+C}{(x^3-8)}+\frac{D}{x-7}+\frac{E}{x+7}$$

$$= \frac{(Ax^2 + Bx + C)(x-7)(x+7)}{(x^3-8)(x-7)(x+7)} + \frac{D(x+7)(x^3-8)}{(x-7)(x+7)(x^3-8)} + \frac{E(x^3-8)(x-7)}{(x+7)(x^3-8)(x-7)}$$

$$2x^2 - x + 4 = (Ax^2 + Bx + C)(x-7)(x+7) + D(x+7)(x^3-8) + E(x^3-8)(x-7)$$

Let x = 0:

$$4 = (C)(-7)(7) + D(7)(-8) + E(-8)(-7)$$
$$4 = -49C - 56D + 56E$$

Let x = 7:

$$2*49 - 7 + 4 = D(7+7)(7^3 - 8)$$
$$95 = 4690D \quad \rightarrow \quad D = 0.02026$$

Let x = -7:

$$2*49 + 7 + 4 = E((-7)^3 - 8)(-7-7)$$
$$109 = 4914E \quad \rightarrow \quad E = 0.02218$$

$$4 = -49C - 56D + 56E \quad \rightarrow \quad C = -0.07944$$

Let x = 1:

$$2 - 1 + 4 = (A + B + C)(-6)(8) + D(8)(-7) + E(-7)(-6)$$
$$5 = -48(A + B + C) - 56D + 42E$$
$$5.203 = -48(A + B + C)$$
$$1.38988 = -48A - 48B$$

Let x = -1:

$$2 + 1 + 4 = (A - B + C)(-8)(6) + D(6)(-9) + E(-9)(-8)$$
$$7 = -48(A - B + C) - 54D + 72E$$
$$6.49708 = -48(A - B + C)$$
$$2.68396 = -48A + 48B$$

$$1.38988 = -48A - 48B \quad \rightarrow \quad \frac{1.38988 + 48A}{-48} = B$$

$$2.68396 = -48A + 48\left(\frac{1.38988 + 48A}{-48}\right)$$

$$2.68396 = -48A - 1.38988 - 48A \quad \rightarrow \quad A = -0.04244$$
$$B = 0.01348$$

$$\int_0^1 \frac{2x^2 - x + 4}{(x^3-8)(x^2-49)} \, dx = \int_0^1 \frac{-0.04244x^2 + 0.01348x - 0.07944}{(x^3-8)} + \frac{0.02026}{x-7} + \frac{0.02218}{x+7} \, dx$$

$$\approx 0.0111$$

Example

Calculate $\int_{5}^{10}\dfrac{x-1}{(x+6)^2(x^2-2)}\,dx$

Solution:

$$\dfrac{x-1}{(x+6)^2(x^2-2)}=\dfrac{A}{(x+6)}+\dfrac{B}{(x+6)^2}+\dfrac{Cx+D}{(x^2-2)}$$

$$=\dfrac{A(x+6)(x^2-2)}{(x+6)^2(x^2-2)}+\dfrac{B(x^2-2)}{(x+6)^2(x^2-2)}+\dfrac{(Cx+D)(x+6)^2}{(x^2-2)(x+6)^2}$$

$$x-1=A(x+6)(x^2-2)+B(x^2-2)+(Cx+D)(x+6)^2$$

Let x = -6:

$$-7=B*34 \quad \rightarrow \quad B=-0.20588$$

Let x = $\sqrt{2}$

$$0.41421=(1.41421C+D)*54.97056$$
$$0.00754=1.41421C+D$$

Let x = $-\sqrt{2}$

$$-2.41421=(-1.41421C+D)*21.02944$$
$$-0.1148=-1.41421C+D$$

$$0.00754-1.41421C=D$$
$$-0.1148=-1.41421C+0.00754-1.41421C \quad \rightarrow \quad C=0.04325$$
$$D=-0.05362$$

Let x = 0:

$$-1=A(6)(-2)+B(-2)+(D)(6)^2$$
$$A=-0.04321$$

$$\int_{5}^{10}\dfrac{x-1}{(x+6)^2(x^2-2)}\,dx=\int_{5}^{10}\dfrac{-0.04321}{(x+6)}+\dfrac{-0.20588}{(x+6)^2}+\dfrac{0.04325x-0.05362}{(x^2-2)}\,dx$$

$$\approx 0.00366$$

Chapter 7
Higher Order Calculus

Most branches of applied math use models with numerous variables or dimensions. In statistics, for instance, a model might contain five or more variables to describe a phenomenon. A model for the percentage of adults diagnosed with depression in a region could rely on two variables—a measure of urban density (x) and the average education (y). These last two variables are independent variables which collectively contribute to the level of depression (z). The actual model could take the form: $f(x, y) = 0.35x - 0.05y + 0.03xy$. What graphical form does the model take? How does each variable contribute to the level of depression?

Multivariate calculus deals with functions containing two or more independent variables. For the more common 3D models, this section of calculus provides methods of computing volumes and monitoring the impact of an individual variable. Many of the operations and rules that applied to single-variable calculus are also valid in multivariate calculus.

Section 7-1 First-Order Partial Derivatives

Many functions have more than one independent variable. Several factors could contribute to the result of a function. For instance, the insurance premium for a super-computer could be: $f(x, y, z) = 6,000 + 75 * x * y + y^2 + 5yz$, where x is the number of processors, y is the number of cooling units, and z is a measure of fire risk. An engineer might need to know how the price of the insurance changes when just one of the independent variables changes. If the company using the computer can reduce the fire risk by one unit, how does the insurance premium change? Any terms in the pricing function that do not include 'z' can be ignored. The term of interest is then "5yz." If z falls by one unit, the price will decrease by -5y dollars.

Partial derivatives describe the behavior of a function with respect to one or more of its independent variables. A partial derivative of a function answers the question, "How do the values of one of the independent variables contribute to the overall changes in the function?" The symbol for a partial derivative is ∂. The expression $\dfrac{\partial f}{\partial x}$ reads "the partial derivative of function f with respect to x." The partial derivative notation is identical to the notation for a regular derivative with the exception that the d's are replaced with twisted d's.

Most of the rules for computing a traditional derivative carry over to partial derivatives. For example, the product rule and chain rule still apply to partial derivatives. The derivative properties for polynomials, trigonometric functions, power functions, and nearly every other type of function are essential in computing partial derivatives. However, the partial derivative is computed only with respect to the variable in the denominator. All other independent variables should be treated as constants.

Example
Calculate the first partial derivative of f with respect to x.
$$f(x, y) = x^2 + 4y$$

Solution:
The other independent variable, y, must be considered a constant value. The derivative of a constant is just zero, so the derivative of any term containing only y and not x is zero. The term "4y" should just be ignored since it does not contain x—the independent variable of interest.

$$\frac{\partial f}{\partial x} = \frac{\partial}{\partial x}\left[x^2\right] + \frac{\partial}{\partial x}\left[4y\right] = 2x + 0 = 2x$$

Example
Compute the first partial derivative of f with respect to y
$$f(x, y) = \cos(y) + 10xy$$

Solution:
Computing the partial derivative with respect to only y means the other variable, x, should be treated like a constant.

$$\frac{\partial f}{\partial y} = -\sin(y) + 10x$$

Example
Compute the following partial derivatives:

    a. $\frac{\partial}{\partial x}\left[18x^5 + xy + 7y\right]$

    b. $\frac{\partial}{\partial x}\left[\sin(x^2) + \tan(xy) + y^{10}\right]$

    c. $\frac{\partial}{\partial z}\left[\ln(xyz) - \cos(z^6) + 5yz\right]$

Solutions:

    a. We need to find the partial derivative of the function with respect to x once. Since we are not computing the derivative with respect to y, the variable y must be treated as a constant.

$$\frac{\partial f}{\partial x} = 18*5*x^4 + y + 0 = 90x^4 + y$$

    b.

$$\frac{\partial f}{\partial x} = \cos(x^2) * \frac{d}{dx}\left[x^2\right] + \sec^2(xy) * \frac{\partial}{\partial x}\left[xy\right] + 0$$
$$= \cos(x^2) * 2x + \sec^2(xy) * y$$

    c.

$$\frac{\partial f}{\partial z} = \frac{1}{xyz} * \frac{\partial}{\partial z}\left[xyz\right] - \left(-\sin(z^6) * \frac{d}{dz}\left[z^6\right]\right) + 5y$$
$$= \frac{1}{xyz} * xy + \sin(z^6) * 6z^5 + 5y$$
$$= \frac{1}{z} + 6\sin(z^6) * z^5 + 5y$$

Section 7-2 Higher-Order Partial Derivatives

In the previous section, you learned how to find the partial derivative of a multivariate function with respect to only one variable. This section shows how to compute the partial derivative of a function with respect to one variable several times, and how to solve a partial derivative with respect to several different variables.

The notation for a higher-order partial derivative describes the number of times the function must be differentiated and with respect to which variables. The syntax for a high-degree partial derivative is $\dfrac{\partial^n f}{\partial x_1 \partial x_2 \partial x_3 \dots}$. The letter 'n' is the quantity of times the function f is differentiated. The independent variables lie in the denominator. The independent variables are listed in reverse order. The function must first be differentiated with respect to x_3, then with respect to x_2, and finally with respect to x_1.

Let's start with second partial derivatives. Suppose we have a function f with two independent variables x and y. The expression $\dfrac{\partial^2 f}{\partial x \partial y}$ reads "the second partial derivative of function f with respect to y and then with respect to x." To compute this derivative, you first need to take the derivative of f with respect to y. Then, you need to take the derivative of the previous result with respect to x. We have a '2' in the numerator to designate two partial derivatives. The partial derivative breaks down as follows:

$$\frac{\partial^2 f}{\partial x \partial y} = \frac{\partial}{\partial x}\left[\frac{\partial f}{\partial y}\right] = \left(f_y\right)_x = f_{yx}$$

The large notation for partial derivatives reads in reverse from right to left. The more concise notation f_{yx} lists the variables in order of their differentiation from left to right.

It is also possible to partially differentiate a function several times with respect to the same variable. So, we could differentiate f with respect to x twice, or we might differentiate with respect to y twice. The higher order partial derivatives take the form:

$$\frac{\partial^2 f}{\partial x \partial x} = \frac{\partial^2 f}{\partial x^2} = \frac{\partial}{\partial x}\left[\frac{\partial f}{\partial x}\right] = \left(f_x\right)_x = f_{xx}$$

$$\frac{\partial^2 f}{\partial y \partial y} = \frac{\partial^2 f}{\partial y^2} = \frac{\partial}{\partial y}\left[\frac{\partial f}{\partial y}\right] = \left(f_y\right)_y = f_{yy}$$

When differentiating a variable several consecutive times, note the quantity of differentiations in the denominator by "raising" that variable to a power. For instance, in the first equation above, the notation x^2 on the bottom signifies that variable x will be differentiated twice.

Example

You are given $f(x,y) = 12xy + 8x^3 - 9xy^4$. Find the second partial derivative of f with respect to x and then with respect to y.

Solution:
The partial derivative we need to calculate is

$$\frac{\partial^2 f}{\partial y \partial x} = \frac{\partial}{\partial y}\left[\frac{\partial f}{\partial x}\right] = (f_x)_y = f_{xy}$$

We need to first compute the partial derivative with respect to x...

$$\frac{\partial f}{\partial x} = 12y + 24x^2 - 9y^4$$

Then, evaluate the partial derivative of the above result with respect to y...

$$\frac{\partial^2 f}{\partial y \partial x} = \frac{\partial}{\partial y}\left[12y + 24x^2 - 9y^4\right] = 12 - 36y^3$$

Example

Find the second partial derivatives for this function: $f(x,y) = \sin(xy) + 25x^5 + x^3 y$

a. $\dfrac{\partial^2 f}{\partial x \partial y}$ **b.** $\dfrac{\partial^2 f}{\partial y \partial y}$ **c.** $\dfrac{\partial^2 f}{\partial y \partial x}$ **d.** $\dfrac{\partial^2 f}{\partial x \partial x}$

Solutions:
a.

$$\frac{\partial^2 f}{\partial x \partial y} = \frac{\partial}{\partial x}\left[\frac{\partial f}{\partial y}\right]$$

$$\frac{\partial f}{\partial y} = \cos(xy)*\frac{\partial}{\partial y}[xy] + 0 + x^3 = \cos(xy)*x + x^3$$

$$\frac{\partial^2 f}{\partial x \partial y} = \frac{\partial}{\partial x}\left[\cos(xy)*x + x^3\right]$$
$$= \cos(xy)*1 - \sin(xy)*y*x + 3x^2$$
$$= \cos(xy) - \sin(xy)*xy + 3x^2$$

b.

$$\frac{\partial^2 f}{\partial y \partial y} = \frac{\partial}{\partial y}\left[\frac{\partial f}{\partial y}\right] = \frac{\partial}{\partial y}\left[\cos(xy)*x + x^3\right] = \cos(xy)*0 - \sin(xy)*x*x + 0$$
$$= -\sin(xy)*x^2$$

c.

$$\frac{\partial^2 f}{\partial y \partial x} = \frac{\partial}{\partial y}\left[\frac{\partial f}{\partial x}\right]$$

$$\frac{\partial f}{\partial x} = \cos(xy) * y + 125x^4 + 3x^2 y$$

$$\frac{\partial^2 f}{\partial y \partial x} = \frac{\partial}{\partial y}\left[\cos(xy) * y + 125x^4 + 3x^2 y\right]$$

$$= \cos(xy) * 1 - \sin(xy) * x * y + 0 + 3x^2$$

$$= \cos(xy) - \sin(xy) * xy + 3x^2$$

d.

$$\frac{\partial^2 f}{\partial x \partial x} = \frac{\partial}{\partial x}\left[\frac{\partial f}{\partial x}\right] = \frac{\partial}{\partial x}\left[\cos(xy) * y + 125x^4 + 3x^2 y\right]$$

$$= \cos(xy) * 0 - \sin(xy) * y * y + 500x^3 + 6xy$$

$$= -\sin(xy) * y^2 + 500x^3 + 6xy$$

Example

Compute the second-order partial derivatives of the following functions with respect to x twice.

    a. $f(x, y) = \cos(xy^2) + \ln(11x^3)$

    b. $f(x, y) = \tan^{-1}(3xy)$

Solutions:

    a.

$$\frac{\partial^2 f}{\partial x^2} = \frac{\partial}{\partial x}\left[\frac{\partial f}{\partial x}\right] = \frac{\partial}{\partial x}\left[\frac{\partial}{\partial x}\left[\cos(xy^2) + \ln(11x^3)\right]\right]$$

$$= \frac{\partial}{\partial x}\left[-\sin(xy^2) * y^2 + \frac{1}{11x^3} * \frac{\partial}{\partial x}\left[11x^3\right]\right]$$

$$= \frac{\partial}{\partial x}\left[-\sin(xy^2) * y^2 + \frac{1}{11x^3} * 33x^2\right]$$

$$= \frac{\partial}{\partial x}\left[-\sin(xy^2) * y^2 + 3x^{-1}\right]$$

$$= \frac{\partial}{\partial x}\left[-\sin(xy^2) * y^2\right] + \frac{\partial}{\partial x}\left[3x^{-1}\right]$$

$$= -\cos(xy^2) * y^2 * y^2 - 3x^{-2} = -\cos(xy^2) * y^4 - \frac{3}{x^2}$$

b.

$$\frac{\partial^2 f}{\partial x^2} = \frac{\partial}{\partial x}\left[\frac{\partial f}{\partial x}\right] = \frac{\partial}{\partial x}\left[\frac{\partial}{\partial x}\left[\tan^{-1}(3xy)\right]\right]$$

$$= \frac{\partial}{\partial x}\left[\frac{1}{1+(3xy)^2}*\frac{\partial}{\partial x}[3xy]\right] = \frac{\partial}{\partial x}\left[\frac{3y}{1+9x^2y^2}\right] = \frac{\partial}{\partial x}\left[3y(1+9x^2y^2)^{-1}\right]$$

$$= -3y(1+9x^2y^2)^{-2}*\frac{\partial}{\partial x}[1+9x^2y^2] = \frac{-3y}{(1+9x^2y^2)^2}*18xy^2$$

$$= \frac{-54xy^3}{(1+9x^2y^2)^2}$$

Example

Compute these mixed partial derivatives:

a. Given: $f(x,y) = e^{4x}*7xy$, Find: $\dfrac{\partial^2 f}{\partial y \partial x}$

b. Given: $f(x,y) = 8x^4y^2 + e^{yx^2} + \sin(x^3)$, Find: $\dfrac{\partial^3 f}{\partial y \partial x \partial y}$

Solutions:

a.

$$\frac{\partial^2 f}{\partial y \partial x} = \frac{\partial}{\partial y}\left[\frac{\partial f}{\partial x}\right]$$

$$\frac{\partial f}{\partial x} = e^{4x}*7y + e^{4x}*4*7xy = 7ye^{4x} + 28e^{4x}xy$$

$$\frac{\partial^2 f}{\partial y \partial x} = \frac{\partial}{\partial y}\left[7ye^{4x} + 28e^{4x}xy\right] = 7e^{4x} + 28e^{4x}x$$

b.

$$\frac{\partial^3 f}{\partial y \partial x \partial y} = \frac{\partial}{\partial y}\left[\frac{\partial}{\partial x}\left[\frac{\partial f}{\partial y}\right]\right]$$

$$\frac{\partial f}{\partial y} = 16x^4y + e^{yx^2}*\frac{\partial}{\partial y}[yx^2] + 0 = 16x^4y + x^2e^{yx^2}$$

$$\frac{\partial}{\partial x}\left[\frac{\partial f}{\partial y}\right] = \frac{\partial}{\partial x}\left[16x^4y + x^2e^{yx^2}\right] = 64x^3y + x^2 * e^{yx^2} * 2yx + 2x * e^{yx^2}$$

$$\frac{\partial^3 f}{\partial y \partial x \partial y} = \frac{\partial}{\partial y}\left[64x^3y + x^2 * e^{yx^2} * 2yx + 2x * e^{yx^2}\right]$$

$$= 64x^3 + \frac{\partial}{\partial y}\left[2x^3 * e^{yx^2} * y\right] + 2x * e^{yx^2} * x^2$$

$$= 64x^3 + \left(2x^3 * e^{yx^2} * 1 + 2x^3 * e^{yx^2} * x^2 * y\right) + 2x * e^{yx^2} * x^2$$

$$= 64x^3 + 2x^3 e^{yx^2} + 2x^5 y * e^{yx^2} + 2x^3 e^{yx^2}$$

$$= 64x^3 + 4x^3 e^{yx^2} + 2x^5 y * e^{yx^2}$$

Example

Compute these higher order partial derivatives:

a. Given: $f(x,y) = -3x^6 y^3 + x^4 y^4$, Find: $\dfrac{\partial^3 f}{\partial y^2 \partial x}$

b. Given: $f(x,y) = \cos(x) * y + e^{3xy}$, Find $\dfrac{\partial^3 f}{\partial x^2 \partial y}$

Solutions:

a.

$$\frac{\partial^3 f}{\partial y^2 \partial x} = \frac{\partial^2}{\partial y^2}\left[\frac{\partial f}{\partial x}\right] = \frac{\partial}{\partial y}\left[\frac{\partial}{\partial y}\left[\frac{\partial f}{\partial x}\right]\right]$$

$$\frac{\partial f}{\partial x} = -18x^5 y^3 + 4x^3 y^4$$

$$\frac{\partial}{\partial y}\left[\frac{\partial f}{\partial x}\right] = \frac{\partial}{\partial y}\left[-18x^5 y^3 + 4x^3 y^4\right] = -54x^5 y^2 + 16x^3 y^3$$

$$\frac{\partial^3 f}{\partial y^2 \partial x} = \frac{\partial}{\partial y}\left[-54x^5 y^2 + 16x^3 y^3\right] = -108x^5 y + 48x^3 y^2$$

b.

$$\frac{\partial^3 f}{\partial x^2 \partial y} = \frac{\partial^2}{\partial x^2}\left[\frac{\partial f}{\partial y}\right] = \frac{\partial}{\partial x}\left[\frac{\partial}{\partial x}\left[\frac{\partial f}{\partial y}\right]\right]$$

$$\frac{\partial f}{\partial y} = \cos(x) + e^{3xy} * 3x$$

$$\frac{\partial}{\partial x}\left[\frac{\partial f}{\partial y}\right] = \frac{\partial}{\partial x}\left[\cos(x) + e^{3xy} * 3x\right] = -\sin(x) + e^{3xy} * 3 + e^{3xy} * 3y * 3x$$

$$= -\sin(x) + 3e^{3xy} + 9xye^{3xy}$$

$$\frac{\partial^3 f}{\partial x^2 \partial y} = \frac{\partial}{\partial x}\left[-\sin(x) + 3e^{3xy} + 9xye^{3xy}\right]$$

$$= -\cos(x) + 3e^{3xy} * 3y + 9y(xe^{3xy} * 3y + e^{3xy})$$

$$= -\cos(x) + 18ye^{3xy} + 27y^2xe^{3xy}$$

Section 7-3 Three-Dimensional Surfaces

Surfaces are generated by 3D functions of the form $f(x, y) = z$. The independent variables x and y are the coordinates on the flat x-y plane. The domain of a 3D function is a subset of the x-y plane. For most 3D functions, the domain is not explicitly specified. You must determine which x- and y-values produce a real number for the output. The dependent variable z is the height of the function above point (x, y). The range of f is the set of all z-values which the function spans.

Example

You are given $f(x, y) = \sqrt{3x + 2y}$. Find:

a. $f(3, 5)$ **b.** The points (x, y) for which the function is defined **c.** The range

Solutions:

a. $f(3, 5) = \sqrt{3*3 + 2*5} = \sqrt{19} \approx 4.3589$

b. The function is defined when the expression under the square root is greater than or equal to zero. That is, the points (x, y) must satisfy: $3x + 2y \geq 0$. In formal notation, the domain is: $\{(x, y) : 3x + 2y \geq 0\}$, which reads "the set of all points (x, y) for which $3x + 2y \geq 0$."

c. The variables x and y could extend to positive infinity. Consequently, the expression under the square root could reach infinity, and the square root itself will near positive infinity. The range of f is the same as the range of a square root function: $[0, \infty)$

Example
Sketch the graph for $f(x, y) = 4 - 5x - 6y$

Solution:
Replace f with z and move all three variables to the same side.
$z = 4 - 5x - 6y$
$z + 5x + 6y = 4$

Set two of the variables to zero, and observe the effect on the remaining non-zero variable.

let y = z = 0
$$0 + 5x + 6*0 = 4$$
$$5x = 4$$
$$x = 4/5 \quad \rightarrow \text{x-intercept: } (0.8, 0, 0)$$

let x = z = 0
$$0 + 5*0 + 6y = 4$$
$$6y = 4$$
$$y = 4/6 \quad \rightarrow \text{y-intercept: } (0, 0.6667, 0)$$

let x = y = 0
$$z + 5*0 + 6*0 = 4$$
$$z = 4 \quad \rightarrow \text{z-intercept: } (0, 0, 4)$$

Graph of the first octant of f:

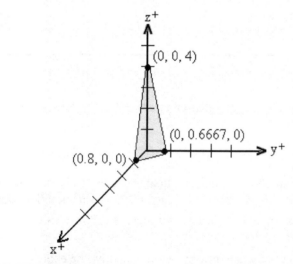

A function of the form $f(x, y) = ax + by + c$ is linear and resembles a plane.

Traces may be developed to better visualize a 3D function. A *trace* is the result of intersecting a plane with part of the 3D surface. Traces are typically single coils or gradually rounding curves. They are two-dimensional in nature. To create a trace, the graph is essentially sliced into vertical or horizontal cross sections. One of the variables must remain constant. For instance, if we desire the traces along the x-axis, allow x to equal the constant c. The function now becomes $f(c, y) = z$. This new graph is the intersection of x = c with $f(x, y) = z$.

Three-dimensional functions will have three sets of traces. Set each of the x-, y- and z-variables to a constant and observe the result. For example, letting x be zero will result in a formula containing only y and z. You can then consider the y-z plane. The graph with just y and z would be two-dimensional. Then, let y be zero and create an equation with just x and z. This will allow you to visualize the x-z plane. Setting z to a constant allows you to visualize a slice of the graph on the x-y plane.

Example

Consider the equation $\dfrac{x^2}{25} + \dfrac{y^2}{16} = \dfrac{z^2}{4}$. Find the traces for this surface, and mentally picture the graph.

Solution:
Let x = 0,

$$\frac{y^2}{16} = \frac{z^2}{4} \quad \rightarrow \quad 4*\frac{y^2}{16} = 4*\frac{z^2}{4} \quad \rightarrow \quad \frac{y^2}{4} = z^2 \quad \rightarrow \quad \sqrt{z^2} = \sqrt{\frac{y^2}{4}}$$

$$z = \pm\sqrt{\frac{y^2}{4}} = \pm\frac{y}{2} = \pm0.5y$$

*The trace at x = 0 consists of two lines in the y-z plane, which cross the origin.

Let y = 0,

$$\frac{x^2}{25} = \frac{z^2}{4} \quad \rightarrow \quad 4*\frac{x^2}{25} = 4*\frac{z^2}{4} \quad \rightarrow \quad \frac{4}{25}x^2 = z^2 \quad \rightarrow \quad \sqrt{z^2} = \sqrt{\frac{4}{25}x^2}$$

$$z = \pm\sqrt{\frac{4}{25}x^2} = \pm\frac{2}{5}x = \pm0.4x$$

*The trace at y = 0 consists of two lines in the x-z plane, which cross the origin.

Let z = 3,

$$\frac{x^2}{25} + \frac{y^2}{16} = \frac{3^2}{4} \quad \rightarrow \quad \frac{x^2}{25} + \frac{y^2}{16} = 2.25$$

*The above equation is that of an ellipse. The horizontal traces must be ellipses.

The figure resembles a double-cone:

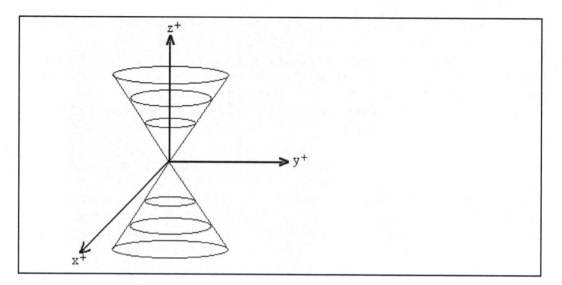

<u>Quadrics</u>

A *quadric* is a three-dimensional function of degree 2. Most quadrics have elliptical or parabolic traces. The common quadrics are described below:

Ellipsoid

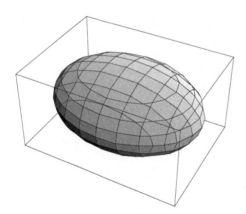

Equation: $\dfrac{x^2}{a^2} + \dfrac{y^2}{b^2} + \dfrac{z^2}{c^2} = 1$

Horizontal Traces: Ellipses
Vertical Traces: Ellipses
*When $a = b = c$, a sphere results

Cone

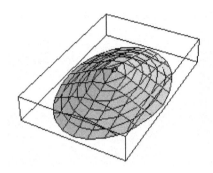

Equation: $\dfrac{z^2}{c^2} = \dfrac{x^2}{a^2} + \dfrac{y^2}{b^2}$

Horizontal Traces: Ellipses

Vertical Traces: (a.) Hyperbolas within the planes $x = d$ and $y = d$, where
$d \neq 0$.

(b.) Lines within the planes $x = 0$ and $y = 0$.

Hyperboloid of One Sheet

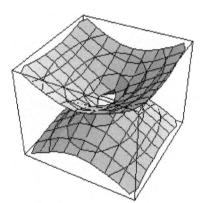

Equation: $\dfrac{x^2}{a^2} + \dfrac{y^2}{b^2} - \dfrac{z^2}{c^2} = 1$

Horizontal Traces: Ellipses

Vertical Traces: Hyperbolas

*The hyperboloid of one sheet is centered along the axis of the variable with a negative coefficient (in this case, the z-axis).

Hyperboloid of Two Sheets

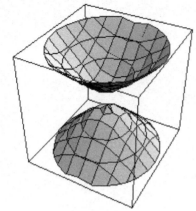

Equation: $-\dfrac{x^2}{a^2} - \dfrac{y^2}{b^2} + \dfrac{z^2}{c^2} = 1$

Horizontal Traces: Ellipses
Vertical Traces: Hyperbolas

Elliptic Paraboloid

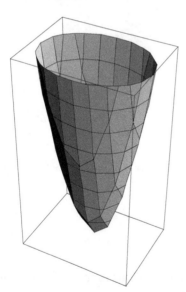

Equation: $\dfrac{z}{c} = \dfrac{x^2}{a^2} + \dfrac{y^2}{b^2}$

Horizontal Traces: Ellipses
Vertical Traces: Parabolas
*The paraboloid is centered on the axis of the variable of degree 1 (in this case, the z-axis).

Hyperbolic Paraboloid

Equation: $\dfrac{z}{c} = \dfrac{x^2}{a^2} - \dfrac{y^2}{b^2}$

Horizontal Traces: Hyperbolas
Vertical Traces: Parabolas

Section 7-4 Double Integrals

A *double integral* provides the volume under a surface. Calculating a double integral entails integrating another integral. We are essentially finding the area of an area. The surface is a 3D function, such as f(x, y) = z. The function has two independent variables that provide the coordinates on the flat x-y plane. The function then provides the height (z-value) at the point (x, y) on the surface. Positive volume exists above the x-y plane, while negative volume lies below the plane. In general, a double integral has the form:

$$\int_c^d \int_a^b f(x,y)\ dx\ dy$$

To compute a double integral, first complete the inner integral, and then calculate the outer integral. Evaluating the inner integral will result in a new function defined solely in terms of the outer integral's variable. That is, the inner variable should completely disappear after evaluating the inner integral. In the expression above, function f(x, y) is the integrand. The expression requires us to integrate first with respect to x and then with respect to y. The bounds on x are 'a' to 'b,' while the bounds on independent variable y are from 'c' to 'd.'

In the simplest case, the bounds on the x- and y- variables are constants. When this is true, you are evaluating the volume above a rectangular section of the x-y plane. In addition, you could switch the variables of integration if the bounds are constants; you can integrate first with respect to x or first with respect to y.

Example

Calculate the volume under the surface $f(x, y) = 4x + y$ for $2 < x < 5$ and $1 < y < 3$.

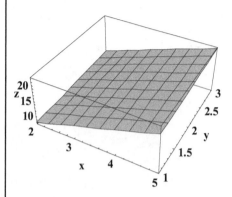

Solution:

The integral we must compute is shown below. Since the x- and y-bounds for the volume are not defined in terms of each other, the order of the independent variables is not a factor in the nested integrals. The inner integral could be based on y rather than x.

$$\text{volume} = \int_1^3 \int_2^5 0.5x + 0.8y \ dx \ dy$$

$$= \int_1^3 \left[0.5 * \frac{1}{2} x^2 + 0.8yx \right]_{x=2}^{x=5} dy$$

$$= \int_1^3 \left(0.5 * \frac{1}{2} * 5^2 + 0.8y * 5 \right) - \left(0.5 * \frac{1}{2} * 2^2 + 0.8y * 2 \right) dy$$

$$= \int_1^3 (6.25 + 4y) - (1 + 1.6y) \ dy$$

$$= \int_1^3 5.25 + 2.4y \ dy$$

$$= \left[5.25y + 2.4 * \frac{1}{2} y^2 \right]_{y=1}^{y=3}$$

$$= \left(5.25 * 3 + 2.4 * \frac{1}{2} * 3^2 \right) - \left(5.25 * 1 + 2.4 * \frac{1}{2} * 1^2 \right) = 26.55 - 6.45 = 20.1 \ u.^3$$

Example

Calculate the double integral:

$$\int_{10}^{20} \int_0^5 0.5x + 0.8y \ dx \ dy$$

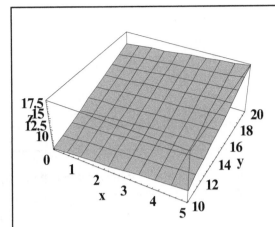

Solution:

$$\int_0^5 0.5x + 0.8y \ dx = \left[0.5 * \frac{1}{2} x^2 + 0.8yx \right]_{x=0}^{x=5} = 0.5 * \frac{1}{2} * 5^2 + 0.8y * 5 = \frac{25}{4} + 4y$$

$$\int_{10}^{20} \frac{25}{4} + 4y \ dy = \left[\frac{25}{4} y + 2y^2 \right]_{y=10}^{y=20} = \left(\frac{25}{4} * 20 + 2 * 20^2 \right) - \left(\frac{25}{4} * 10 + 2 * 10^2 \right) = 662.5$$

Example

Evaluate the following double integral:

$$\int_0^5 \int_3^7 2x^2 + 4xy \ dx \ dy$$

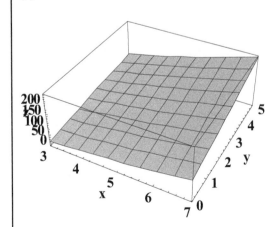

Solution:

$$\int \int = \int_0^5 \left[2 * \frac{1}{3} x^3 + 4 * \frac{1}{2} x^2 y \right]_{x=3}^{x=7} dy$$

$$= \int_0^5 \left(\frac{2}{3}7^3 + 2*7^2 y \right) - \left(\frac{2}{3}3^3 + 2*3^2 y \right) dy$$

$$= \int_0^5 228.6667 + 98y - 18 - 18y \ dy$$

$$= \int_0^5 210.6667 + 80y \ dy = \left[210.6667y + 80*\frac{1}{2}y^2 \right]_{y=0}^{y=5} = \textbf{2,053.3333 u.}^3$$

The inner integral could have bounds that are functions. These inner bounds will utilize the outer integral's variable. Suppose a double integral appears as

$$\int_c^d \int_{g(y)}^{h(y)} f(x,y) \ dx \ dy$$

The bounds for x are two functions, with the minimum set at g(y) and the maximum value equal to h(y). These bounds are not constants but vary depending on the value of y. Evaluating the inside integral yields a new function that has only variable y. Finally, compute the outer integral with respect to the second variable. The bounds on the outermost integral must be constants. The non-constant bounds allow for non-rectangular regions on the x-y plane. The regions could be triangles, partial discs, and many other undefined shapes.

Suppose you need to double-integrate a function above this triangular section of the x-y plane:

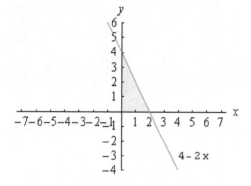

The region is enclosed by the x- and y- axes, along with the line $y = 4 - 2x$. We know the range for variable x, [0, 2], and the range for y, [0, 4]. The outer integral could use either variable x or y, since the bounds for these variables are known constants. What variable should we use for the inner integral? The line in its current form provides y-values, so the inner integral should be respect to y. The double integral could be

$$\int_0^2 \int_0^{4-2x} f(x,y) \ dy \ dx$$

The range for variable y stretches from the x-axis (y = 0) up to the line of interest. Finally, we will let x run from 0 to 2. Let's assume f is a simple plane with $f(x,y) = 3x + y$. The integration becomes

$$\int_0^2 \int_0^{4-2x} 3x + y \ dy \ dx = \int_0^2 \left[3xy + \frac{1}{2} y^2 \right]_{y=0}^{y=4-2x} dx$$

Evaluate the integral in the same manner as if the bounds were constants. You need to find the anti-derivative of the integrand first with respect to y. This anti-derivative must be evaluated from y = 0 up to $y = 4 - 2x$. Simply plug the upper bound into the anti-derivative to produce

$$\int_0^2 \left(3x(4-2x) + \frac{1}{2}(4-2x)^2 \right) - \left(3x*0 + \frac{1}{2} * 0^2 \right) dx$$

$$\int_0^2 12x - 6x^2 + \frac{1}{2}(4-2x)^2 \ dx$$

Now we have a single integral that holds only one independent variable—x. Compute this integral to find the volume under the 3D surface and within the triangular region.

You can often switch the order of integration when the bounds are functions. In the example above, you could integrate first with respect to x and then with respect to y. If we choose this path, we must define the bounds for x in terms of functions utilizing y. Solve for x in the line equation:

$$y = 4 - 2x \ \rightarrow \ y - 4 = -2x \ \rightarrow \ x = \frac{y-4}{-2} \ \rightarrow \ x = \frac{-1}{2} y + 2$$

The bounds for x span 0 to the line $x = \frac{-1}{2} y + 2$. The double integral will appear as:

$$\int_0^4 \int_0^{-0.5y+2} f(x,y) \ dx \ dy$$

The inner integral is now with respect to variable x, with bounds depending on y. The result of this integral will match the volume computed with the original bounds.

Example

Consider the surface defined by $f(x,y) = 3xy^2 + 0.25y^3$. Find the volume under the surface for $y < \frac{1}{2}x - 2$, $6 < x < 8$, and $y > 0$.

Solution:

$$\int_6^8 \int_0^{(1/2)x-2} 3xy^2 + 0.25y^3 \ dy \ dx$$

The bounds for x are clearly defined in the problem description, so the outer integral will utilize variable x. The variable y depends on x, so the inner integral should be with respect to y.

$$\int\int = \int_6^8 \left[3x * \frac{1}{3}y^3 + 0.25 * \frac{1}{4}y^4 \right]_{y=0}^{y=(1/2)x-2} dx$$

$$= \int_6^8 x*((1/2)x-2)^3 + \frac{1}{16}((1/2)x-2)^4 \ dx$$

Break into 2 integrals...

$$= \int_6^8 x*((1/2)x-2)^3 \ dx + \int_6^8 \frac{1}{16}((1/2)x-2)^4 \ dx$$

First integral...

$$x*\left(\frac{1}{2}x-2\right)^3 = x*\left(\frac{1}{2}x-2\right)\left(\frac{1}{2}x-2\right)\left(\frac{1}{2}x-2\right)$$

$$= x*\left(\frac{1}{4}x^2 - x - x + 4\right)\left(\frac{1}{2}x-2\right)$$

$$= x*\left(\frac{1}{4}x^2 - 2x + 4\right)\left(\frac{1}{2}x-2\right)$$

$$= x*\left(\frac{1}{8}x^3 - \frac{1}{2}x^2 - x^2 + 4x + 2x - 8\right)$$

$$\int_6^8 \frac{1}{8}x^4 - \frac{3}{2}x^3 + 6x^2 - 8x \ dx$$

$$= \left[\frac{1}{8}*\frac{1}{5}x^5 - \frac{3}{2}*\frac{1}{4}x^4 + 6*\frac{1}{3}x^3 - 8*\frac{1}{2}x^2 \right]_{x=6}^{x=8}$$

$$= \frac{1}{40}(8^5 - 6^5) - \frac{3}{8}(8^4 - 6^4) + 2(8^3 - 6^3) - 4(8^2 - 6^2)$$

$$= 624.8 - 1,050 + 592 - 112 = 54.8 \ u.^3$$

Second integral...

Let $u = \dfrac{1}{2}x - 2$

$du = \dfrac{1}{2}dx \quad \rightarrow \quad \dfrac{1}{8}du = \dfrac{1}{16}dx$

When x = 8, u = 2
When x = 6, u = 1

$\displaystyle\int_{1}^{2} u^4 * \dfrac{1}{8}\ du = \dfrac{1}{8} * \left[\dfrac{1}{5}u^5\right]_{1}^{2} = \dfrac{1}{40}(2^5 - 1^5) = \dfrac{1}{40}(32 - 1) = \dfrac{31}{40}\ \text{u.}^3$

Total volume = $54.8 + 31/40 =$ **55.575 u.**^{3}

Example

Find the volume under the surface $f(x,y) = 7y^2 + 10x^2 y$ for $\dfrac{1}{4}x^2 < y < -\dfrac{3}{4}x + 3$.

Solution:
Since the bounds for y are defined in terms of x, the inner integral should be with respect to y. We also need to find the bounds for x, which will be used in the outer integral:

find the points of intersection for $\dfrac{1}{4}x^2$ and $-\dfrac{3}{4}x + 3$ ...

$$\dfrac{1}{4}x^2 = -\dfrac{3}{4}x + 3$$

$$\downarrow$$

$$\dfrac{1}{4}x^2 + \dfrac{3}{4}x - 3 = 0$$

$$x = \dfrac{-3/4 \pm \sqrt{(3/4)^2 - 4*(1/4)*(-3)}}{2*(1/4)}$$

$$\downarrow$$

$$x = \dfrac{-3/4 \pm \sqrt{3.5625}}{(1/2)} \quad \rightarrow \quad x \approx 2.27492 \text{ and } x \approx -5.27492$$

$$\int_{-5.27492}^{2.27492} \int_{0.25x^2}^{-0.75x+3} 7y^2 + 10x^2 y\ dy\ dx$$

$$\downarrow$$

$$\int_{-5.27492}^{2.27492} \left[7 * \dfrac{1}{3}y^3 + 10x^2 * \dfrac{1}{2}y^2\right]_{y=0.25x^2}^{y=-0.75x+3} dx$$

$$\int_{-5.27492}^{2.27492} \left(\frac{7}{3}(-0.75x+3)^3 + 5x^2(-0.75x+3)^2 \right) - \left(\frac{7}{3}(0.25x^2)^3 + 5x^2(0.25x^2)^2 \right) \ dx$$

$$(-0.75x+3)^2 = (-0.75x+3)(-0.75x+3) = 0.5625x^2 - 4.5x + 9$$

$$(-0.75x+3)^3 = (0.5625x^2 - 4.5x + 9)(-0.75x+3)$$
$$= -0.421875x^3 + 1.6875x^2 + 3.375x^2 - 13.5x - 6.75x + 27$$
$$= -0.421875x^3 + 5.0625x^2 - 20.25x + 27$$

$$\frac{7}{3}(-0.75x+3)^3 = -0.984375x^3 + 11.8125x^2 - 47.25x + 63$$

$$5x^2(-0.75x+3)^2 = 2.8125x^4 - 22.5x^3 + 45x^2$$

$$\frac{7}{3}(-0.75x+3)^3 + 5x^2(-0.75x+3)^2 = 2.8125x^4 - 23.48438x^3 + 56.8125x^2 - 47.25x + 63$$

$$\int_{-5.27492}^{2.27492} \left(\frac{7}{3}(-0.75x+3)^3 + 5x^2(-0.75x+3)^2 \right) - \left(0.03646x^6 + 0.3125x^6 \right) \ dx$$

$$\int_{-5.27492}^{2.27492} -0.34896x^6 + 2.8125x^4 - 23.48438x^3 + 56.8125x^2 - 47.25x + 63 \ dx$$

$$\left[\frac{-0.34896}{7}x^7 + \frac{2.8125}{5}x^5 - \frac{23.48438}{4}x^4 + \frac{56.8125}{3}x^3 - \frac{47.25}{2}x^2 + 63x \right]_{-5.27492}^{2.27492}$$
$$= 105.31744 - -4947.076 = 5{,}052$$

Appendices

Appendix A: The Greek Alphabet

Uppercase Letters:

A = Alpha

B = Beta

X = Chi

Δ = Delta

E = Epsilon

Φ = Phi

Γ = Gamma

H = Eta

I = Iota

K = Kappa

Λ = Lambda

M = Mu

N = Nu

O = Omicron

Π = Pi

Θ = Theta

P = Rho

Σ = Sigma

T = Tau

Y = Upsilon

Ω = Omega

Ξ = Xi

Ψ = Psi

Z = Zeta

Lowercase Letters:

α = alpha

β = beta

χ = chi

δ = delta

ε = epsilon

φ = phi

γ = gamma

η = eta

ι = iota

κ = kappa

λ = lambda

μ = mu

ν = nu

o = omicron

π = pi

θ = theta

ρ = rho

σ = sigma

τ = tau

υ = upsilon

ω = omega

ξ = xi

ψ = psi

ζ = zeta

Appendix B: Extra Math Symbols

    Mathematics is often a universal language. Two people with different speaking languages can still understand the same math problem. A set of common symbols was developed for communicating in math. These symbols are essential to writing proofs and understanding theorems.

Symbol	Meaning
$=$	"is exactly equal to"
$\approx$	"is approximately equal to"
$\equiv$	"is logically equivalent to"
Δ	delta, which represents a change
$\therefore$	"therefore"
$:$	"such that" or "under the condition of"
$\in$	"is an element of"
$\ni$	"such that"
$\{\ \}$	represents a set of elements
iff	"if and only if;" the argument is true both ways (If the premise is true, then the conclusion is true. And, if the conclusion is true, then the premise must also be true.)
$\Leftrightarrow$	Has the same meaning as iff
$\exists$	"there exists"
$\forall$	"for all" (also the anarchy symbol)
$\rightarrow$	"maps" (for example, $f : x \rightarrow y$ is notation for "function f maps x onto y")
$\cup$	"union"
$\cap$	"intersection"
$\subseteq$	"subset" (For instance, the expression $A \subseteq B$ translates to "A is a subset of B." All the elements in set A also exist in set B, but not all the items in B necessarily lie in A.)
R	the set of all real numbers
Z	the set of all integers
Z+	the set of all positive integers
Z-	the set of all negative integers
I	the set of all imaginary numbers
N	the set of all natural numbers
Q	the set of all rational numbers

Appendix C: Trigonometric Identities

$$\sin^2(\theta) + \cos^2(\theta) = 1$$
$$\cos^2(\theta) - \sin^2(\theta) = \cos(2\theta)$$
$$\sin(a+b) = \sin(a)*\cos(b) + \cos(a)*\sin(b)$$
$$\sin(a-b) = \sin(a)*\cos(b) - \cos(a)*\sin(b)$$
$$\cos(a+b) = \cos(a)*\cos(b) - \sin(a)*\sin(b)$$
$$\cos(a-b) = \cos(a)*\cos(b) + \sin(a)*\sin(b)$$
$$\tan(a+b) = \frac{\tan(a) + \tan(b)}{1 - \tan(a)*\tan(b)}$$
$$\tan(a-b) = \frac{\tan(a) - \tan(b)}{1 + \tan(a)*\tan(b)}$$
$$1 + \tan^2(\theta) = \sec^2(\theta)$$
$$\cot^2(\theta) + 1 = \csc^2(\theta)$$
$$\tan(\theta) + \cot(\theta) = (\sec(\theta))(\csc(\theta))$$

Half-Angle Identities:
$$\sin^2(\theta) = \frac{1}{2}(1 - \cos(2\theta))$$
$$\cos^2(\theta) = \frac{1}{2}(1 + \cos(2\theta))$$

Double Angle Formulas:
$$\sin(2\theta) = 2*\sin(\theta)*\cos(\theta)$$
$$\cos(2\theta) = \cos^2(\theta) - \sin^2(\theta)$$

Pythagorean Identity:
$$\sin^2(a+b) + \cos^2(a+b) = 1$$

Index